THE INDEPENDENCE OF SCOTLAND

The Independence of Scotland

Self-government and the Shifting Politics of Union

MICHAEL KEATING

OXFORD
UNIVERSITY PRESS

OXFORD
UNIVERSITY PRESS

Great Clarendon Street, Oxford OX2 6DP

Oxford University Press is a department of the University of Oxford.
It furthers the University's objective of excellence in research, scholarship,
and education by publishing worldwide in

Oxford New York

Auckland Cape Town Dar es Salaam Hong Kong Karachi
Kuala Lumpur Madrid Melbourne Mexico City Nairobi
New Delhi Shanghai Taipei Toronto

With offices in

Argentina Austria Brazil Chile Czech Republic France Greece
Guatemala Hungary Italy Japan Poland Portugal Singapore
South Korea Switzerland Thailand Turkey Ukraine Vietnam

Oxford is a registered trade mark of Oxford University Press
in the UK and in certain other countries

Published in the United States
by Oxford University Press Inc., New York

British Library Cataloguing in Publication Data

Data available

Library of Congress Cataloging in Publication Data

Data available

Library of Congress Control Number: 2009926747

Typeset by SPI Publisher Services, Pondicherry, India
Printed in Great Britain
on acid-free paper by
the MPG Books Group, Bodmin and King's Lynn

ISBN 978-0-19-954595-7

3 5 7 9 10 8 6 4 2

Contents

Preface   vi
List of Figures   ix
List of Abbreviations   x

1. State and Nation   1

2. Understanding the Union   17

3. The Strange Death of Unionist Scotland   45

4. Becoming Independent   79

5. The Political Economy of Independence: Large States and
   Small Nations   101

6. Constitutional Futures: State and Nation in the Twenty-First
   Century   125

7. Beyond Devolution: Evolutionary Change   143

8. Scotland and the Future of Union   173

Notes   181
Bibliography   187
Index   207

Preface

This started out as a book about Scottish independence, prompted by the Scottish National Party victory in the elections of 2007, the promise of a referendum by 2010, and the remarkably low key of the debate surrounding all this, both in Scotland and in England. There has not been a serious intellectual analysis on the meaning and implications of independence; and I know of no country where a secessionist movement exists in which the majority of the host state appears so unfazed about the prospects of its dissolution. Yet in the writing, the project has expanded. If it is true that the Anglo-Scottish Union is dissolving then we need to know more about how that Union was constructed and how it worked. Chapter 1 insists, as an antidote to British exceptionalism, that the relationship between state and nation has rarely been a simple one anywhere and that multiple forms of polity have existed in history. Both unionist and nationalist teleologies, seeing the end of history in one nation state or the other, are thus misleading. So are simple explanations for the supposed demise of the Union, whether from internal or external causes. Rather, we must analyse the Union and its trajectory at four levels: functional change, mass opinion, elite strategies, and the moulding effects of institutions. Chapter 2 argues that the secret of the Union was the recognition of national diversity within a unitary state in which the position of Scotland has regularly been negotiated. It was understood rather differently on each side of the border, an 'anomaly' that partly explains its historic success. Union was buttressed by a distinctive ideology, more familiar in Scotland than in England, and by elaborate institutional mechanisms for brokering Scottish interests within the United Kingdom.

These devices have come under strain from developments in the wider political economy, while the mystique of Union has been broken and its ideological crisis is revealed by the tortuous efforts to reinvent Britishness (Chapter 3). This has created the opportunity structure for a rival nation-building project focused on Scotland. It is important to note that none of this depends on social, economic, or cultural differentiation or even on large differences in political values. Scotland has never needed to be different from England in order to exist, but it provides a historic and institutional frame and a focus of identity for the construction and reconstruction of a spatially focused political community. Yet this cannot take the form of a nation state, for much the same reasons that the British national project is in trouble. Rather, we are seeing the building of new forms of political community, loosely bounded and nested in broader unions. The mass public has become more Scottish in identity and supportive of more self-government, but hesitates on the threshold of independence. Supporters of independence themselves seek to locate their project within wider structures. So, while traditional unionism may be spent, everyone still seems to talk the language of union.

Chapter 4 considers the legal, political, and institutional implications of independence. Scotland is perhaps unique in facing no serious legal or constitutional bar to independence, nor much opposition in principle within the host state. The mechanics are more difficult and I argue that, total independence being impossible in the modern world, the key issue is how to manage interdependency in the (British) Isles, Europe, the Atlantic community, and the world. Even more difficult is the political economy of independence, discussed in Chapter 5. There is evidence that small independent nations can thrive in European and global markets, but there are important choices to be made among the very different social and economic models on offer. This debate has hardly started and there is a tendency to mix and match desirable policies at will, irrespective of their compatibility. For some years, I have argued that we have moved from a world of absolute sovereignty to a post-sovereignty era, in which power is shared at multiple levels and self-determination does not necessarily imply statehood (Keating 2001*a*, 2001*b*). Scotland is a site for these debates, but there have been few attempts to sketch out what a post-sovereign, third way between independence and devolution would look like. This task has taken up two chapters. It is not just a matter of looking at individual powers as has often been done, but of marking out a direction of travel.

As unionism has adapted and accepted devolution, so many nationalists would settle for something less than independence. Yet there remains a division of principle between neo-unionists, who start from the premise of a single UK (or British) citizenship, in its civil, political, and social dimensions, and neo-nationalists, who start with the presumption of Scottish self-determination and ask how it can fit into the wider order. This distinction underpins the debates about fiscal autonomy, devolution of social policy, the infamous West Lothian Question, relations with Europe, and the constitution of the British centre. The standard constitutional models of the unitary state, federalism in its various forms, or confederalism do not fit the United Kingdom well, but their underlying principles are still relevant. Neo-unionists are inspired by notions of decentralization in unity, or cooperative federalism, while neo-nationalists are inclined to confederal ideas. These contrasting perspectives do not, on the other hand, prevent practical compromises. Plurinational states are doomed to a certain existential uncertainty over matters of sovereignty and to a lack of consensus on their ultimate destiny, but constitutional practice can work around this to prevent constant deadlock.

It would not be the first time in history that a policy or reform had been agreed by different parties for different reasons, and indeed devolution itself rests upon such a bargain.

Some years ago, an anonymous *Economist* review of my *Nations against the State* noted that I had asked the right questions but not given the 'answer': should Scotland, Catalonia, and Quebec become independent or not? Readers looking for such 'answers' might well stop here. We are dealing with complex issues reducible neither to the certainties of the old nation state nor to those of free-market dogma. History has not, despite the triumphalist moment of the early 1990s, ended. Political order is being rebuilt in myriad ways across the globe and Scotland, like other societies, is evolving. Its direction of travel in recent decades has been towards self-government and rebuilding the nation, but the destination is unknown. It has become a cliché to describe devolution as a process, not an event; but institutions, once established, do take on a life of their own. All parties are now committed to reopening the 1999 provision, but a new union settlement needs to be agreed at two levels, within Scotland and at Westminster. The sticking point at Westminster will probably not be the degree of Scottish self-government, a matter to which both mass opinion and political leaders in England appear indifferent, but Scottish influence at the centre. Hence my provocative suggestion that it could be the English, in defence of their unitary conception of the constitution, and not the Scots, who are more used to multilevel politics, who finally break the Union.

In writing this book I have benefited from discussions with colleagues in political science, sociology, history, and law, in Scotland, Catalonia, the Basque Country, Galicia, Ontario, Quebec, and at the European University Institute. In the best scholarly tradition we have thrashed out ideas to the point that we no longer know who was first responsible for which idea – and to try and name them would merely risk missing somebody out. Their contribution is gratefully, if anonymously, acknowledged. I have tried out my ideas and benefited from feedback in presentations at the University of Aberdeen; University of Edinburgh; Queen's University of Belfast; Goldsmiths, University of London; Xunta de Galicia, Santiago de Compostela; Centre d'Estudis Jordi Pujol, Barcelona; Pentsamundua, Bilbao; Grup Blanquerna (Majorca); and the American Political Science Association in Boston. All these have reinforced my conviction that Scotland can only be understood in a comparative perspective since, while it may be distinct, it is far from being unique.

Aberdeen and Florence   Michael Keating
December 2008

List of Figures

2.1 Scottish GDP as percentage of United Kingdom, 1924–2006   33

3.1 National identity, Scotland, 1992–2006   62

3.2 Support for independence in Scotland, 1999–2007   74

5.1 Eighty-five per cent North Sea oil revenue as percentage of
Scottish non-oil GDP   108

5.2 UK and Scottish fiscal deficits, 1992–2006 (% GDP)   109

5.3 Selected % tax rates, 2006–7   116

5.4 GDP growth, 1980–2006   117

List of Abbreviations

ADQ	*Parti Action Démocratique du Québec*
CFP	Common Fisheries Policy
CoR	Committee of the Regions
ECHR	European Convention for the Protection of Human Rights and Fundamental Freedoms
GDP	Gross Domestic Product
GERS	Government Expenditure and Revenues in Scotland
GVA	Gross Value Added
JMC	Joint Ministerial Committees
NAFTA	North American Free Trade Agreement
PQ	Parti Québécois
PR	Proportional Representation
SNP	Scottish National Party
SSAS	Scottish Social Attitudes Survey
VAT	Value Added Tax
WEU	Western European Union
WLQ	West Lothian Question

1

State and Nation

THE END OF BRITAIN?

Since the 1990s a whole genre of literature has emerged about the question of Britain and the crisis of the Union. Nairn (2000, 2007), picking up a theme he first deployed a generation earlier, writes of 'After Britain'. Bryant (2006: 58) questions whether 'a British national identity can be reconstructed'. Colley (2003: 275), having traced the process of forging a British nation, concludes that 'a substantial rethinking of what it means to be British can no longer be evaded'. For McLean and McMillan (2005), unionism (if not the Union) has expired. Weight (2002: 1) asks 'why the people of Britain stopped thinking of themselves as British'. Haseler (1996: 3) believes that 'we are coming to the end of Britain'. Colls (2002) looks to the re-emergence of an English nation from the ruins of union. On the more polemical edges of political writing, Redwood (1999) thinks that Britain is finished because of Europe, while Heffer (1999) has called for the independence of England. Scruton (2000) believes that there never was a British nation and laments the destruction of the English one.

There is a striking contrast with a previous generation in the social sciences and history when everything seemed to point to integration and harmony. So Blondel (1974: 20) could write that 'Britain is probably the most homogeneous of all industrial countries' on the grounds that the non-English parts were too small to matter. Finer (1974: 137) wrote that 'Like many of the new states today, Britain too had its "nationalities" problem, its "language" problem, its "religious" problem, not to speak of its "constitutional" problem. These are problems no more.' Certainly Scotland was recognized as somehow 'different', with a strong identity about which its people could be sensitive; but this was largely confined to the non-political spheres of sport, culture, and religion. Politics seemed to follow the normal British two-party pattern, and the great issues of the day were the same on both sides of the border.

For mainstream social science, the Anglo–British union was a case of functional integration, through economic exchange, the creation of a single market, mergers of firms and trade unions, and free movement of labour. Political integration marched in step, as a common national identity was forged through shared experience. Party competition was based on class alignments within agreed rules of the game in which the shape of the polity itself was not an issue. Institutional integration was ensured by a single Parliament and government, whose distinctive Scottish aspects were at best a secondary consideration.

Historians, while aware of the difficult Anglo–Scottish relations over the centuries, tended to show the period since the Union, or at least since 1745, as one of progressive integration allied with modernization and progress. The self-congratulatory Whig history that saw British constitutional evolution as a lesson to the world incorporated a complacent acceptance of the benefits of union under English domination. Even after the Whig historians had gone out of fashion or retreated in the face of criticism (Butterfield 1968), the teleology of the Union remained largely unquestioned.

The shock of a resurgent Scottish nationalism in the 1970s provoked a sharp reaction. Many English scholars refused to take it seriously, arguing that nationalist voting was a mere 'protest', implying that it represented a form of deviant behaviour, while voting for Labour or Conservative was somehow normal. As the reality of nationalism became apparent, some scholars abruptly changed tack to argue that England and Scotland had never really been integrated, that the Union was a mere veneer so that, as soon as external circumstances and internal calculations changed, it was bound to fall apart. Proffered explanations are legion; but most of them seem to depend on a winding back of the historical clock, so that the artificial or historically contingent skein of Britishness is shed, with an automatic default to pre-British identities in the nations of these islands. The problem here is that pre-British identities were not fully national in the modern sense (Kidd 1999) and should be seen, rather, as the seeds of alternative modernizing projects that never came to fruition. Scotland existed before the Union but not as a modern state and society, so that what emerged from its collapse would be something else and deeply moulded by the experience of the Union itself. Moreover, British identity, far from being a temporary overlay, did have a depth and conviction that prevent us regarding it as a historical convenience, to be dropped as soon as it ceased to be profitable.

One set of explanations for the decline of the Union focuses on Britain's external relations and the diminishing instrumental value and emotional hold of the Union at both mass and elite level. A common device is to take Linda Colley's account (1992) of the rise of popular Britishness, forged in war with France and Protestantism, and show how these factors are no longer relevant (Bryant 2006). Colley herself writes (2003: 6):

> As an invented nation heavily dependent for its '*raison d'être*' on a broadly Protestant culture, on the threat and tonic of recurrent war, particularly war with France, and on the triumphs, profits and Otherness represented by a massive

overseas empire, Britain is bound now to be under immense pressure.... We can understand the nature of present debates and controversies only if we recognise that the factors that provided for the forging of a British nation in the past have largely ceased to operate.

This approach is open to several objections. Protestantism was divisive within the United Kingdom, and Presbyterianism was a marker of Scottish cultural and institutional distinctiveness. From 1689, there were two different religious establishments within the United Kingdom, and by 1922, there were four. This very diversity, in defiance of Westphalian principles,[1] was a vital pillar of the Union, although it came too late to save the Irish one.[2] War with the neighbours was the common European experience, not a British peculiarity. France and Germany were forged as modern nations in opposition to each other from the Napoleonic era. National identities are not picked up and dropped so easily but rather, forged in one era, can become self-sustaining and adapt to new circumstances and new issues. So France, united by Catholicism, was further unified by the Republic, especially after the 1870s when the anti-clerical Third Republic forged a new secular identity. Germany was united and nationalized in spite of religious divisions.

An older version is that the United Kingdom was the creature of the Empire and, after its disappearance, lost both its instrumental appeal and its ideological underpinnings (Marquand 1995; Weight 2002; Gardiner 2004). The argument is plausible but tends to be drawn at too general and broad a level and downplays the depth and reality of Britishness itself and of unionism as a doctrine (Aughey 2001; Ward 2005). Scots did participate disproportionately in the Empire (Fry 2001; Devine 2003) so that there was no frustrated upward mobility such as is credited with favouring nationalism in some other cases. Yet there were episodes of Scottish nationalism in the late nineteenth and early twentieth centuries, usually placed within a broader imperial narrative. The demise of the Empire did indeed force Britain (I leave aside the more difficult question of the United Kingdom) to reconstruct itself as a nation state, but few people in the 1940s or 1950s, with the foundation of the welfare state, would have considered this particularly problematic; on the contrary, these were bleak times for anti-unionists. Decolonization did not immediately put in question the nature of the metropolitan state in the way it did, for example, in Spain after 1898 or France in the 1950s and 1960s.[3] This is all the more remarkable since the first breach in the Empire was made not at the periphery but in the very centre, in Ireland, a country that had for over a hundred years been part of the metropolitan state itself.

Another external explanation is that Britain has come apart under the influence of European integration as Scots have embraced Europe while the English reject it (Weight 2002). The question of Europe does indeed touch the debate about Scotland's place in the United Kingdom, as we shall see, but in a complex manner. Polls show Scots to be almost as Eurosceptic as the English, and the nationalists are hardly an exception. So Euroscepticism is something that we could expect to unite the United Kingdom or at least Great Britain and, given its exploitation by both main parties, but especially the Conservatives, to underpin a revived British nationalism.

Internal explanations are also legion. One is that the destruction of the welfare state has broken an essential bond of Britishness, especially among the working class. There is a great deal to be said for the argument that the welfare state was critical in building Scottish working class support for the Union, and was decisive in turning Labour and the trade unions away from lingering nationalist sympathies from the 1930s and 1940s. Yet it is not true that the welfare state has been dismantled. On the contrary, it resisted most Thatcherite assaults and now enjoys record levels of spending. There have been shifts in priorities, notably away from publicly provided housing and on unemployment regimes, but this is hardly enough to explain a disengagement from statewide solidarity. Nor is there much evidence that this statewide solidarity itself has disappeared, or at least that it preceded the decline of unionism as would be necessary to give it causal primacy. The hypothesis that English voters have abandoned their belief in the welfare state, while Scots have clung to it, can also largely be rejected. Neither Scottish nor English voters have rejected basic welfare values; surveys show Scots only marginally to the left of the English as a whole, and even that difference is due to southern England, rather than Scotland, being the outlier from the UK mean (Rosie and Bond 2007).

The decline of class identities might also be an element in the demise of unionism. In the early twentieth century, Scottish Labour was rather particularist and only aligned with the rest of Britain after the First World War, taking the working class into the British political system (Keating and Bleiman 1979). Working class solidarity was, in principle, universal, but in practice followed the boundaries of the British state, as Labour opposition to European integration in the years after the Second World War showed. Yet it is not clear why the decline of class should work in favour of a renewed Scottishness. The relationship between class and national identity is complex, and they should not be seen as mere substitutes for one another in different historical periods.

A similar problem arises with the demise of unionism on the right. The decline of the Scottish Conservative and Unionist Party[4] has been presented as one of the explanations of the decline of the Union. Yet the party across Britain has been able to adapt its ideology and appeal to different economic doctrines and to embrace newly emerging social strata. There seems no *a priori* reason why 1980s Conservatism, even in its Thatcherite version, should not have appealed to a new middle class in Scotland.

One explanation has to do with changing identities and the increased salience of Scottishness. On the Linz–Moreno scale, asking people about which identities they prioritize, there has been a shift towards a stronger Scottish and a weaker British identity (Paterson 2002a). Those prioritizing a Scottish identity went up from 56 per cent in 1979 to 76 per cent in 2005, while the British identifiers declined from 38 to 15 per cent. More recently, there is evidence of English people beginning to prioritize an English identity and pride in Britain weakening (Heath 2005; Curtice 2005). Yet the relationship between identity and support for Scottish independence is a very complex one (Bechhofer and McCrone 2007). Scottishness is much more widespread than support for independence and embraces people with all manner of political orientations. Indeed, as we shall see, it was an important ingredient in unionism itself.

Purely instrumental analyses reduce the question to economic advantage. One such theory is based on relative deprivation, arguing that Scots have turned against the Union because they are getting less out of it than are the English. Hechter (1975) presented the most exaggerated version of relative deprivation theory, to the effect that Scotland was an 'internal colony' exploited by English capital and the state – an idea that has not withstood serious scrutiny (Page 1978; McCrone 2001b) and which Hechter himself (1985) was later to turn on its head. Others argue that Scots make shorter-term calculations and have turned nationalist since the 1970s because the economy is doing badly (Weight 2002). Yet Scottish nationalism, if anything, does badly during periods when Scotland's economy is performing rather poorly (as in the 1930s, 1950s, and 1980s), while it strengthened during times of relative prosperity (such as the mid-1970s and the 1990s).[5] This is perfectly rational, since in bad times many Scots feel that they need the support of the centre more. In any case, Scotland acceded to the Union for more than economic reasons, and unionism was to put down deeper roots.

COMPLEX EXPLANATION

These explanations all have an unsatisfactorily *ad hoc* character to them. They do not travel well across time, if we examine the historical record, or across space, putting Britain in a comparative context. Indeed, they usually smack of the exceptionalism that has so often characterized British history (discussed in the following paragraphs). They also seek to explain a complex process of political restructuring and shifting patterns of identity with factors cast at an extremely general level, which are assumed to impact on the whole nation in a more or less undifferentiated manner. Yet Scottish society is complex and stratified like others, and changes in the environment can be expected to have a differential impact within it. Too much work on the Union has been reductionist in focus. Integrationist narratives have shown territorial identities as giving way to class cleavages at a higher level, with functional differentials triumphing over older national alignments. The more recent analyses have tended to another form of reductionism, in assuming that the erosion of integrative pressures means that Scotland will default to an older territorial identity. We need a more sensitive and complex frame of analysis, allowing us to trace integrationist and disintegrationist tendencies and the building and re-building of national identities over time. The argument developed here analyses the Union and its challenges at four interlinked levels: functional change, mass opinion, elite strategy, and institutions. The evolution of the Union needs to be understood in a historical context taking into account both historical experience and the interpretation and re-interpretation of that experience. None of these levels is determinant on its own, but they interact with, and mutually influence, each other.

Functionalist accounts of the Union focus on deep processes in the economy and social structures, which shape or even determine the political superstructure. Modernist sociology from Durkheim (1964) long argued that territorial distinctiveness would be eroded in the course of modernization, giving way to a differentiation of social roles linked to the modern division of labour, notably class. Similar thinking informed functionalist and neo-functionalist accounts of European integration, where they have been found wanting. Recent work in political geography and territorial politics, however, disputes the notion that territory and function are competing principles of social, economic, or political organization (Keating 1988, 1998; Paasi 2002). Rather, various functional systems adapt to and adapt the territorial frameworks in which they operate, at state, sub-state, and suprastate levels. A process of spatial rescaling is presently changing the relationship between territory and function across a range of fields. As we will see, the economy is not an aspatial system with the same impacts everywhere as predicated by the neoclassical model, but a social system that adapts to circumstances and in particular to locality. After an era of globalization in the nineteenth and early twentieth centuries, economies were bound between the wars into national protectionism. In recent years, they have been both globalizing and localizing, with important effects on the nation state as the framework for public policy. Social solidarity, previously linked to the nation state, is being recast at new levels. Culture and identity are undergoing both a de-territorialization and a re-territorialization with new spatial horizons.

Public opinion is not a homogeneous mass but is structured by social and ideological divisions, which may coincide or cross-cut each other; they include class, sector, gender, locality, and national identity. Social divisions in turn are not quite the same as political cleavages, but they become so (structuring political competition) only because of the activities of parties in exploiting differences, aggregating interests, and in constructing ideologies that can incorporate them in a reasonably coherent whole (Bartolini 2005). So political alignments are the product of functional or class conflicts in specific places, whose outcomes are refracted by the context in which they take place. Nationalism needs to be placed in this framework. It cannot be divorced from attitudes and interests in social and economic issues, or reduced merely to these interests. Different sections of the population respond differently to nationalist appeals, touching on emotive, economic, cultural, or other interests, in specific circumstances. National identity is notoriously complex, and it is not uncommon for people to have more than one. Its meaning also changes according to time and place, taking on varied cultural, political, and economic implications. Across much of Europe, the emerging working class in the late nineteenth and early twentieth century were pulled by the competing forces of class and territorial or nationality politics. In some cases, class politics triumphed, while in others the national issue eclipsed all others. In the Basque Country and Catalonia, both principles flourished, leaving a particular legacy to modern politics. Britain provides a particularly complex example of the linkage of class and national politics, in a context in which there were two possible levels of nation-building, that of the state and of the constituent nations. Irish politics went strongly towards the nation-building pole; Scotland has been more ambivalent.

Both functional change and mass opinion are responsive to the strategic and tactical behaviour of elites. Since the resurgence of territorial politics in the 1970s, some scholars have drawn attention to the persistence of a territorial dimension even in the most unitary of states and the importance of state strategy, or territorial management, in explaining how states come together *and* how they stay together (Rokkan and Urwin 1982, 1983; Bulpitt 1983; Keating 1988). Territorial management strategies include party–political incorporation; centre–periphery intermediation through political and bureaucratic channels including clientelistic networks; policy concessions, notably but not exclusively in economic policy; and institutional decentralization. For their part, actors on the periphery may pursue territorial autonomy or may prefer to seek privileged access to the centre. Systems of territorial management will incorporate both, in different measures. Changing internal and external conditions alter the strategic interests and calculations of both central and peripheral actors. For example, the selective creation and closing of many national markets in the late nineteenth century made centres into peripheries and vice versa, as did the opening of European and global markets a hundred years later. Tariff policy was thus a key issue in territorial politics in the first era of globalization, creating new constellations of territorial and sectoral interests. Penetration of the state into territories, as it extends its reach, threatens the old system of intermediation, creating a crisis of territorial representation, a challenge to the state, and a reconfiguration of territorial politics. Such crises occurred in the late nineteenth century and again in the late 1960s and early 1970s, not just in the United Kingdom but across western Europe (Keating 1988). In the latter case, one cause was the new phase of territorial management represented by modernizing regional policies, intended to integrate declining and underdeveloped territories into national economies within the overall Keynesian strategy of macroeconomic management. These were presented as essentially technical and of benefit to all by maximizing national output yet, delivered by the central state, they disrupted existing patterns of territorial intermediation. This produced reactions within the regions and a new wave of territorial mobilization, itself taking various forms, from a defence of old modes of production to alternative policies for development. In more recent years, European integration has similarly destabilized modes of territorial management, depriving states of key instruments of accommodation and creating new alliances of winners and losers (Jones and Keating 1995). Territorial distinctiveness is thus not something overcome once for all, but creates and recreates itself in each generation.

This brings us to the role of institutions in shaping territorial politics. The unitary state in its starkest form provides a single arena for politics, forcing demands to the centre. Nation-building states like France sought to use institutions such as education, the military, and the administration to build not only a unitary state machinery but also a uniform sense of identity. Even here, however, practical realities necessitated some means for adapting to territorial diversity. The British state was more accommodating, and the survival of institutions such as the Church, the law, and the education and local government systems has been widely credited with the resilience of Scottish national identity in the absence of strong linguistic or cultural markers. They sustain the banal nationalism (Billig 1995) of everyday life and put economic and social questions in a Scottish frame. Institutions have been, at different times, assimilationist and differentiating, but they may not always have their intended effects. So in many parts of western Europe, including the United Kingdom, regional policy and planning mechanisms put in place in the 1960s to incorporate peripheral territories into the national economic and social space had the effect of emphasizing the territorial dimensions of policy and encouraging citizens to articulate their demands in a territorial framework (Keating 1988).

The interaction among functional change, mass attitudes, and elite strategies within institutional parameters must be understood as a historical process unfolding over time. History is important in the immediate sense that decisions taken at one time serve to change the institutional parameters for decisions in the next period (Mahoney and Rueschemeyer 2003; Pierson 2004). We must, however, be wary of nationalist teleologies, which purport to show the direction of historical evolution and its final point in the nation state. These may be British unionist, as the old Whig history of progress and union; or Scottish nationalist, as in Nairn's persistent view (1977, 2000, 2007) that Scotland, having missed the historical train of statehood in the nineteenth century, will have to catch up now. In recent years, scholars have emphasized the different forms of polity that had existed at different times and places, with the nation state as only one option among others.

There is a tendency in most countries of Europe to write history, sociology, and politics from the inside out, that is to describe and analyse the state and the nation on its own terms, rather than as part of a wider whole. Combined with the focus on ideal-types of the 'normal' nation state, this leads to a recurrent tendency to exceptionalism, by which one's own country is an outlier, not conforming to the 'normal' rules of national development. Typically, it is claimed that this or that country did not have a bourgeois revolution, or remained internally rather diverse. The United Kingdom is not immune to this tendency, although historians over recent years have made progress in relating the histories of the 'British Isles' (Pocock 1975; Kearney 1995; Davies 1999), and putting them in a European context (Scott 2000). No country's development can ever correspond to that of the ideal-types, since these are mere generalizations from the sum of individual experiences, but this does not condemn us to exceptionalism. We can still use social science theories sensitively to interpret cases, while recognizing their historical specificity. The United Kingdom may be very different from France, but its historic experience has things in common with, for example, Spain.

History is important in another sense, too often neglected by political scientists: as a field of struggle and means of interpreting and coping with the present. Historians know that their agenda is often shaped by present-day concerns, and historical arguments, for example, about the Union of 1707, are often driven by attitudes to the Union in 2008. History often resembles a lumber-room of items that can be dragged out, refurbished, and re-assembled for present purposes; and Scottish history is no exception. We have already noted one example in the tendency of some observers to assume that because the Union is weakening it can never really have existed. There are endless arguments about the old Scottish state and whether it ever successfully asserted sovereignty, as well as about Scotland's historical European vocation.

The evolution of the Union over three hundred years has itself been shaped partly by changing representations of its original purpose. Its ambiguities and silences (for example over the question of sovereignty) have provided fuel for legal and constitutional debates.

Historical accounts are also handicapped by the different forms of knowledge that we have of different periods, and by the dangers of anachronism. There were no opinion polls before the mid-twentieth century, so that mass opinion must be inferred from the indirect information available; and in any case mass opinion did not have the role it has in a modern polity. Concepts of statehood and political order in the eighteenth century are not what they were in the twentieth century, and in the present century they are changing again. So while it is justifiable to trace a Scottish polity and sense of common identity back to the Middle Ages, it is a mistake to confound this with modern nationalism or to assume that a timeless Scottish frame is available to take over whenever the British one fails. Scottish identity is, rather, reforged and re-invested with political significance in different historical epochs. What we are seeing at present is a new Scottish nation-building project, contrasted with the old Union and in competition with an attempt at rebuilding a British nation. This is taking place in circumstances far removed from the classic nation- and state-building era of the nineteenth century.

STATES, NATIONS, AND POLITIES

Modern social science has been thirled to a model of the nation state, from which it has difficulty in escaping (Keating 2008*b*, 2009*c*). This represents the state as a stable set of boundaries within which are contained a spatially bounded economy, a society united by identity and culture, a set of governing and representative institutions, and, in more recent times, a system of social protection. It is seen as a historically evolved reality, the product variously of power politics, functional integration, and international norms about the location of power. It is also presented, in political theory, as a normatively desirable form of polity. A single, shared identity provides the unified *demos* that both underpins democracy (Mill 1972) and sustains social solidarity (Miller 1995). The borders and structure of the state lock in the main social and economic actors, preventing free-riding and defections and encouraging social dialogue. Yet the term is used in two rather different senses: one referring to its external boundaries and political reach and the other to its internal composition. In much of social science, and particularly international relations, it simply denotes the sovereign state such as is (misleadingly) said to have emerged from the Peace of Westphalia in 1648 and is the building-block of the system of international relations. In its other meaning, it suggests that nation and state coincide in space. We might combine the two meanings to create a Weberian ideal-type of a state in which the boundaries of sovereignty and identity coincide perfectly. Like all ideal-types, however, such a model should not be mistaken for a description of reality.

It jars with the sociological fact that some states contain more than one group whose members see themselves as a nation.[6] Such multinational states are now widely recognized as posing particular problems and demanding specific forms of government, including federalism, power-sharing, and recognition of cultural difference. The 'Jacobin' form of democracy, with its assumption of a single *demos*, has to be abandoned in favour of a more complex and pluralist understanding of democracy, citizenship, and solidarity. Our case, however, is even more complex since it belongs in a group of countries in which the terms themselves are often contested and take on different meanings in different parts of the state. Elsewhere, I have used the term 'plurinational' to capture such situations (Keating 2001*a*). In the United Kingdom, state and nation have long been in tension, and neither has a shared meaning. The term 'nation' is applied both to the whole and to its constituent parts, while the theory of the state is less developed than in most European countries. The non-English parts have an intermediary level of political identification between the citizen and the state, while in England the state is largely identified with its largest component. Within the peripheral nations themselves, these multiple identities are felt rather differently by different parts of the population. These ambiguities may explain the success of the Union for three hundred years, yet they also explain its weakness and contain the seeds of its own transformation. The essentially asymmetrical nature of nationality sentiments also explains why conventional federal solutions are as difficult as are unitary state forms.

State and nation are historically and spatially contingent, the product of history but not determined by it. Some theories of state-building are functionalist, notably Karl Deutsch's insistence (1966) on social communication theory in the creation of communities of identity; it is these communities that create governments rather than the other way around. Charles Tilly (1975), by contrast, stressed the role of force in the creation of European states, with the extractive capacity then being used to establish more extensive forms of administration and services. Later, however, he argued that coercion was just one element, with capital (economic factors) also playing a large role in moulding different forms of state (Tilly 1990). Spruyt (1994) showed how various forms of authority, including empires, large states, small states, and city-states, were possible in particular historical epochs. In the early modern period, trading city-states were viable, able to mobilize economic resources to negotiate autonomy. Changing conditions of war, munitions, and the rise of mass armies then gave the advantage to large land-based states or to maritime empires. In the twenty-first century, the old identities among territory, society, economy, and political institutions are changing as these institutions are, at least partially, territorially unbundled to allow the creation of more novel political forms (Keating 1988, 2001a). There is now a substantial literature on the various forms of polity that have existed in history (Ferguson and Mansbach 1996). The European state system is thus historically contingent and not pre-determined, as is the nature of the state itself. So in the early twenty-first century, if the nation states falter or are transformed, there is no particular reason to believe that they will be replaced by other entities of the same nature, just at a larger (European) or smaller (such as Scottish) scale.

Nations are also historically contingent. Nation-building (not always the same thing as state-building) is not a one-off event but a work in progress, and nations can be deconstructed as well as constructed. This is not to say that they can be conjured up at will. Benedict Anderson's famous expressions (1983) about imagined communities should not be misinterpreted as 'imaginary' communities; nation is a sociological category rooted in institutions, identities, and social practices. There has been a lot of ink spilled on the question of the antiquity of nations, whether they are modern or perennial, and whether they preceded the state or were formed by it. Too often these have generalized from a specific case or group of cases, or have confused an ideal-type with the historical reality.

So there are multiple paths to both statehood and nationality. In the course of the nineteenth century, during the so-called awakening of the nations, there was an increasing tendency to see the end point of nationality claims as the creation of an independent state, but it was not until the First World War that the idea gained almost universal acceptance. Nationality movements learnt from each other and adapted to the international environment, sharing the idea of statehood as the highest political form as well as the best guarantee of security. They also had to fit into the categories recognized by the international system. As it happens, this was also the period in which the modern social sciences emerged, their language, categories, normative assumptions, and data-sets moulded by the nation state. From the late twentieth century, however, these categories have themselves been changing, under the influence of global transformation, especially within Europe. This not only points to a different future. It has also provided a reappraisal of the past, an appreciation of the historical contingency of the nation state, and a recognition of the varied institutional forms that nations may assume.

Rokkan and Urwin (1983) distinguish four types of territorial polity. The unitary state recognizes only one political community and centralizes all authority. Mechanical federalism recognizes only one political or cultural community but divides power and authority between central and regional governments, the latter based on functional or even arbitrary criteria, as in Germany; it is imposed from above by constitutional means. Organic federalism refers to a system in which power is similarly divided, but the constituent units are based on political, historical, or cultural communities with their own identities. The 'union state' is a polity that is territorially differentiated, preserving pre-union constitutional elements but not formally federal. 'Incorporation of parts of its territory has been achieved through treaty and agreement; consequently territorial integration is less than perfect. While administrative standardization prevails over most of the territory, the union structure entails the survival in some areas of variations based upon pre-union rights and infrastructures' (Rokkan and Urwin 1983: 181). The categories are, in many respects, questionable. Mechanical federalism does not have to be imposed from above. Organic federalism bears a strong resemblance to the union state category, as cases such as Canada show. Yet the notion of a union as a complex polity retaining the traces of its component parts is a powerful one, echoing British vocabulary in practice, and has been reintroduced in the debate about the United Kingdom and other plurinational polities (Mitchell 1996; Keating 2001*a*).

An earlier formulation comes from Georg Jellinek (1981), who in the late nineteenth century criticized the dominant legal doctrine that the only units of jurisdiction were states and provinces within them, arguing that there was a wide array of entities in between. There were states, each with its own territory, subjects, and government. Some were sovereign and independent. Others were non-sovereign but counted as states because, equipped with the bureaucratic infrastructure and possessing the title of kingdom, republic, or free state, they could easily continue if necessary without the parent state. An example was Bavaria. At the other extreme were protectorates, with their own territories and subjects but no governments, such as Bosnia-Herzegovina and Alsace-Lorraine. Fragments of state (*Staatsfragmente*) were territories that had only some of the attributes of states. So the Austrian Länder had their own laws and parliaments but not executive power; Iceland had its own constitution but was governed by a Danish minister; Croatia had much of the infrastructure, but lacked its own citizenship and its government was nominated by Hungary. Finland was more contentious since some people considered it a non-sovereign state, while Jellinek saw it as a fragment within the Russian Empire. Fragments of state in turn could be divided into stronger and weaker categories, of which Jellinek outlined four. In the weakest, the centre creates and changes the constitutions of units; in the next, the units have limited powers over their own constitutions; in a stronger form, the constitutions of the units can only be changed by their own laws; in the strongest, the units have full constituent power, able to change their internal constitutions at will. They may enjoy certain of the international privileges of states such as membership in the International Postal Union. Again, Jellinek's categories, which perhaps betray an excessive legal formalism in contrast to Rokkan and Urwin's behavioural approach, can be questioned; but he too is pointing to the way in which different forms of polity have existed in the past and can exist in the future, disentangling the various elements that have been brought together in the concept of the nation state. Scotland pre-devolution might, in Jellinek's terms, be seen as a fragment of state, while since 1999 as a non-sovereign state.[7]

The changed international security regime and the spread of free trade, especially in Europe, have put in question the previous identification of large consolidated nation states with security and economic welfare. This has prompted new interest in the city-states, trading nations, and open systems of the past. Catalan political leaders have refurbished their history as a self-governing trading nation nested within a loose monarchy and empire to show their aptness to play in the new European dispensation (Moreno and Martí 1977; Lobo 1997; Albareda and Gifre 1999). Basque leaders have re-emphasized their traditions of shared sovereignty and pact-ism to fashion ideas for a semi-independent status (Lagasabaster et al. 1999; Gurtubay 2001). Welsh nationalists have rediscovered conceptions of community in contrast with statehood, also rooted in ideas of shared sovereignty. The development of the European Union has posed further questions about the relationship between nationality and political authority and rekindled interest in these ideas. For some, it is just an association of states, whose sovereignty remains unabridged; for others, it is a federation in the making. An increasing number of scholars, however, argue that it cannot be understood using the terminology of statehood, whether intergovernmental or federal. It is, rather, a distinct political and legal order to be understood on its own terms. This has led to a wave of writings about European futures, and also to a search among former types of polity for ideas that might lend themselves to present questions. This is not a matter of anachronistically putting back the clock, but rather of examining historically specific experiences and learning how they might be adapted for present purposes. The European order is in one sense new, but it is only unprecedented if our precedents are confined to the era of the nation state. In its mixture of unity and diversity, domination and power-sharing, it resembles in some ways pre-modern forms of polity.

Zielonka (2006) and Colomer (2006) have recently retrieved the concept of empire as a way of capturing the emerging transnational realities. Again, it would be a mistake to confuse concepts with reality or to preach a return to mediaevalism or the Holy Roman Empire. The term 'empire' itself became discredited in the twentieth century by its association with the colonial era of European domination in Asia and Africa. In another sense, however, empire is a form of polity that is not necessarily based on domination or dictatorship. It is, rather, a complex polity in which the various parts can have a different relationship to the whole and in which citizenship is differentiated, while retaining common elements. Historians have revisited the experience of the Habsburg and even Ottoman empires as forms of polity that, while not democratic, were for much of their history more pluralistic than the west European nation state.

Similarly, monarchies have often been better at managing multinational polities than have republics, since the principle of popular sovereignty in the latter implies defining the people (or *demos*) and establishing a unity of rights and duties. Rose (1982) has identified the key role of the monarchy, symbolized by the 'mace' in unifying the United Kingdom. Reformers, from the nineteenth-century radicals to the Charter 88 movement of the late twentieth century, have deplored these pre-democratic features of the constitution and called variously for a republic, the principle of popular sovereignty, and a written constitution. Yet it is arguably the flexibility of the ancient constitution that has permitted an accommodation of different national realities in a way that has escaped Spain, where democratic regimes have struggled to reconcile popular sovereignty and equality with national diversity.

So there was political life before the consolidated nation state, and there will be political life after it. The United Kingdom is not an exception to some rule about statehood and nationality, but rather a specific example of the complexities of these concepts and their evolution over time. The next two chapters examine these specificities, and the nature of the Anglo-Scottish Union, and the way in which it is being transformed in our times. Before we consider the unravelling of the Union, we need to understand the nature and practice of unionism as a particular form of constitutionalism.

2

Understanding the Union

STATE AND UNION

On 1 May 1807, the centenary of the Anglo-Scottish Treaty of Union was celebrated, in the midst of war, with a grand ball in Edinburgh, the hall festooned with elegant transparencies depicting St. George, St. Andrew and St. Patrick, and a band of pipers playing *Rule Britannia, Hearts of Oak, Britons Strike Home* and *God Save the King* (*Scotsman*, 1 May 1907). Britishness, in the midst of the long struggle with Napoleonic France, was at a high point. A hundred years later, there was more circumspection. A proposal that the Convention of Royal Burghs should organize a celebration was opposed by some on the grounds that Scottish interests had lately been neglected, but was carried by a large majority who argued that the Union, far from erasing Scottish nationality, had been the means of preserving it (*Times*, 31 January 1907). As the day approached, the Lord Provost of Edinburgh declared that 'the two hundred years which have elapsed since the Union have witnessed changes almost fabulous in the social, economic and political condition of Scotland. Not even the bitterest opponent of Union would desire a return to the old conditions' (*Scotsman*, 3 April 1907). In 2007, on the eve of elections that were to return a nationalist government to the restored Scottish Parliament, the anniversary passed almost unnoticed. Nationalists saw little to celebrate, while unionists seemed to lack a message. Neither the triumphant Britishness of 1807 nor the more nuanced argument of 1907 seemed appropriate in the new conditions.

The argument that follows is that a British nation was built following the Union, alongside a British state, but that the process was a long one and was incomplete compared with integrated European nations like France, although not with cases like Spain or Belgium. Contradictory visions of state and nation have coexisted but have usually been managed by incremental adjustment or a renegotiation of its terms in alternate phases of assimilation and of differentiation, without elaborating a clear doctrine or consistent institutional design. This is partly a matter of timing. As Bulpitt (1983) remarked, the British union came too late for the 'Celtic' territories to be able to regard themselves as natural and inevitable associates of England but too early for the processes of social and political assimilation that might have created a unitary state, too early for federal ideas to have been available, and too early for an ideology of bourgeois nationalism. Key elements in the Union have been functional integration; the preservation of the old English constitution, explaining the tendency in English thought to deny a rupture in 1707 and to think of the state as unitary; an accommodation of Scotland within the unitary state, helped by the informal nature of the constitution; a limited amount of socialization and nation-building, which have waxed and waned over time; the periodic reconstruction of a Scottish nation as a rival or as a part of British identity; practices of territorial management; and a balance of economic advantage, which sustained instrumental support. These have been underpinned by a unionist ideology, which differs from its continental counterparts in accepting the plurinational nature of the polity, sustaining a sense of Scottish distinctiveness while channelling it to the institutions of the central state.

It is not my intention here to rehearse the history of the Union and its making, a matter argued over for many years in the usual cycle of interpretation and revisionist re-interpretation (Ferguson 1977; Riley 1978; Scott 1992; Fry 2006; Whatley 2006; Macinnes 2007). These debates, however, have moulded political arguments about Scotland's place in the United Kingdom down to the present. Unionists and nationalists make recurrent appeals to the true meaning of Union, whether as annexation by England; a corrupt bargain by treacherous Scottish elites (Burns' parcel of rogues); the creation of a common British ideal; or a union of equals. Formally it took the form of a treaty between the parliaments of England and Scotland, although there was a great deal of coercion involved and it was hardly a voluntary compact between equals; while there were no opinion polls in the eighteenth century, observers are agreed about the hostility of the population. Yet the form of the Union is critical to its subsequent understanding since it underpins the Scottish doctrine that it can always be renegotiated. It formally abolished both parliaments, but in practice left the English one intact, with the addition of Scottish members and peers. In what was described as an incorporating (but not assimilating) union, most Scottish institutions were maintained, including the Church, local government and the legal system. Existing provisions for the monarchy and religion were affirmed. This was nothing like a modern constitution. There was no reference to sovereignty. A vague clause indicated that matters of 'public right' could be handled by the central Parliament but matters of 'private right' could be resolved only 'for the evident utility of the subjects within Scotland'; yet pleas for a federal union, which could have given this institutional form, were rejected. The result was a constitution that could be interpreted in two ways. For the English, it was a mere expansion of the existing state and constitution, as shown by their continuing use of the words 'England' and 'English' with reference to it. For Scots, it was a union of nations, which some saw as the core of a new British nation, while others saw in it a protection of their own national status in a dangerous world.

The settlement of 1707 may look untidy to modern eyes, but it was very much of its time. The integrated nation state did not yet exist and large parts of Europe were under imperial regimes, which typically consisted of patch-works of territories each with a different relationship to the centre. Spain was a monarchy but neither a nation nor a state (Artola 1999), although in 1714 Catalonia and the other territories of the Aragonese crown lost their self-governing status. Even France was a complex of jurisdictions, privileges, and exceptions which, despite the centralizing efforts of the monarchy, lasted until the Revolution (Braudel 1986). Germany and Italy were not unified until the last third of the nineteenth century.

Yet, while avoiding the perils of exceptionalism, it is necessary to recognize a distinctive path for nation- and state-building in the United Kingdom. In some European cases, the nation came before the state and gave rise to it, usually in the nineteenth century. In others, the state came first and forged the nation within it over a long period, this being the usual explanation for France. More generally, in western Europe at least, nation and state were constructed together, with the one sustaining the other. Territories were integrated institutionally, the state penetrated society, cultures and languages were unified, and national identity forged (Deutsch 1966). After the French Revolution, the doctrine of popular sovereignty reinforced both the nation (since this defined who the people were) and the state (as the vehicle of this sovereignty). The nation state thus came to represent the coincidence within the same territorial boundaries of identity, a shared culture, a polity, a system of representation, an economy and a civil society. This in turn provided the framework of democracy based on trust and shared values, and later for social solidarity and the welfare state.

Oddly, the comparative literature on state- and nation-building consistently brackets England/Britain with France as one of the first nation states, con-trasting these with the latecomers like Italy and Germany or the uncompleted nation states like Spain or Belgium. Stein Rokkan (1980), in his conceptual map of Europe, identifies the Atlantic periphery as the first part of Europe to engage in state-building and sees England as one of the earliest examples. Yet, while correctly noting that England never really assimilated the peripheral territories of Ireland, Scotland, and Wales, he goes on to include the United Kingdom as a unitary state formed in the Middle Ages (Rokkan 1980: 170). Anthony Smith (1999), who sees nations as based on 'ethnic cores', identifies one such in southern England, subsequently embracing the rest of Britain. Liah Greenfeld (1992) sees England as the first nation in modernity and, although she is careful not to confuse it with Britain, does suggest that it became and remained a state. The problem with these approaches is that they try to explain two very different things – the forging of England, and the United Kingdom – with the same theoretical apparatus. This is not merely inconsistent but contradictory, since if a strong and unitary English nation was forged in mediaeval or early modern times, this should militate against its absorption in a multinational state. A similar cognitive dissonance seems to affect English-domiciled Europeans (like Blondel and Finer, each cited in Chapter 1), who try to reconcile their vision of the United Kingdom as a homogeneous unitary state with their knowledge that there are nations beyond England. Ralf Dahrendorf (1982), in his lectures *On Britain,* managed a brief reference to the non-English parts and to devolution but insisted that Britain had managed to avoid a 'national question'.[1]

Scottish historians (and some non-Scots) who have examined the Union, on the other hand, are agreed that it did not immediately create Britons out of English and Scots. There is less agreement on what happened subsequently. Until the 1960s, scholars tended to argue, explicitly or implicitly, that a British nation was forged. For others, especially those writing in the light of developments in recent decades, nation-building never took place, and the Union remained a marriage of convenience, of purely instrumental value, variously for the Scots or for the English (Haseler 1996).[2] Since the 1990s the debate has been dominated by Linda Colley's work (1992), arguing that during the eighteenth and early nineteenth centuries a sense of common Britishness was forged from common Protestantism and war with France. The disappearance of these factors in turn explains the loosening of the tie (Weight 2002). Critics have questioned the analysis, noting that Protestantism was divisive within the British Isles (Aughey 2001), while war with the neighbours has been the common European experience since the end of the Roman Empire. More crucially, Colley's explanation for the demise of Britishness is underdetermined, since national identities are, by most accounts, self-sustaining, surviving the conditions in which they were created. Both Spanish and French identities were forged by Catholicism but are resilient in the face of secularization. Colley's argument also seems to assume that, if Britishness weakens, the default identities of England and Scotland will reassert themselves automatically. Yet this undermines the original argument about integration by suggesting that the mechanism is less one of socialization ('forging the nation') than of instrumental advantage. We need at least to know why Scottish national identity should have survived and flourished within the Union.

FUNCTIONAL INTEGRATION

A long tradition of modernization theory argued that nation states were forged by a process of functional integration, with the creation of national markets, the spread of common language and values and the displacement of territory by function as the main principle of social differentiation. There is a lot of evidence that this did occur in Britain. Industrialization and urbanization had a similar impact across England, Wales, and Scotland, creating one of the first recognizably modern societies. McCrone (2001*b*) has shown that by the mid-nineteenth century Scotland had an industrial and occupational structure close to the British median, a position that it has retained ever since. Social class became the defining feature of social relations, taking similar forms in the three nations of Great Britain. Scotland and England were linked by communications from the railway age (Birch 1977), and there was free movement of population, although this mostly took the form of Scots moving to London rather than the other way around. Efforts to explain the survival of Scotland as a nation by its structure of production or class system thus do not work well. Dickson et al. (1980), like some other authors, claim that Scotland's industrial structure from the late nineteenth century was dominated by heavy industry, but this is to generalize from the experience of the west-central region. Hechter's notion (1975) that it was an internal colony of the British state, assigned a subordinate position in the division of labour, has been widely discredited (Page 1978). His later revision, that Scotland was an over-developed periphery, trying to save the theory by reversing its meaning, was no more successful (McCrone 2001*b*).

Linguistic assimilation was already well under way before the Union of 1707. The Scottish crown had not looked with favour on Gaelic, which had already retreated to the Highlands and Islands. Scots, the language of Court and law, was undermined by the removal of the Court to London in 1603 and the failure to produce a Scots Bible until 1983. It survived as a series of local dialects, of poetry and some prose but was never standardized in the way Catalan was, for example, and did not provide the basis for a vernacular education. This was to have important effects on the development of Scottish national consciousness and, later, on nationalism, weakening its cultural underpinnings but broadening its potential appeal. Language remains a differentiating factor in the weaker form of accent as Scotland, unlike most of England, retains a full range of vernacular accents across the class spectrum; but this is not the subject of political mobilization the way language is in other small nations.

Changes in relative populations helped homogeneity, as England's population increased ninefold between 1701 and 2001 while Scotland's increased just fivefold and stabilized from the mid-twentieth century (Lee 2005). England's population went from five times that of Scotland in 1707 to ten times in 2001. Its share of the UK population was consistently dominant, at 82 per cent in 1707, 80 per cent after the Irish Union of 1800, and 86 per cent in 2001. This English predominance shaped the workings of the polity as well as both internal and external perceptions of the Union as a greater England. Yet functional integration did not obliterate a Scottish sense of identity. Rather, nation, class, and sector interacted as principles of political mobilization, mediating each other's effects. Scottishness remained as a resource to be used by political actors at critical times and was recreated by institutions and practices within the Union that sustained a distinct Scottish arena and ensured that politics would continue to have a Scottish dimension.

BUILDING THE POLITY

It has often been noted that Britain lacks a coherent concept of the state such as found in continental European countries (Dyson 1980). This is not to say that the state does not exist or act; rather that it is poorly theorized and not seen as something above and distinct from society. Indeed, British and Americans tend to prefer talking about 'government' except in certain specific contexts. In Britain, this has allowed a certain ambivalence about the relation between state and nation and some very loose usages of the concept of the nation state. In France, by contrast, the nation and state are regarded as strictly co-extensive, while in plurinational Spain the fact that they are not has caused endless anguish and conflict. There is a more substantive implication as well, since in Britain the scope of government has historically been less extensive than elsewhere, leaving many matters of regulation and organization to civil society or the common law. Under the Union these could be differentiated territorially, allowing Scottish professions, the universities or sporting bodies to manage their own affairs. Religion was not separated from the state, but Scotland kept its own church, whose relation to the state was different from that of its English counterpart. There was no large standing army and no compulsory military service before the First World War. Unlike other European countries, Britain never established a large centralized bureaucracy or field administration, so that management of public affairs was in the hands of local elites. In Scotland this took the form of boards, gradually giving way from the late nineteenth century to elected local governments and a professional public service. Jim Bulpitt (1983) described the resulting regime as a 'dual polity', in which the centre occupied itself with high politics of foreign affairs and finance, while management of the localities and nations was entrusted to local collaborators. Lindsay Paterson (1994) sees an effective autonomy for Scotland compared with other European peripheries and localities, despite the lack of federal self-government.

This system of informal government was challenged at times of state expansion, as government increased its tasks and engaged in purposive modernization. From the 1870s the enlargement of government encountered local opposition, notably over control of education, resolved by the establishment of the Scotch (later Scottish) Education Department in 1870. In 1885, a Secretary (of State) for Scotland was appointed and gradually took over domestic administration for Scotland, representing the central government in Scotland and Scotland in the central government. In the early twentieth century and again after the Second World War, the state advanced, government increased its penetration of society and the relationship between Scottish society and British government was again strained. Such central-peripheral clashes (which occurred also in other European countries) were resolved sometimes by more centralization and assimilation but more often by a readjustment of the Union and administrative decentralization. In this way, the periphery was accommodated without federalizing the state or affecting the central constitution. Territorial politics were kept out of Westminster except for the period between the 1870s and the First World War, when the Irish Party held a substantial block of seats, which they used to constrain minority Liberal governments and, from time to time, to obstruct parliamentary business in pursuit of land reform and home rule. The example of the Irish Party was not taken up in Scotland and Wales, despite some moves to do so (Morgan 1980).

Democratization, with the steady extension of the vote, gradually created a common citizenship. In 1884, the franchise rules were standardized across the United Kingdom. This did not mean that votes had the same weight throughout the state. Scotland's share of parliamentary seats was lower than its population share until 1885 but thereafter it rose as relative population declined. For most of the twentieth century, Scotland was over-represented in Parliament (McLean 1995; Rossiter et al. 1997) and, when the task of drawing electoral boundaries was entrusted to an independent commission in 1948, separate commissions were set up for the constituent nations. The Scottish Commission long operated with a minimum of 71 seats but, curiously, was allowed to create more (it created an additional one in 1983). So a formally equal franchise allowed for a continued element of territorial differentiation and representation.

EMPIRE AND MONARCHY

State-building in the United Kingdom was intrinsically bound up with the making of Empire. Scotland, having failed in its own efforts with the Darien scheme, was invited into the English Empire in 1707 and, after the loss of the American colonies, Scots were prominent in the 'second Empire' in Asia and Africa. Curiously, the role of Scotland in the Empire was neglected in national narratives during the second half of the twentieth century, the high point of British national consciousness. Devine (2008*b*) notes that between 1937 and 2001 no major study of Scotland's role in the imperial project was published. Perhaps Scots of a more nationalistic and/or left-wing bent chose not to dwell on imperialism, preferring more progressive narratives of Britishness. A few, it is true, presented Scotland as a colonial victim of England. This theme was most prominent during the heyday of anti-colonial liberation movements in the 1950s and 1960s and echoes ideas found in other stateless nations of Europe, including Brittany and Languedoc (Lafont 1967), Galicia, Catalonia, the Basque Country (de Pablo and Mees 2005) and Ireland (Howe 2000). Hechter's endorsement (1975) of the idea has already been mentioned, while Haseler (1996) comes close, seeing the United Kingdom as effectively a greater England.[3] Such analyses, however, did not survive decolonization and the emergence of a Third World to which the peripheral parts of European states manifestly did not belong. Since devolution, the theme of Empire has returned in a series of works showing how, far from being colonized, Scots made a disproportionate contribution to the Empire – although differing in interpretation, from Fry's emphasis (2001) on peaceful commerce to Devine's documentation (2003) of Scots complicity in the less savoury aspects of imperialism.

The influence of Empire on British history of the nineteenth and twentieth centuries is so vast that it is easy to attribute almost anything to its rise and fall. It is important, therefore, to be careful about tracing its effects and to avoid the temptations of exceptionalism. France, Spain, the Netherlands and Belgium also had overseas empires; their experience sometimes paralleled, and sometimes differed from, the British. The construction of Empire diverted attention from the construction of a British state and nation in a way that was echoed in Spain but not in France, which managed through the nineteenth century to forge a unitary nation and later even tried to apply the same principles (with an almost complete lack of success) through its empire. The United Kingdom assembled its empire in a piecemeal fashion, often preferring indirect rule through local elites as it had often done at home.

Constitutional practice was *ad hoc* and it was never clear, especially in the case of Ireland, where the Empire ended and the metropolitan homeland began.[4] As the settler dominions gained self-government from 1867 onwards, they emerged as neither part of the state nor really foreign. Their constitutional status was not resolved until the Statute of Westminster in 1931, and even then there were continual arguments, often started by the Irish Free State pushing the boundaries of its 1922 settlement. During the early twentieth century, ideas of imperial federation became fashionable, confined though they were to the white dominions (and possibly India in some distant future). This provided a framework both for unionists, for whom Britain would remain the mother country, and for Scottish home rulers, who could envisage Scotland as an autonomous member of such a federation. Even after the idea of imperial federation had disappeared, some Scottish nationalists saw the Empire as an external support system for a self-governing nation, much in the way Europe is used in this century (Finlay 1992).

Empire may also have provided the salient common identity for Britons in the late nineteenth century although, in the absence of survey data, we really do not know. The cult of imperialism was common throughout the United Kingdom and seems to have had strong appeal in Scotland. The Empire was one institution that was universally described as British, even by normally insensitive English commentators. It was associated with monarchy, the military, civic ceremonial and patriotic fervour, and a cult of superiority and honour, elements normally linked to emerging national identities and which reached a peak around the Boer War. The monarchy was both domestic and imperial and represented commonality and sovereignty to such an extent that it became the sticking point in the Anglo-Irish negotiations of 1921–2 and the cause of the Irish Civil War. Yet beneath this, as in empires generally, there was scope for diversity and multiple identities. Indeed, the monarchy is perhaps the most ingenious of the unionist devices, serving symbolically and constitutionally to unite the United Kingdom while recognizing its diversity. The Royal Family, at least from Queen Victoria onwards, has taken care to cultivate its Scottishness, even if couched in the increasingly antiquated accents of the old ruling class. The annual sojourn to Balmoral has become obligatory, and Prime Ministers are expected to wait attendance there. The monarch even manages the challenge of apparently changing religion on crossing the border, attending services in the Church of Scotland, although doubtless taking a permissive Anglican view on the need for doctrinal conformity.

Citizenship in the British Empire was a muddle and its legacies are still with us in the differentiated rights of British passport-holders (Heater 2006). It could not be tied to a territorially-delimited state and, until the second half of the twentieth century, British governments saw no need to restrict free movement and settlement; indeed this would have damaged the imperial ideal itself. This had domestic repercussions since, although citizenship rights were identical throughout the United Kingdom from the nineteenth century, they were not based on strong notions of a common *demos*. Popular sovereignty could not work in an empire where some peoples were manifestly privileged over others,[5] but the issue could be fudged with the old formula of Monarch-in-Parliament. All of this militated against the creation of a homogeneous British nation state.

Empire also shaped the political economy of union, at least from the mid-eighteenth century. Scotland became part of a global free trading area, in which it was to find a lucrative niche, at least until the First World War (see following text). Its economy adapted to imperial markets and, especially on the west coast, was able to make the transition from the tobacco trade, to cotton, to engineering and shipbuilding, in response to changing imperial and global conditions. Empire further provided an outlet for qualified and upwardly mobile young people who, in other multinational polities, provided an excluded and frustrated nucleus for nationalist and revolutionary agitation.

FORGING THE NATION

Nineteenth- and twentieth-century nation-builders set great store on symbols, including flags, anthems, and celebrations. While in other states these have striven to project a unitary identity, in Britain they have also celebrated diversity; the Union flag itself was a combination of the emblems of the constituent nations. Monarchs have usually sought to present themselves as both English and Scottish, although annoyance was regularly caused by the habit of numbering them in succession to English monarchs only, notably in 1903 and 1953 (Finlay 1997). The army is one of the few institutions invariably referred to as British, even in England; but unionists are among the most fervent defenders of the distinct Scottish regiments.

There were recurrent efforts at assimilation. During the eighteenth century, the term 'North Britain' was coined while some intellectuals (including famously David Hume) sought to disguise their Scottish accents. Yet while some Scots were still giving their address as North Britain in the 1890s,[6] the English never adopted the term 'Briton' (let alone 'South Britain') and continued to use the term 'England' for the whole. By the late nineteenth century, rising Scottish consciousness had made this less politically acceptable. Prime Minister Lord Salisbury was regularly criticized for using 'England' for 'Great

Britain' (Finlay 1997), and during the First World War such reminders became common (Weight 2002); but it was not until the 1960s that political leaders learned to avoid the offence.[7] The result was that Scots developed a dual identity as Scots and British, while the English largely confounded the two. As Bryce (1887) wrote, 'An Englishman has but one patriotism because England and the United Kingdom are to him practically the same thing.' English insensitivity to terminology continues to this day but, while it can be infuriating to Scots, it gives us one key to understanding the Union. For English people some of the time, Britain is greater England and there is no tension between the two. At other times, Scotland is a dispensable part of the apparatus, whose secession would leave the essence of the state untouched. Only on rare occasions are they called on to resolve the contradiction. For Scots, on the other hand, Britain allows a dual identity, protecting their own national identity but giving the benefits of a larger polity. That this is a radically different interpretation from that in England has been a problem only at times of political tension.

It would be a mistake to think that Britishness was no more than imperialism and thus bound to disappear with the Empire. Mass warfare in the twentieth century had mobilizing effects as it did in other European states. Military conscription enlisted a large part of the male population, while women were drawn in large numbers into war-related occupations. Patriotism was exalted during the First World War, although the reference point was often still the Empire. By the Second World War, the homeland was the focus of loyalty, and patriotism was reinforced by the idea that the fight was in a just cause. Conscious efforts were made by government and the BBC to portray the nation as 'Britain' and avoid using 'England' as a synonym (Nicholas 1998; Webster 2005), although Haggith (1998) argues that propaganda films confined their images to the English countryside. Afterwards, memorials for the wars sprang up in towns and villages across the country, and annual ceremonies commemorated the dead. The post-war Labour Government drew on these wells of patriotism and collectivism in the Festival of Britain, the welfare state and the nationalization of industry (where nation clearly refers to Britain).

Education was less prominent as a nation-building device than in other European countries. There has never been a British ministry of education, the English and Scottish systems have maintained their autonomy and there was until the late twentieth century considerable autonomy at the local and school levels. A critical moment came in the early 1870s, on the eve of universal education, when a proposal for a British education act was defeated and a separate Scottish one introduced. So the landmark Butler Act of 1944, building a new and avowedly more democratic education system on the basis of the popular mobilization during the war, applied only to England, with Scotland going its own way. Patriotism did inform the teaching programme, but as education expanded from the late nineteenth century this was focused on the broader imperial identity. As late as the 1950s, classrooms displayed maps with large portions of the globe coloured in pink, and Empire (later Commonwealth) Day was the main occasion for patriotic display. Only in the late twentieth century did the issue of education as a means of promoting a distinct, non-imperial citizenship and national identity emerge, and that mainly in England (see Chapter 3).

The mass media reflect the same balance of assimilation and distinctiveness. Scotland has always had its own quality newspapers but firmly committed in the nineteenth century to Union and Empire. Within this allegiance, they sustained a certain cultural Scottishness and attention to Scottish issues and managed to limit the appeal of London papers. The popular press followed suit, presenting a couthy and stereotypical Scottishness to match a unionist political message (the extreme example being the *Sunday Post*). At other times they have been opportunistic, playing the Scottish card when it was profitable. In the twentieth century, the BBC was consciously founded as a British institution committed, under its Scottish founding Director General John Reith, to the Union and to enlightening the public. It made the transition from Empire to nation more easily than some other institutions. Commercial television from the 1950s was regionalized (Scotland was covered by two regions and part of a third) but its news content was provided from a common source, supplemented with specialized local bulletins.

A conventional view of British politics (and the subject of innumerable undergraduate examination questions) was Peter Pulzer's aphorism about class being the only thing that mattered in electoral politics, a view that Pulzer (1972) himself qualified heavily in the second edition of his book. In fact the relationship between class and electoral choice was always strongly mediated by offerings of the political parties and the institutional context of elections, and the territorial construction of political issues and cleavages.

In Scotland, the early labour movement emerged locally, imbued with a Scottish cultural identity, and was drawn to nationalist politics, especially around the First World War (Keating and Bleiman 1979). After the war, however, the Scottish Labour leadership threw in its lot with its English counterparts, recognizing the weakness of the Scottish economy, the dependence on British markets and, in times of recession, the British state. Scottish trade unions merged with English ones and the movement as a whole sought to become an interlocutor with the centre, in alliance with a Labour Party that had also committed itself to the British connection. There was rural unrest in the Highlands but, given the small size of the population, this did not, as in

Ireland, underpin an independent politics.[8] We know less about how far the mass of working class people were socialized into a common British identity in the industrial era. The labour movement retained an undertow of Scottishness, taking the form of arguing for specific Scottish arrangements within the union state, attention to Scottish needs and, periodically, calls for Scottish home rule.

The upper classes of the United Kingdom also managed to sustain local and wider identities. Scottish aristocrats after the Union took to sending their sons to English public schools or to schools founded in Scotland on the same model, where they learnt English accents and manners. For Haseler (1996) and Clark (1995) this represents Anglicization, while Colley (1992) sees it as evidence of Britishness; she even insists that their tendency to talk of 'England' reflected a habit of using the term for the whole island. In fact, they seem to have managed to Anglicize their manner and way of thinking to fit into the dominant mores of the ruling class, while not alienating themselves from their own people to the extent that happened in Ireland and Wales, where there was a marked religious difference. They thus remained, well into the twentieth century, an integrating factor in the Union. From the 1950s, they were even strengthening their presence within the Conservative Party (Keating 1975), although social and economic changes, together with the decline of deference, were undermining their position in the wider society.

The commercial and industrial bourgeoisie were more Scottish in manner and accent until the twentieth century, when they, like other non-metropolitan bourgeoisies, sought to enter the landed classes and sent their children to public schools. Their role in sustaining a Scottishness consistent with a wider British identity and in promoting a particular concept of union has been highlighted by Morton (1999) and McCrone (2001*a*). This was a case of material self-interest finding its ideological expression in a balance between assimilation and particularism. A similar dilemma confronted other non-central bourgeoisies in Europe, notably in Catalonia, where a dynamic indigenous business class was torn between a Spanish state, which they needed but which could not accommodate them, and a Catalan nationalism that promised them autonomy but at the risk of losing Spanish markets; during the Civil War, they were torn both ways. It was resolved in Scotland largely by the decline of the indigenous bourgeoisie as industrial firms closed or were taken over by English and foreign enterprises after the First World War; after the Second World War the industrialist class almost disappeared with nationalization and the decline of the heavy industries (Scott and Hughes 1980; Harvie 1995; McCrone 2001*b*).

The development of party politics was at one time thought to follow the same homogenizing trajectory as class integration. A duopoly between

Tories/Conservatives and Whigs/Liberals gave way smoothly to a Conservative vs. Labour one without changing the basic rules of the game. Nineteenth-century Scotland was a bastion of Liberalism, but during the twentieth the differences seemed to shrink steadily and what remained might be attributed to nothing more than the differential distribution of social classes. A convergence in voting behaviour, however, is not necessarily evidence of convergence in political attitudes. It might equally be that the parties had learnt to make differential appeals in different parts of Britain, in order to build the parliamentary majorities needed for governing.

Scottish Conservatism was indeed a different animal from its English counterpart, growing in the twentieth century by absorption of the Liberal Unionists and even preferring the Unionist[9] name until 1965, while presenting candidates under various labels (Conservative, Liberal Unionist, National Liberal or even Conservative and Liberal). It retained two traditions: an urban one rooted in the industrial and commercial middle classes and working class Protestants; and a rural one based on the landed classes and social deference. This coalition was firmly in favour of the Anglo-Scottish Union and remained a powerful force in Scottish politics until the 1960s (Fry 1987; Mitchell 1990). Labour across the United Kingdom drew on the working class but tapped the Scottish Catholic working class vote only after the Irish settlement of 1922; it then made big inroads into the Irish Catholic middle class during the heightened sectarianism of the 1930s. Up to the late twentieth century, it could use the rhetoric of class solidarity against nationalist competition within Scotland, while also purveying a strong Britishness in relation to the rest of the world. Both parties incorporated a Scottish appeal, especially from the mid-twentieth century, promising to bring more largesse from London in return for political support. Parties, then, both served distinct Scottish interests and helped to integrate these into the wider British politics, combining their broad class and ideological appeals with a recognition of a distinct political market in Scotland – more distinct in some periods than in others.

The twentieth century brought an additional integrative factor in the welfare state, based on common British identity and social solidarity. Writing under the post-war Labour Government, T.H. Marshall (1992) saw this as a third phase of rights following the conquest of legal and political rights. The resulting 'social citizenship' helped national integration by including the working class in the political nation and reconciling it to the capitalist system. The term 'national' was freely used for initiatives like the health service and social insurance, with the clear meaning of British. Curiously, Marshall ignored the multinational nature of the British state, reasoning as though England and Britain were the same and constituted a unitary and homogeneous nation. Labour politicians and trade union leaders sometimes suggested that social solidarity was founded upon class and rhetorically attacked nationalism as dividing the working class or as a form of false consciousness. The fact that only in sections of the left was this extended to a genuine cosmopolitanism that would give the workers of the world the same rights, however, exposed the British national assumptions on which the mainstream was working. As we shall see, these assumptions have themselves now been challenged as social solidarity has become attached also to Scottish national identity (McEwen 2006; Keating 2009*a*).

THE ECONOMICS OF UNION

Economics was not the determining factor in the Union of 1707 and, in so far as the Scottish interests were concerned, the stakes were defensive, to stave off English retaliation and exclusion from markets rather than to enjoy new opportunities. In the early years, Scotland appears to have done rather badly from Union, but after 1760 there was an economic take-off (Devine 2005) and during the nineteenth century Scotland's commerce and industry gained greatly from access to imperial markets and the British free trade regime. By the end of the century, Clydeside was the world's industrial powerhouse, geared to exports of heavy goods (Campbell 1980), and the Union was being defended as an economic godsend.

It is difficult to calculate exactly how well Scotland has done in the longer run, since until the 1960s the data were difficult to assemble and numerous estimates and assumptions had to be made. Producing a time series is even more tricky, since the successive measures of performance, including National Income, Gross Domestic Product (GDP) and Gross Value Added (GVA), are not exactly equivalent. While these differences create problems for comparison over time, however, they do not prevent us from making comparisons at any one point in time. Since there is no reason to think that the successive measures systematically distort the Scotland/England comparison, we can then see the relative productive output of Scotland and the rest of the United Kingdom since the beginning of the twentieth century. Some of the earliest calculations are reported in Crammond (1912), based admittedly on approximations. These show Scotland in a rather consistent balance, with its population, income, and share of common expenditure all around 10 per cent. Lee (2005) shows Scottish earnings at between 10 and 25 per cent below those of England and Wales (Ireland being lower again), perhaps because of the larger share of rents in Scottish national income.[10] Indeed there were suggestions already that Scotland remained competitive only by maintaining low wages, a strategy that was under challenge with the rise of UK-wide pay bargaining (Campbell 1980). Calculating the fiscal balance is also difficult. Mackinnon (1907) complained that Scotland contributed a disproportionate share of UK taxes, but this seems to be a complaint about the low share from Ireland rather than from England. Separating out 'domestic' from 'imperial' expenditure,[11] Crammond (1912) calculated that Scotland in 1899–1900 was contributing some 10.84 per cent of the latter, for a population of 10.7 per cent, suggesting an almost perfect balance. By 1909–10, however, Scotland moved into deficit, contributing only 9.67 per cent to imperial expenditure. The main factors here appear to be a downturn in the Scottish economy, together with the increase in expenditure on education and the Lloyd George pension scheme, the first suggestion that Scotland could not meet the demands of the developing welfare state out of its own resources. Its deficit, on the other hand, paled beside that of Ireland.

Calculations from the 1920s made by Campbell (1954, 1955) still rely on approximations. During the First World War, Scotland did quite well and in its aftermath had a national income over 95 per cent of the UK average, despite the recession of 1921. From the late 1920s, however, it entered a serious slump; indeed, signs of falling competitiveness had been present as early as 1914 amid the triumphalism of Scottish industrialists (Campbell 1980). During the 1930s there was continued stagnation even while recovery occurred over much of England, and a drift south of jobs and investment. Scottish income *per capita* fell to 87 per cent of the UK average (Campbell 1954, 1955). Locally-owned industry closed down or sold out, and the Scottish industrial economy became more dependent on English and foreign capital and on British industrial policy, fiscal subsidies and protectionism. Lee (1995) suggests that Scotland's contribution to income tax receipts, which had overtaken the UK average during the boom of 1919–22, had slumped to 60 per cent of the *per capita* average by 1926. There was another spurt of Scottish growth during and after the Second World War, but then Scotland's relative position drifted downwards until the mid-1960s (Figure 2.1).

This was not due to a functional or sectoral differentiation of the Scottish economy. In fact, Scottish industrial structure has since the nineteenth century been close to the British mean (McCrone 2001*b*). Rather, within most sectors it had more low-productivity specialities and firms. Although the differential between Scotland and England was rather small by international standards, it transformed the politics of the Union for decades and shifted the focus of attention towards action at the centre and integration into a broader British system of social protection. From the early 1960s, government intervened with an elaborate range of regional policy measures designed to link Scotland back into the growing sectors of the British economy (see following text).

Figure 2.1 Scottish GDP as percentage of United Kingdom, 1924–2006

Sources: Lythe and Majmudar (1982) GDP factor cost, 1954–79. Office of National Statistics, GVA 1996–2004. McCrone (1965, 1969). *Regional Trends*, various years. *Abstract of Regional Statistics*, various years.

This active engagement of the state in economic management did improve economic performance (McCrone 1965, 1969) and tied Scotland more tightly into Union while recognizing its special problems. Yet while unionism was thus strengthened its promise was transformed, from offering access to expanding markets, to being a source of aid for a dependent and insufficient territorial economy.

It is sometimes assumed that falling support for the Union in Scotland is the result of economic hardship (for example Weight 2002). The historical evidence, however, shows that when Scotland is doing relatively well, ideas of nationalism or home rule thrive, while when it is doing badly Scots tend to cleave to the Union. The slump of 1921–2 killed off the lively home rule movement that had flourished around the First World War and convinced the labour movement that safety lay in the UK connection (Keating and Bleiman 1979). Unionism dominated Scottish politics during the 1930s, the foundation of the Scottish National Party and the activities of a few colourful nationalists merely highlighting lack of interest within the political mainstream. A spurt of home rule feeling after the Second World War petered out in the harder times of the 1950s, and nationalism did not revive until the late 1960s and early 1970s when the Scottish economy was doing relatively well. It died off again in the recession of the 1980s only to revive in the following decade. This is not really so surprising. In so far as support for the Union is instrumental and based on calculation of advantage, then we would expect it to fall when Scots feel more confident of their ability to go it alone. In lean times Scotland reverts to the politics of dependency and territorial management – although this may not be true in future.

MANAGING THE UNION

The Anglo-Scottish Union is a complex set of institutions and practices, to be understood through the lens of British informal and unwritten constitutionalism. There has been state-building and nation-building, but it is limited and partial. While this is true of many multinational states, the British case is unusual in having developed a doctrine and practice of unionism that recognizes both national diversity and political unity. Straddling these two principles has not been easy, and the Union has experienced phases of integration and of differentiation, of acceptance and of challenge. In the early years, it was deeply unpopular in Scotland and, while it is true that the lives of most Scots were not immediately changed, there was resentment over violations of the Treaty such as the restoration of lay patronage in the Church and the abolition of heritable jurisdictions. Jacobite rebellions in 1715 and 1745 challenged the Union[12] although they may also have rallied much of Presbyterian Scotland to it. By the end of the eighteenth century, support for union appears to have consolidated and among the intellectual ferment of the Scottish Enlightenment there was no questioning of its beneficent effects.

Thereafter, periods of integration and assimilation alternated with phases of differentiation. Expansion of the state in the late nineteenth century and dissatisfaction with Scottish administration, land agitation in the Highlands, and the aspirations of the early labour movement led to a reassertion of Scottish demands including more consideration for Scotland and, in some cases, a renegotiation of the Union. Home rule was not achieved, but administrative assimilation was halted and Scottish identity reasserted. From the 1960s, the Union came under further challenge from a revived nationalist movement and changes in the external environment and internal workings of the British state.

British government territorial management was a notable failure in Ireland and, so far, largely successful in Scotland. One reason for the contrast is the reliance in Scotland on local collaborators, with credibility within the society but reliably loyal to the Union. In the early years, Scotland was run by a Secretary of State, but the office was abolished following the 1745 rebellion. Thereafter, Scotland was governed by a manager who, in return for delivering parliamentary votes to the government in power, had a free hand in the distribution of patronage and the supervision of the administrative boards. The fall of the most celebrated manager, Henry Dundas, in 1828 produced a vacuum in Scottish administration, provoking increasing criticism from local government and business. After the threat to Scotland's own education system was fought off in the early 1870s, the Scotch (later Scottish) Education Department was established and in 1885 a Scottish Office and Secretary for Scotland took over general supervision of Scottish affairs. Expanding its role over the ensuing century, the Scottish Office became responsible for most domestic policy in Scotland with the notable exceptions of taxation and social security (Mitchell 2003). The Secretary of State developed a threefold role: to manage matters that historically were organized separately in Scotland; to bend British policy to Scottish circumstances; and to lobby for Scotland in the Cabinet (Midwinter et al. 1991).

The Union left the Scottish legal system intact, with Parliament passing separate Scottish laws in various fields. Scottish MPs, while loyal to the British parties, developed a distinct role. Most of them focused on Scottish affairs, dealing with Scottish legislation and, when promoted to government, serving in the Scottish Office. A minority consciously sought a wider UK role and avoided Scottish matters (Keating 1975). There thus developed a distinct Scottish sphere of government, administration, legislation, and parliamentary business, nestled within the British system. Kellas (1973) described this as a Scottish political system, providing a measure of self-government within the British state. Others disagreed, noting that Cabinet government prevailed, the Secretary of State was a member of the ruling party, and Scottish legislation was decided by the whole House of Commons in which Scottish MPs were regularly outvoted (Mackintosh 1973; Midwinter et al. 1991; Keating 2005). The result was a typically unionist arrangement, in which recognition was given to Scottish distinctiveness, and many Scottish concerns accommodated, but without surrendering the authority of Parliament. For the dominant parties during most of the twentieth century, this was a good bargain, since it preserved the Scottish sphere while providing access to the centre, where resources could be mobilized for Scotland's benefit. They could point to the gains from regional policy and public spending consistently above English levels. The invisibility of territorial politics at the UK level only helped them, since it allowed discreet lobbying and bending of priorities without drawing the attention of English MPs to Scotland's advantage.[13]

In the twentieth century, the most salient aspect of territorial management was regional policy. The first moves came in the 1930s with the designation of Distressed Areas and the Scottish Economic Council (later Scottish Council, Development and Industry), founded to study, plan, and press for action. During the Second World War, Tom Johnston, previously a radical and home ruler, turned to technocratic solutions to Scotland's problems, in alliance with the British state. After the war, the Scottish Office gradually expanded its economic responsibilities and in 1965 Scotland was designated one of the planning regions for the Labour Government's National Plan. By 1974 the whole country was eligible for regional aid, and the following year a Scottish Development Agency (for which many people had been pressing since the 1930s) was established.

Regional policy was aimed not at creating a distinct Scottish economy but at modernizing Scotland's productive structure and integrating it into the UK, European, and global markets as part of a 'spatial Keynesianism' appealing to both centre and periphery. It served to develop the regions, reduce congestion in the booming areas and bring into use idle resources, so boosting overall UK production. Socially, it represented the territorial dimension of the welfare state. Politically, it helped diffuse discontent in the nations and regions and bind their politics into the centre. These objectives were to prove difficult to reconcile when economic conditions changed. Nor did economic integration through regional policy entail political integration, as functionalist theories might imply. On the contrary, selective intervention served to raise the salience of Scotland as a space for economic planning and action and to create the notion of a 'Scottish economy' even while it was increasingly integrated into UK and global markets, a phenomenon also visible in other parts of Europe (Keating 1988, 1998). Once again, we see the two sides of Union, at once binding Scotland to England and preserving its distinct identity. Parties now competed over which could do more for the Scottish economy and, when the background conditions changed with the discovery of North Sea oil and changing ideas about regional development, the unionist case came under serious challenge.

THE IDEOLOGY AND DOCTRINE OF UNION

Nation-building everywhere uses historical materials even, as Renan (1992) famously remarked, to the point of getting them wrong. It is typically built on a teleological narrative of the nation, from its seeds in antiquity to its inevitable flowering in the present or future, and is accompanied by a set of values, whether social, religious, or political. The English national narrative has drawn heavily on myths of liberty and individualism, often laced with references to the ancient Saxons and reinforced by the revolutions of the seventeenth century. Scottish myths are not so different, drawing on the mediaeval heroes of independence and tracing liberty to the religious struggles of the early modern period (Ferguson 1998). Finding a British myth is more difficult, although there were ephemeral efforts to rediscover the ancient Britons of classical times.

British Whig historiography presents constitutional development as a continuous progress from its origins in the English Parliament. The unions of 1536, 1707, and 1801 are treated as mere incidents after which English history continues. So Erskine May's (1906) *The Constitutional History of England* is presented as an effort 'to trace the progress and development of the British constitution' (p. iv), arguing that 'nothing in the history of our constitution is more remarkable than the permanence of every institution forming part of the government of the country' (p. 273). Trevelyan (1926) wrongly claimed that the Union involved the absorption of Scotland's Parliament and Privy Council in those of England. Maitland (1908), despite writing explicitly about the unions and revolutions of 1688–9, 1707, and 1801, insists that the United Kingdom Parliament has developed continuously from the old English one. One result of this was that constitutional historians saw the United Kingdom as the product only of English constitutional practice, arguing that parliamentary sovereignty was absolute since this had been established in sixteenth- and seventeenth-century England (Dicey 1912; Dicey and Rait 1920).[14]

After the Union, many Scottish Whigs colluded in this narrative, adopting English constitutional history as their own while stripping it of its more chauvinistic and exceptionalist elements (Kidd 1993; Finlay 1998; Pittock 1999; Devine 2008*a*). Denial that Scotland has contributed anything to the constitution is a powerful element in unionism but co-exists with a recognition of social and cultural distinctiveness. Indeed, Great Britain has sustained a series of unionist stories, corresponding to the mixed strategy of assimilation and distinctiveness that has characterized political and institutional practice. Sir Walter Scott is now recognized as among the pre-eminent unionist ideologues. His novels, which inspired generations of romantic writers throughout Europe, celebrate pre-Union Scotland, allowing credit to all sides in the religious wars and Union debates but carrying an underlying message of progress under the settlement of 1707. The Union, in Scott, is an honourable bargain, preserving Scottish identity while bringing the blessings of a greater Britain and healing the divisions of the past. His subsequently much-mocked extravaganza of 1822, when King George IV was dressed up in

Highland gear for a progress through Edinburgh, symbolically united both
parts of Scotland and the whole of Great Britain. Other ideologues went even
further, appropriating William Wallace and Robert Bruce, the heroes of the
mediaeval independence struggle, to the unionist cause, the argument being
that only their defence of Scottish rights had allowed the nation to enter the
Union as an equal partner in 1707 (Morton 1999).

Unionism as an ideology and a political practice is committed to the unity
of Britain and traditionally against any measure of self-government. It
emphasizes the absolute sovereignty of the Westminster Parliament as the
supreme constitutional principle. Yet unlike state-nationalists in other
European countries, unionists fully accept national cultural diversity, administrative decentralization and Scotland's distinct civil institutions (Kidd
2008). Ward's portraits (2005) of prominent unionists provide insight into
this ideology and statecraft across the United Kingdom. The Lord Provost of
Edinburgh quoted at the beginning of this chapter capped his eulogy of the
Union with a strong plea for Scottish MPs to press on government the 'just
claims of Scotland'. This stance has been described by Morton (1999) as
'unionist nationalism', a striking and deliberately paradoxical phrase to
capture the insistence on Scottish distinctiveness within the Union. It would
be more accurate, however, to label it more simply as 'unionism', since British
unionism has never been assimilating and is distinct precisely in recognizing
national diversity. Nationalism, on the other hand, refers to a programme
for political self-government, something that unionists have explicitly
rejected.

The whole edifice is crowned by a British patriotism, presented as more
enlightened and less aggressive than the nationalisms facing it from within or
without. Conservative unionism tends to be traditionalist, based on Burkean
notions of respect for the past and the wisdom of ages (although its Irish
version presents an altogether harsher aspect). On the Labour side, unionism
is linked to a denigration of nationalism as divisive, the need for broader
forms of solidarity, an emphasis on class (at least in the past) and a strong
centralized state to redistribute resources (Walker 2002). From another angle,
however, we might see unionism itself as a form of nationalism, asserting the
primacy of a British nation, a feature that becomes more obvious when it is
faced with challenges from within (from Scottish nationalism) and without
(from European integration).

The central doctrine of the Union, the absolute sovereignty of Parliament,
allows for considerable variation in practice across the constituent nations, on
the argument that none of this can affect the basic principles of authority. It
also, by avoiding the concept of popular sovereignty, makes it unnecessary to
define the 'people'. Yet the doctrine itself has never been uncontested in

Scotland. Dicey and Rait (1920) insisted that the Westminster Parliament inherited all the prerogatives of the English Parliament and can therefore legislate on anything, including the constitution itself. Others have countered that the Union is a fundamental law and cannot be changed by a parliament that was its creation. Both English and Scottish parliaments were abolished in 1707 and, since the Scottish one had never asserted the principle of absolute sovereignty, the new one could not have inherited it (MacCormick 1999, 2000; McLean and McMillan 2005). Many scholars have emphasized the distinct tradition of popular sovereignty and balanced government in Scotland (Kidd 1993; Ferguson 1998) and the specific reservations in the Union Treaty itself. It is always difficult in such cases to appeal to the original intent of the constitution-makers; in this case it is likely that they were concerned among other things to protect the Church of Scotland from the sort of state regulation to which the Church of England is subject. It is more important to see how doctrines have evolved in practice and are understood over time, as well as the way in which a distinctive constitutional doctrine was kept alive in Scotland even during the era of unionist hegemony.

The idea of limited sovereignty survived long enough for Lord Cooper in the Court of Session to find in 1953 that Parliament was not unlimited, although this celebrated case for long remained no more than a legal curiosity.[15] MacCormick (1999) details the two rival views of the constitution and, while inclining to the view that the Union represented the foundation of the constitution and was thus superior law, admits that this has not been the prevailing doctrine. Dicey (1961) can certainly be accused of over-reach in his doctrine of parliamentary sovereignty, since he even suggested that the 1931 Statute of Westminster, declaring that Parliament would no longer legislate for the Dominions (thus in effect giving them independence), could be superseded by subsequent Westminster legislation, a position that nobody would share today. He also had a tendency to write of England and the English constitution, which might have been the usual insensitivity to the nature of the state, if it were not for the fact that he was well aware of the constitutional issue in Ireland and Scotland. Rather, it seemed to reflect an assumption that only English constitutional practice was relevant to the Union, a proposition that could certainly be challenged. Political scientists and some lawyers have also argued that the concept of the Union as a partnership of nations should be regarded as one of the conventions on which so much British political practice is based (Tierney 2004).[16] At its weakest, the argument is that political prudence should inculcate in British politicians a sensitivity to Scottish differences. Even Dicey, in the same sentence in which he likened the Act of Union[17] to the Dentists Act, conceded that it would be 'political madness to tamper gratuitously' with it. Nor was

Dicey himself consistent, as he supported Irish unionists in their defiance of Parliament's concession of home rule before the First World War. Challenges to the Union from the 1960s have led to a renewed interest in Scottish constitutional traditions and arguments that they should be included in any account of the British unwritten constitution (Keating 2001a; MacCormick 1999, 2000; Walker 2000; Tierney 2004). In the late 1980s the Campaign for a Scottish Assembly (1988) produced a Claim of Right, deliberately based on the Scottish covenant tradition, insisting that sovereignty belonged to the Scottish people. That it gained the assent of the entire Scottish Parliamentary Labour Party, with the single exception of Tam Dalyell, might be read as an endorsement of the claim or, more likely, as an indication that they did not take it seriously.

This ambiguity was the efficient secret of the Union, but also its weak point. As Colls (2002) puts it, unionists never allowed the wires of nationality and statehood to be crossed. Scotland could have as much of its historic and cultural identity as it wanted, together with its own civil society and even administration, but never an elected parliament, since this, resting on the principle of nationality, would inevitably assume sovereignty for itself and challenge the one fundamental principle of Union. This was a staple of Dicey's argument (1912) against Irish Home Rule and was later taken up by Wilson (1970) and Dalyell (1977) in the context of the devolution debates of the 1970s. There may be something to their argument; but it rests upon the hope that these two dimensions of Scottishness (or Irishness before it) can be kept apart indefinitely. This was not to be.

REMAKING SCOTLAND

The evolving Union settlement did not merely sustain the British state and nation. It also served to maintain and develop a Scottish nationality, which was contained within it but always presented a potential challenge. Davidson (2000) has controversially asserted that the Scottish nation was invented subsequently to 1707 by and within the Union. This may be intended as a provocation to nationalists and a corrective to primordial views of the nation, since there was of course a Scottish nation before 1707. It would be less controversial to note that Scotland, like other nations, does not stand still and has been redefined several times over the centuries. The Union is an inescapable part of the context for this, as is the changing international order.

Whether or not the idea of the nation was created in modernity, it is certain that the nation as we know it is profoundly shaped by the experience of social and economic change that swept western societies in the nineteenth and twentieth centuries. It is in this period that the *modern* nation is forged, integrating its diverse components into a coherent, if rarely homogeneous, whole. As already noted, there was once a tendency to see Scotland as having been integrated successfully into a British nation. When the resurgence of Scottish nationalism forced a reappraisal of these ideas, it was often presented as an ethnic outlier, resisting incorporation and therefore somehow exceptional and needing a special explanation.[18] This leads to the argument that, in order to exist at all, Scotland must somehow be 'different' (meaning in practice different from England).[19] In another vein, Nairn (1977, 2000) has long argued that it somehow missed its historical destiny in the nineteenth century, by not becoming a normal nation state.

More recent scholarship presents Scotland not as a historical exception or an ethnic fragment but as a European nation that has gone through most of the usual processes of modernization (Keating 2001*b*; McCrone 2001*b*), including internal integration and nation-building around common symbols and institutions. To the puzzlement of some outside observers, this is not based on language or the more obvious ethnic identifiers, but on historical memories, symbols, myths, and institutions. This is a 'banal nationalism' (Billig 1995) in which small daily reminders serve to keep alive the collective consciousness, becoming overt and strident only when it is challenged. Scotland is not defined, *pace* Anthony Smith (1999), by an 'ethnic core' to which other elements are assimilated but by a civic identity that built upon diverse elements. The culturally distinct Highlands and Lowlands have been accommodated within a common Scottish identity since the nineteenth century, as the predominance of the population has shifted south and Highland imagery (including tartan, kilt, and bagpipes) has diffused to the whole of Scotland. The influx of Irish immigrants from the mid-nineteenth century challenged understandings of Scotland as an essentially Protestant country and opened up a sectarian cleavage, especially in the urban areas of western Scotland, that persisted until the mid-twentieth century. The evidence shows that this population is now thoroughly Scottish in identity; indeed it may be that these families went from a predominantly Irish Catholic identity to a Scottish one without passing through a British phase. Italians and eastern Europeans have similarly been socialized. Newer immigrants, including Muslims, have negotiated their own accommodations with Scottish identity, again often without going through a British phase (Hussein and Miller 2006).

To argue that nationality must necessarily take the form of a state, however, is to invoke a non-existent historical rule. Unionism cultivated a non-politicized Scottish identity, in which the symbols of nationality were pressed into the service of the British state. It stretched to cover a practical Scottish politics, focused on policy and administration. In the middle of the nineteenth century the National Association for the Vindication of Scottish Rights complained of administrative neglect and the decay of Scottish institutions. Practical businesspeople and local government leaders were behind the campaign for a Secretary for Scotland, a Scottish Grand Committee and more time for Scottish legislation in Parliament. During the twentieth century, economic questions took on a greater importance, in the face of industrial decline and recession. From the 1930s, a Scottish territorial lobby emerged in which business, trade unions and political parties cooperated to promote a common economic interest in industrial development, regional policy and public spending. The whole edifice of administrative devolution discussed earlier served to reinforce the idea of a Scottish arena of public life, contained within the greater British one.

This could for a long time be accommodated within the broad tent of unionism but this was periodically challenged by a nationalist alternative. As in other cases, we can trace forms of proto-nationalism back a long way; indeed, something like it has never been far below the surface of Scottish life. Some authors have detected strong nationalist tones in the programme of the Jacobite rebels of the eighteenth century (Pittock 1999), although their aim was to restore the Stuarts to the thrones of three kingdoms, the most important of which by far was that of England. Demands for administrative reform during the nineteenth century have similarly been seen as a form of proto-nationalism; but episodes like the National Association for the Vindication of Scottish Rights in the 1850s were firmly within the unionist tradition, asking for more consideration for Scottish issues at Westminster and in Whitehall.

Nationalism in its modern form, demanding an elected Scottish Parliament, is the product of the late nineteenth century (Powell 2002), when it emerged in parallel with similar movements across Europe.[20] A Scottish Home Rule Association was set up in 1886 following Gladstone's conversion to Irish Home Rule, and another one after the First World War, with support from advanced liberals, the labour movement and land reformers. Initial demands focused on Home Rule, that is, self-government within the United Kingdom of the sort offered to Ireland by Gladstonian Liberals. The movement has often been dismissed as not real nationalism since it was not separatist (Nairn 1977), but this is to assume that nationalism must be state-seeking (McCrone 2001*b*; Keating 2001*a*). Scotland was not alone in generating forms of non-separatist nationalism in the nineteenth century;

Hroch (1985) has argued that nationalist revivals in the nineteenth century went through a series of stages, not all ending up demanding a fully-fledged state. Indeed, few of the European nationalities movements before the First World War, including in the Habsburg Empire, were pressing for independent statehood. The same can be said of the mainstream of Irish nationalism and even of early Sinn Féin. Scottish Home Rule was often placed in the context of Empire, with Scotland a self-governing Dominion like Canada or Australia, or as a component of a putative imperial federation, in constant search for a middle ground between unionism and separatism. Twenty home rule bills or motions were presented to Parliament between 1889 and 1927 and, under Liberal or Labour governments, usually supported (Mitchell 1996). The agitation reached a peak in the immediate aftermath of the First World War and fell away rapidly.

The failure of the last bill provoked a break between home rulers and supporters of full independence, and in 1928 the first explicitly nationalist party was formed, to transmute in 1932 into the Scottish National Party (SNP). The middle ground was already being undermined after the Imperial Conference of 1926 agreed to a new definition of Dominion Status, which, after the Statute of Westminster in 1935, effectively meant independence. The Irish settlement of 1922 ruled out a federal United Kingdom, and interest in constitutional change on the part of the British political class quickly died out. Even now the division between separatists and home rulers was not entirely clear-cut. Figures like John MacCormick could move between activism in the SNP and involvement in all-party movements for home rule, and the meaning of independence itself was not always obvious. Perhaps only in the 1950s and 1960s, with the Empire gone and the European Union yet to come, was a clear independence project on offer, and this was at a time when support for the nationalist party was at a very low point.

Yet for all their ambivalence, home rule and nationalist movements served periodically to repoliticize Scottish identity, to challenge the unionist settle-ment and to force unionist governments to extend recognition of Scottish distinctiveness and administrative, if not political, devolution. They exposed a weakness in the unionist settlement, since Scottish opinion, whenever it has been tested in an opinion poll, an election where it was an issue, or by referendum, has without exception shown itself in favour of self-government, usually within a federal United Kingdom. Home rule ideas also persisted widely in the political class. For its entire existence, with the exception of the years 1958–74, the Labour Party has officially been committed to devolution for Scotland; the Liberals have supported it since Gladstone's time; and there is a Conservative home rule tradition that never quite died out. Yet, faced with the challenges of governing the United Kingdom, these parties always came down for unionism and the Westminster model. Morton (1999) argues that 'unionist nationalism' was effectively killed by the advance of the state against the autonomous civil society after 1860; in fact, unionism (as it is better described) had another hundred years of life as the state itself adapted to recognize Scottish distinctiveness.

3

The Strange Death of Unionist Scotland

THE UNION AT 300

In May 2007, the third centenary of the Anglo-Scottish Union occurred to almost no rejoicing and public ceremonial. The Convention of Scottish Local Authorities (successor of the Convention of Royal Burghs) passed no resolution of congratulation, and there were no official balls. An election for the Scottish Parliament was pending, the Scottish National Party (SNP) saw no reason to celebrate the Union, and its opponents scarcely knew whether or how to do so. Polls gave conflicting readings on the state of public opinion; but perhaps the most striking finding is that so many people could live with the Union or without it. An opinion poll (ICM, January 2007) showed that only a little over a third of voters expected the Union (of England, Wales, Scotland, and Northern Ireland) to last more than fifty years, while half declared themselves favourable to Scottish independence. The electors seemed equally unmoved by the nationalist promises of plenty after independence was achieved, and by the dire prophecies of doom from their unionist opponents. One third thought that Scotland would be worse off without England, while slightly more thought that it would be better off. More striking still is the reaction in England, which closely mirrored Scottish attitudes. Only a third of English voters thought that the Union would survive more than another fifty years, while two fifths thought that at least one part would leave within twenty years. About half of English voters supported Scotland becoming an independent country.[1] Most English people thought that Scottish independence would make no difference to England's prosperity, and only a fifth thought that it would be worse off.[2] Another ICM poll later in the year asked specifically about the union between England and Scotland and, while the figures supporting Scottish independence were lower, they were again identical on both sides of the border (ICM, December 2007).[3] These are not random findings but echo surveys conducted over recent years. In international comparison this is a remarkable thing. Nationality conflicts in Spain, Canada, and Belgium (to mention only comparable liberal democracies) stir powerful passions on the sides of both minority nations and the state majority, who see secession as an existential threat to their political identity and being.

Clearly something important had happened in the intervening centuries, but it is not at all clear what or why. Critics of the Union argued in 2007, as they always had, that the events of 1707 were a shady bargain between corrupt elites against the wishes and interests of the people. Defenders, however, no longer extolled the glories of the British people (or race as they would say in the nineteenth century) and their civilizing mission. Prime Minister Tony Blair and his soon-to-be successor Gordon Brown certainly talked a lot about British values, but these tended to the platitudinous or to universal notions like democracy and fairness, and it was difficult to see the connection between them and a specific form of the state. For the most part, however, unionists stuck to instrumental arguments about the economics of independence or about the inconvenience of borders. The economic arguments could play either way, depending on factors such as the price of oil, while inveighing against borders was hardly consistent with the government's assiduous strengthening of the UK border with the rest of the world, including the European Union. The resort to instrumental arguments in itself suggests a shift away from an affective attachment to a British nation to a more negotiated form of order. Yet, while unionism may have faded, it is not giving way to a hegemonic Scottish counter-project for a smaller nation state. There is a lot of ambivalence in public opinion, and the direction of institutional change is unclear. We could be heading towards a new constellation of states within the United Kingdom, or a renegotiated Union.

THE REINVENTION OF TERRITORY

The revival of sub-state nationalism and regionalism in the developed West from the 1970s took many observers by surprise since modernization had been supposed to eliminate such historical remnants. Many scholars sought to explain the phenomenon as retarded modernization, or the belated birth pangs of the new industrial order. After the 'delayed modernization' hypothesis had been deployed so many times, however (in the late nineteenth century, between the wars and again in the 1970s), others began to suspect that something was wrong with it and to think how modernization itself can generate new territorial cleavages or revive old ones (Tarrow et al. 1978; Keating 1988). Territorial politics thus ceased to be an anomaly in the modern world but a central and normal part of political life.

At the end of the twentieth century, a new wave of modernization theory predicted the 'end of territory' (Badie 1995) and a 'borderless world'

(Ohmae 1995) as communications and production technology dissolved the constraints of space and time. This coincided with, and at times linked to, hubristic narratives of the end of history itself, as all previous forms of politics were absorbed into the US model of liberal capitalism. Again, however, a counter-note has been struck, this time by the literature on spatial rescaling, which emphasizes the reconstruction of territorial systems, at new levels, above, below, and across states. This re-territorialization is in part a response to functional change, of which the examples of economy and culture are among the most obvious. While the economy has indeed restructured at the European and global levels, it has also shown strong tendencies to localization (Storper 1997; Scott 1998). The interaction between the local and the global and the diminished importance of the nation state framework are at the centre of the 'new regionalism' (Keating 1998). In this new vision, territory is not important simply because of the availability of raw materials and proximity to markets, as in the past, but because of the importance of local networks, social practices, and institutions, and the capacity of societies to innovate. It is striking that the most advanced industries and those most reliant on the new technology of communication, such as financial services and software production, are among the most localized. Similarly, culture and languages, while going global, are also localizing, given the need for physical communities and institutions for cultural production, diffusion, and education.

European integration and the single market have reinforced these effects. Borders have not been abolished, but they no longer bound the full range of systems traditionally associated with the nation state. The various domains of economic management, cultural integration and welfare have migrated to different territorial levels, and so are delinked from each other, breaking down and opening out state-based political arenas (Bartolini 2005; Ferrera 2006). Some see this as a threat to the capacity for collective action, democratic efficacy, and the social solidarity with which they associate the nation state. The ability of the state to forge social compromises between capital and labour is undermined as investors can easily exit from national politics by relocating, while workers are less mobile. Old-style territorial management and regional redistribution are no longer possible, depending as they did on a strong state framework. The shared national sentiment that underpinned solidarity is eroded, as new and revived identities emerge at spatial and sectoral levels.

Yet, spatial rescaling is never driven by purely functional imperatives. Politics will out and, confronted with global change, movements will emerge to rebuild governing institutions and political communities at new levels. The European Union is one effort to recapture the capacity for social and economic regulation at the supranational level, while the widespread adoption of regional devolution in Europe serves the same role at the sub-state level. Political mobilization around territorial and cultural identities is another response. In some cases, these emerging territories are based on historic nations and regions; but this is no mere reversion to the past since the past communities of memory no longer exist in their original forms. Rather, they are the sites for the construction of new forms of polity, some based on exclusion and isolation but others that are themselves expressions of universal and modern values. The aspiration in the latter is to rebuild 'global societies' containing within them the full range of social institutions and actors, rather than ethnic or cultural fragments (Langlois 1991). In practice, however, they are weakly bounded communities that are unlikely to become nation states in the classic nineteenth- and twentieth-century sense, since it is precisely the erosion of this model of statehood that has allowed them to emerge. Political, economic, cultural, and social borders can never correspond more than approximately, and the emerging systems are embedded in global and European networks. It is in this way that we can understand in comparative context the re-emergence of Scotland as an economic, social, and political space, a salient frame of reference for politics and institution-building, but not the sole form of reference as was the old nation state.

It is important to note that this argument about re-territorialization does not depend on an underlying social and economic differentiation of territories. This explains the paradox that, while Scotland has continued to converge with England on many social and economic indicators, its politics are diverging (Kendrick, Bechhofer, and McCrone 1985; Kendrick 1989). Social structures are similar, and homogeneity is reinforced by secularization and the advance of post-industrial values. Scotland is not even marked by a distinctive language or way of life. Yet it has become the site of a strong nationalist movement and a conflict over the shape of the polity. The issue at stake is not how to be different, but what are the boundaries of the political community and the institutions for shaping a social and economic project. The conflict is not so much about cultural or ethnic differentiation but rather over competing projects for the rebuilding of political communities at new levels and the search for institutions that can reconcile economic competitiveness and social solidarity within new spaces.

This transformation of the national question away from ethnic differentiation might, in some respects, seem to help accommodation between states and stateless nations, since it lowers the stakes and diffuses the issue across a variety of systems, making the old issue of independence less relevant. On the other hand, the very fact that stateless nations are constructing themselves as political communities based on universal values, rather than ethnic fragments based on particularism, may make accommodation more difficult. Stateless nation-builders are now claiming the same normative ground as the state itself and, as states are weakened by the process of global and European transformation, they seek to guard their prerogatives more closely. This is what Dion (1991), in the case of Quebec, has called 'de Tocqueville's paradox', the rise of nationalism along with cultural convergence.

THE POLITICAL ECONOMY OF UNION

During the nineteenth century, economic arguments seemed strongly to favour union as the heavy industries of the Scottish lowlands thrived in imperial markets. Its industrial bourgeoisie was firmly wedded to the Empire and Union, source of its prosperity. The working class occasionally showed nationalist inclinations, but the labour movement was equally unwilling to risk its welfare and was strongly committed to free trade. After the First World War, these calculations changed rapidly. Scotland's heavy industries were hit hard by the Depression and, unlike in the south and midlands of England, there was no general recovery in the 1930s. Some observers, looking at the rise of a generation of nationalist literati and the foundation of the first nationalist parties, have concluded that depression and nationalism were linked. In fact, the contrary was true. Business looked to government in London for help through tariff protection and subsidies and merged their businesses into UK-wide conglomerates and cartels. Labour ended its flirtation with nationalism and also turned to the centre for help. Scottish economic interests still pointed to the Union, but for very different reasons than before, and with different implications. Previously an outlet for a dynamic industrial sector, the UK (after the failure of schemes for Empire economic union) was a source of assistance. Henceforth, Scotland was an economic dependency of the United Kingdom; leaders from politics, administration, and both sides of industry made the extraction of resources from the centre the mainstay of their political strategy. As erstwhile Home Ruler Tom Johnston (1952: 14) noted in his memoirs:

> For many years past, I have become ... uneasy lest we should get political power without our first having ... an adequate economy to administer. What purport would there be in getting a Scots Parliament in Edinburgh if it has to administer an emigration system, a glorified Poor Law and a graveyard?

It was this thinking that underlay the focus of regional policy from the 1950s to the 1970s, and the strategy of managed dependency, which reached its peak in the late 1970s. The 1980s, however, inflicted a series of blows on Scotland's industrial economy as the global recession was intensified by the deflationary policies of the Thatcher government. All the major industrial plants brought to Scotland under the earlier regional policies closed. While this could be exploited by the nationalists as evidence of neglect on the part of British policy-makers, they were not the immediate political beneficiaries. Rather, the industrial crisis sparked a familiar coalition of territorial defence, including business, unions, politicians, and civil society and focused on a campaign to defend the steel plant at Ravenscraig. The Labour Party retreated into a state-led protectionist policy under the rubric of the Alternative Economic Strategy, which left little room for autonomous territorial initiatives (Jones and Keating 1985). Remarkably, at the very time that North Sea oil revenues reached their peak, equivalent to over half of the non-oil Scottish economy (Figure 5.1), the nationalist vote fell steadily and the oil issue faded from prominence. It was in this period, however, that the foundations were laid for a new economic representation of Scotland. The Ravenscraig campaign secured no more than a short prolongation of its existence, but the demise of the old heavy industries paved the way for fresh thinking about economic development and removed an incubus from any future home rule administration.

The 1990s saw a major international change in scholarly thinking about regional development. Previous approaches had emphasized diversionary policies, steering investment into needy regions through regulations and subsidies, investment in physical infrastructure, and the promotion of growth poles focused on large plants in growing sectors, which could attract networks of suppliers around them. These were the policies characteristic of Scotland in the 1960s and 1970s; and indeed, Scotland had been a leader in the field. The new wisdom accepts the importance of inward investment and incorporation into the global economy, but puts much more emphasis on entrepreneurship and innovation. It aims to reinforce spatial networks of economic dynamism in line with the new regionalist thinking on the importance of territory. The instruments are institution- and network-building, promotion of new firms, education, research, and technology transfer. These are public goods that can be supplied at the sub-state level. At the same time, emphasis has shifted from the integration of regions into statewide markets according to a national division of labour, towards the promotion of inter-regional competition in European and global markets. The result is a decline in traditional state-based regional policy and the decentralization of development efforts to the regions themselves. Whether regions really do compete with each other is not entirely undisputed, and the new regionalist thinking has come under some strong criticism (Lovering 1999). There is no doubt, however, that it has affected thinking among policy-makers at European, UK, and Scottish levels, as elsewhere in Europe and North America. In the devolution proposals of the 1970s, economic development was reserved to the UK Government and the Secretary of State for Scotland. In the 1998 Scotland Act, it is devolved. So even as the Scottish economy is internationalized and absorbed into UK, European, and global chains, economic development strategy is more appropriately handled at the devolved level, along with the instruments for its realization. This undermines some of the old unionist arguments about the need for centralized government in order to balance territorial demands and look after the interests of Scotland.

Just as the growth of a Scottish political consciousness cannot be explained by distinct values or culture, so also the concern with a 'Scottish economy' cannot be explained by a distinctive form of Scottish capitalism or productive structure. The decades following the First World War saw a steady decline in Scottish ownership across the economy in favour of British and multinational capital (Baird et al. 2007). By the 1970s there was serious concern about the loss of local ownership, and suggestions were made about the need to limit takeovers in the interests of the domestic economy (Firn 1975; Ashcroft and Love 1993). A broad Scottish lobby was mobilized to defend the Scottish banks and firms like Anderson Strathclyde. Although the government and the Monopolies Commission officially took no cognizance of the regional impact of mergers, there did seem to be some discreet political pressure to retain Scottish ownership. The Scottish Development Agency sought to bring business headquarters to Scotland to overcome the 'branch plant' syndrome. By the end of the 1990s, however, this concern had largely disappeared. Even the nationalists welcomed inward investment and accepted mergers and takeovers, although preferring to keep headquarters' functions in Scotland. This, too, follows international and academic thinking, which placed much less emphasis on ownership as a factor in regional development.

There is a strong argument to the effect that the economic advantages of union have been exhausted and that political choices within Scotland are now more important than linkages with the United Kingdom (Ross 2007). There may not be a distinct Scottish economy even to the extent that there was in the nineteenth century. The sectoral structure of the Scottish economy is remarkably similar to the UK mean, with manufacturing employment at 10.1 and 11.8 per cent, respectively, and financial services at 18 and 20 per cent. Agriculture shows a bigger proportionate difference, but the absolute figures are very low, at 1.6 and 0.9 per cent employment, respectively. The proportion of the population receiving their income from wages and salaries is identical, as is the proportion receiving benefits (Office for National Statistics 2008). There is, however, a Scottish economic debate since the economic issue has been framed as a territorial one. The politics of managed dependency has consequently given way to strategies for autonomy. At the same time, the latest phase of modernization has fundamentally altered social relations in Scotland, eroding the old class structure and undermining the old unionist certainties (Paterson, Bechhofer, and McCrone 2004).

SOCIAL CLASS AND SOCIAL CHANGE

Three pillars of the old Union – the landed classes, the industrial bourgeoisie and the labour movement – have undergone radical changes and, while not swinging to Scottish nationalism, can no longer count on the niche they occupied under the traditional dispensation. Scotland's landowning class was once a bulwark of the Union, owning estates in all parts of the United Kingdom, sharing a common social formation, and exercising both social and political leadership. The old estates are now transformed into capitalist enterprises, many under foreign ownership and catering to a global market. Even the venerable Scottish Landowners' Association has become the Scottish Rural Property and Business Association which, having lost its old protectors in the Conservative Party, needs to play the Scottish political game. The gentry class is largely absent from the ranks of the Conservative Party in the Scottish Parliament.

The old industrial bourgeoisie and its political representation have suffered with the demise of Scottish-owned business. This had direct repercussions on the Unionist (after 1965 Conservative) Party; the 1976 Fairgreave Report into Conservative Party structure noted the drying-up of financial support as locally-owned business disappeared and recommended the absorption of the party organization into its British counterpart, a process largely complete by the 1990s (Seawright 1999). The old business leadership has also largely disappeared from Scotland's cities, although from the 1980s there were efforts to promote local business leadership in urban renewal. The extensive privat-ization pushed through by Conservative governments in the 1980s and 1990s was not used to revive a Scottish business class (with the odd exception like the Stagecoach firm built on the deregulation of transport). Business repre-sentative organizations remain firmly unionist and suspicious of further devolution, let alone Scottish independence but, with the demise of the Conservatives, no longer have their own political party. Their attitude to devolution has gone from outright opposition, to sullen neutrality to a less grudging acceptance as the new institutions have bedded down and they are being drawn into new Scottish policy networks and playing politics by the new rules. There has also appeared a cohort of business figures, small in number but significant in impact, who lean to the SNP, attracted by its new business-friendly image and promises of a low-tax independent Scotland.

The professional classes occupied their own niche in the old Scottish system, enjoying varying degrees of self-regulation and autonomy. The weakness of the business class may have given them greater prominence while the expansion of state employment increased their numbers. The attacks on the professions and the self-regulating civil society by successive Conservative governments dislodged them from their old niche and created insecurity. As devolution has led to differences in public service provision, with Scotland less committed to marketization and more concerned with equity and partnership, the professions have come to appreciate the importance of the Scottish arena. In 2008, the British Medical Association, meeting in Glasgow, were favourably comparing the Scottish with the English model for the National Health Service.

The old working class has faded. People are less likely to identify with a social class, industrial employment has fallen to a fifth of the workforce, of whom 30 per cent are managerial and professional, and only a tenth in unskilled work (Paterson, Bechhofer, and McCrone 2004). Council housing has declined as owner-occupation has increased from 40 per cent of households in 1982 to 70 per cent in 2005. Trade union membership has also fallen sharply, if not quite so much as in England, and is concentrated in the public sector (Brook 2002). The SNP has made inroads into the working class, although not the organized trade union movement. Trade unions themselves have supported devolution since the 1960s and were prominent in the movement during the 1990s but otherwise remain unionist, supporting a single British market, labour regulation system and framework for social solidarity. Yet the linked worlds of Labour Party, trade unions, and council tenancy that underpinned the party's hegemony from the 1950s and allowed it to represent a distinct Scottish (and largely unionist) interest within a broader British politics are no more. New social movements are less tied to the old assumptions about class and its meaning. This opens the way for new narratives of class, interest, and identity, and for a reframing of the political agenda.

THE WELFARE STATE

The welfare state was another pillar of the modern Union as an expression of British-wide solidarity and redistribution in favour of poorer territories. It is sometimes argued that the retrenchment of the welfare state in the 1980s and

1990s undermined the Union by penalizing Scotland and offending the egalitarian and social democratic principles of the Scottish people (Civardi 2002; King 2007). There may be an element of truth here, but the argument is again drawn at too general a level. The welfare state has not been dismantled, despite the dreams of Conservative zealots in the 1980s. Nor are the Scots massively more favourable to welfare spending than the English. On matters of income distribution and welfare, they are only marginally to the left of voters south of the border and rather closer to those in the north of England than to those in the south (Rosie and Bond 2007). The only clear and consistent Scotland–England difference is on comprehensive education, which the Scots have not abandoned, with those identifying as predominantly Scottish most in favour (Paterson et al. 2001).

Yet the changing politics of welfare have sapped the foundations of Union. The similarity of attitudes on both sides of the border is due to the fact that neither Scots nor English abandoned the old welfare settlement or really embraced Thatcherism. The difference is that the rejection of neo-liberalism has a territorial expression in Scotland and was linked to rising nationalist sentiment and the campaign for self-government, to which it probably gave the extra momentum that previous home rule campaigns had lacked. There is evidence that national identity and attitudes to social equality and welfare are linked. Paterson (2002b) shows that the more people identify as Scottish, the more they agree that 'there is one law for the rich and one for the poor'. Rosie and Bond (2007) show a small but consistent tendency for those identifying as Scottish to espouse more social democratic values. Social solidarity may thus still be rooted in the nation, but increasingly this may be the Scottish rather than the British nation.

Political rhetoric has perhaps unwittingly helped to sever the link between the Union and social solidarity. Conservative politicians during the 1980s and 1990s spoke of Scotland's 'dependency culture', referring to the lack of entre-preneurship and high welfare rolls. Sometimes this was contrasted with a vision of Scotland exemplified by the industrial revolution and Adam Smith – as in Margaret Thatcher's extraordinary portrayal of Smith as a proto-Thatcherite. Had this self-help rhetoric been accompanied by a positive attitude to Scottish self-government, as happened briefly with Edward Heath in the late 1960s, it might have made a consistent message. Instead, it had to co-exist with absolute resistance to constitutional change. New Labour rhet-oric is less hostile to welfare and public services, and represents an effort to reinvent social democracy for a new age. Yet for all its emphasis on community, New Labour has continued to delegitimate the state as a vehicle for expressing it. Its attacks on the public service professionals and dogmatic support for private provision, apart from alienating sections of the Scottish middle classes, have helped to break the connection between the state and social solidarity or public services. When the state ceases to be the institutional expression and foundation for national solidarity, state and nation not surprisingly fall apart. As noted below, there is indeed evidence that pride in British welfare standards has fallen sharply in Scotland.

There is also some evidence for a distinct conception of the welfare state at the elite level in Scotland, more favourable to universalism and sceptical about the reforms pursued under both Conservative and New Labour governments. Paterson's survey (2003) of university academics shows a greater civic commitment in Scotland and a lesser tendency to see the university as apart from society. A survey in 2003 found that just under 60 per cent of medical general practitioners across the UK would like to charge for home visits, while in Scotland the same proportion was opposed (NU Health Care 2003). Scottish medical practitioners show a lesser inclination to private practice than those in England, as shown on a number of occasions (Keating 2005). During the 1980s and 1990s few Scottish schools opted out of local authority control, and the take-up of fund-holding by general practitioners was much lower than in England. These elements together have served to create a moral community and public space in Scotland that is not necessarily to the left of England in a traditional sense, but is deeply imbued with ideas of collective welfare and social responsibility.

THE END OF CLUB GOVERNMENT

The British state has long had a distinctive relationship to civil society. The failure of revolutionary activity in the early nineteenth century and the successful management of the nationalities question outside Ireland meant that it was never necessary to build a centralized state apparatus dominating over society. An unwritten constitution complemented a system of self-regulation in large areas of economic and social life including the City of London, in the legal and medical professions, the universities and business, allowing the state itself to govern with a relatively light touch. The trade unions escaped from legal restriction not by dint of a positive set of rules but in a series of exemptions from restrictive laws. Government at the centre was guided by conventions and unwritten norms. The civil service, drawn from a narrow social background in the elite private ('public') schools and ancient universities, was characterized by the cult of the gifted amateur rather than technical specialization. The same elite backgrounds dominated in the judiciary, the boardrooms of big firms, and much of the political elite, especially in the Conservative Party. The metaphor of 'club government' (Marquand 1981) combined the notion of exclusiveness and coherence with the ethos of the London gentleman's social establishment, and matched Bulpitt's conception of the 'right chaps' who managed the territorial state. Between the 1950s and the 1970s, there was also a broad consensus on policy issues, together with an unwillingness to upset the social balance by confronting either trade unions or business.

Club government was attacked periodically from the left and the right, and widely blamed for Britain's apparently inexorable decline from the late nineteenth century. Labour governments in the 1940s, 1960s, and 1970s extended the role of the state in the management of the economy. Edward Heath's government in the early 1970s sought to introduce modern techniques into the machinery of government. From the 1960s there was a frenzy of institutional reform, covering the health service, local government, the civil service and, later, the universities; but most of this left the essentials of club government at the centre intact. It was only in the 1980s that radical change began, with the policies of Margaret Thatcher consciously breaking with the consensus and abandoning much of the consultation and conciliation of earlier years. Thatcherism was the declared enemy of the state, dedicated to rolling back its frontiers. Yet, while pledged to economic liberalism, it pursued a social authoritarianism domestically and a nationalist rhetoric in external policy (Gamble 1988). Liberalization of the economy was accompanied by centralization over local government and the rise of a massive and intrusive regulatory state (Moran 2003).

Under the Scottish Office system, Scotland was deeply embedded in the old assumptions about consensus, conciliation, and informality. Ministers could carry out the policies of the centre while discreetly signalling their dissent for audiences back home. The latitude given to the professions and other self-regulating bodies applied in Scotland, sometimes with a distinct Scottish dimension. This is not to say that Scotland ran its own affairs before Thatcher – we have already noted that it did not. There was, however, a Scottish set of institutions and practices for the management of its affairs, run by people identifying with Scottish traditions and with an understanding of the politics of the Union. This old polity combined a doctrine of parliamentary sovereignty with the understanding that it would be used with restraint, a lesson lost during the 1980s and 1990s. Conservative attacks on club government therefore hit the old mechanisms of territorial management forcefully, but without putting anything in its place. To the contrary, the old Scottish Office model was continued, even as the government found increasing difficulty finding enough MPs to staff it. The decline of the Conservative Party may also owe something to Thatcherite disdain for the professions, which had their own niche in the old Union settlement. By the late 1990s, the Conservatives were governing with a smaller base of electoral support than any of their predecessors, and without the restraining influence that a closer connection with Scottish civil society, and a body of their own supporters, might have provided. This was 'direct government', against the essence of the old unionism, and could only be expected to provoke a sharp reaction within civil society.

TRANSNATIONALISM AND EUROPEAN INTEGRATION

It is not only the internal dimension of statehood that has been transformed. Like other states, the United Kingdom is losing competences, power, and (arguably) sovereignty to the global level and specifically the European Union. Major powers over market-regulation, trade, competition, agriculture, and the environment have now shifted up to the European level, followed by some classic state-defining functions in foreign affairs and security, and home affairs and justice. Individual rights have been entrenched through the European Convention for the Protection of Human Rights and Fundamental Freedoms (under the Council of Europe), whose application to devolved matters in Scotland is direct. Europe represents a new economic and political union, superimposed on that of 1707, and potentially has a major impact upon it. The general opening of borders in Europe and the shift of competences to multiple levels have broken the old nation state formula in which functions, institutions, and systems of representation were coincident within the same boundaries, turning politics inwards and reinforcing state integration (Bartolini 2005). Right across Europe, this has provoked movements of territorial reassertion and the search for means to act within the new context (Keating 2004; McGarry and Keating 2006). There have been movements to create a Europe of the Regions, a Europe of the Peoples, a Europe of the Cultures, all intended to circumvent the old states and find a new formula for autonomy. Nationalities movements have shifted from a widespread scepticism about European integration to general support (Lynch 1996; Keating 2004). For some, Europe provides the opportunity to become independent at a lower cost and with a secure external support system. In this sense, Europe could play for modern Scotland the role that the Empire did in the nineteenth century. Other nationalities movements are less ambitious, seeing a place for them in the Europe of the Regions, gradually extending their autonomy as European integration deepens. A third group have embraced the notion of post-sovereignty, arguing that European integration makes the whole idea of state sovereignty redundant, and that we should return to older ideas of shared and divided sovereignty at multiple levels (Keating 2001a).

In the early years of the European project, there was widespread hostility in Scotland, on national, class, and ideological grounds. The Labour Party, dominant electorally since the late 1950s, generally opposed membership of the (then) European Communities because of fears for the welfare state, worries about the competitive challenge to industry, and a preoccupation with the loss of sovereignty and the power of national government to manage social and economic progress. These concerns, rooted in ideology and protection of class interests, intersected with a British nationalism that was suspicious of foreign entanglements (Jones and Keating 1985). Labour in Scotland was even more opposed than in England and remained suspicious even when the Labour Government applied for membership in the 1960s. In the 1975 referendum on staying in the Communities, Scotland voted Yes, but by a notably smaller margin than England. The SNP, after pursuing a vaguely pro-European line in the 1950s, turned sharply against in the 1960s and campaigned for a No vote in 1975, although a pro-European minority was given leave to dissent. SNP voters in 1979 were more anti-Europe than those of the other parties (Dardanelli 2005). The Conservatives and Labour pro-Europeans, for their part, presented Europe as a strategy of British modernization and a way to strengthen the state after the loss of Empire and disappointment with the special relationship with the United States. Only Jim Sillars and the ephemeral Scottish Labour Party in the 1970s were able to make a strong link between the unification of Europe and the disintegration of Britain.

In the 1980s, matters changed as Labour and the trade unions embraced Europe in reaction to Thatcherism and in response to Jacques Delors' espousal of a 'social Europe', taking a large swathe of their supporters with them. The SNP changed tack in 1988, partly under the influence of Jim Sillars, and has since been officially pro-European. Both parties make a connection between Europe and Scottish self-government. Labour has joined in the Europe of the Regions movement, seeking influence in Brussels and over the UK position in European negotiations. The Labour-led Scottish Executive after 1999 upgraded Scotland's presence in Brussels, with an Executive office alongside the existing Scotland Europa mission. In 2001 it signed the Flanders Declaration with six other 'constitutional regions' calling for more recognition for regions in the EU policy process, causing some friction with Whitehall. During the deliberations of the Convention on the Future of Europe (2002–3) and after, the Scottish Executive was active in the movement of Legislative Regions pushing for a special status in the making and implementation of European policies. The SNP's policy is simply stated as independence in

Europe, with accession as a full and equal member state of the European Union.

Yet neither party has succeeded in making a coherent link between Europe and Scottish self-government. Labour continues to subordinate European concerns to the UK line, and was careful in government not to depart publicly from the UK position or to present Europe as an alternative framework to the United Kingdom. The SNP is pro-Europe but has espoused an inter-governmental vision, in which the prime role will be played by national governments. Both parties face a Scottish electorate that is exposed to, and shares, much of the Euroscepticism that has dominated public discourse in the United Kingdom since the late 1980s. They are also cross-pressured by sectoral concerns and the impact of European policies. Both were able to play up the impact of EU Structural Funds in Scotland during the 1990s. Reform of the funds, enlargement to the east and improvements in the Scottish economy have now reduced the eligibility for European funding. There is an element of symbolism in all this since these funds were channelled through London, which deducted equivalent amounts from its regular transfers under the principle of non-additionality so that Scotland neither gained from them nor lost out from their reduction; but their presence allowed politicians from all parties to present Europe in a positive light while claiming credit for themselves. European competition policies, which have restricted subsidies for ferries, and especially agriculture and fisheries policies, have attracted less favourable attention. The result is that, when forced to make a clear choice for Europe, neither party has been able to do so, as was shown over the draft Constitutional Treaty from the Convention and the subsequent Lisbon Treaty. While the UK Labour Government put forward some proposals for regional input in Europe, its attitude to the Convention as a whole was highly defensive, and its case for the resulting treaty based almost entirely on what it had stopped rather than what it had built. The SNP, which might have taken advantage of Labour's cautiousness to stake out a stronger pro-Europe stance and demonstrate the need for independence, opposed both the draft Consti-tutional Treaty and Lisbon on the grounds that they continued the hated Common Fisheries Policy. Indeed, the party and the new SNP Government of 2007 demanded a referendum in which they would campaign for rejection, the implication being that an independent Scotland would be prepared to block the entire treaty for the sake of the fisheries sector.

Surveys show that attitudes to the EU in Scotland are complex. The Scottish Social Attitudes Survey (SSAS) measures attitudes to Europe on a five-point scale, with two points denoting Euroscepticism and two points Europhilia, the middle one being neutral. As in the rest of Britain, there is a pervasive Euroscepticism; this is slightly, but consistently, less pronounced in Scotland than in England. Supporters of all parties in Scotland are less Eurosceptic than in England, so this effect is not due to nationalist enthusiasm for Europe. While the previous tendency for nationalists to oppose Europe had disappeared by 1997 (Dardanelli 2005), they are now divided on the issue (McCrone 2006). Those identifying as Scottish are less Eurosceptic than British identifiers; English respondents identifying as English are more Eurosceptic again.

There is some connection between attitudes to Europe and on Scottish constitutional issues, but it is rather loose. The small number of people who favour independence outwith the EU are, not surprisingly, very Eurosceptic, as are the small number who want to have no Scottish Parliament (SSAS 1999, 2000, 2003, 2005). Those favouring independence in the EU are more likely to be Europhiles than those favouring other constitutional options; but only one survey, that of 2003, found that Europhiles actually outnumbered Eurosceptics among the independence-in-Europe camp (35 to 33 per cent: McCrone 2006). Two years later, amid more general Euroscepticism, the best that could be said is that they were less anti-Europe than other groups (47 against 52 per cent: SSAS 2005). Supporters of independence in Europe are less inclined than others to want to withdraw from the EU (although some 5 per cent consistently choose this option) but tend to be moderate Eurosceptics, who want to stay in the EU but reduce its powers. Supporters of independence outwith the EU are more likely to favour withdrawal but, curiously, most of them favour staying in.

A more general question asking whether people favour giving the Scottish Parliament more powers (on a five-point scale) also shows a loose connection with Euroscepticism. Nearly three quarters of those strongly opposed to giving the Scottish Parliament more powers are Eurosceptic, against half of those strongly in favour (SSAS 2005). Most of the electorate, however, take rather centrist positions on both issues. Young people are distinctly less Eurosceptic than their elders, a finding that holds equally for England and Scotland. This all suggests that there is a market for a pro-European policy combined with more Scottish autonomy or independence, and that the SNP has made some progress in convincing its supporters, but that the link is by no means obvious to all. Working class voters, a key part of the nationalist constituency, are inclined less to both Euroscepticism and Europhilia, while small businesspeople, another (albeit less numerous) pool of SNP support, are highly sceptical (McCrone 2006).

The nationalist project to shift the electorate away from supporting Scottish autonomy within a British union to a coherent project of independence within the European Union has therefore had a limited impact, albeit important in some sectors of the population. The SNP must be cautious about associating their project with a European project that gains little more enthusiasm in Scotland than elsewhere in the UK, and especially cautious about stressing the supranational aspects of Europe. On the other hand, Europe may work as a permissive factor to loosen the dependence on the British Union and serve to undermine some of the classic unionist arguments, while the electorate, when considering independence options, may take the EU context for granted. So at a time when Labour politicians were proclaiming that in an independent Scotland people would face border controls and be cut off from their relatives in England, surveys showed that the electorate did not believe them.[4] Many of them are now used to travelling easily in Europe; some would be aware that it was the UK Government that had refused to join the Schengen area of passport-free travel and was even then introducing drastic new border controls for entry and exit.

SHIFTING IDENTITIES

The last thirty years have seen a shift in national identities in Scotland, away from more British ones and towards more Scottish ones. The clearest evidence is provided in the Linz/Moreno question asked at various times since the 1980s, and in the Scottish Social Attitudes Survey since 1992, in which respondents are asked about the degree to which they feel British or Scottish. The responses are shown in Figure 3.1. Given a straight choice between Scottish and British, the proportion choosing Scottish rose from 65 per cent in 1974 to peak at 80 per cent in 2000 and has since fluctuated between 72 and 80 per cent. The decline in Britishness in Scotland is not therefore linked to devolution, although devolution does seem to have affected attitudes south of the border, with increasing numbers making a distinction between Britain and England, and English identifiers overtaking British identifiers there in 2006 (Heath and Roberts 2008).

Further probing reveals that these figures encompass a shifting relationship between Scottishness and other identities. The salience of Scottish identity is shown by the fact that it ranks alongside being a parent (and above gender, class, or marital status) as the most important (Bond 2006), which is not the case in England or Wales (Bond and Rosie 2006). There is a link with class in that Scots, particularly those identifying as Scottish, have been more likely to describe themselves as working class, irrespective of their objective occupational class (Brown et al. 1999; Surridge 2003) – although most people are now reluctant to place themselves in a social class at all. Not surprisingly, SNP voters overwhelmingly prioritize their Scottish identity (i.e. feeling only Scottish or more Scottish than British), but so do two thirds of Labour voters,

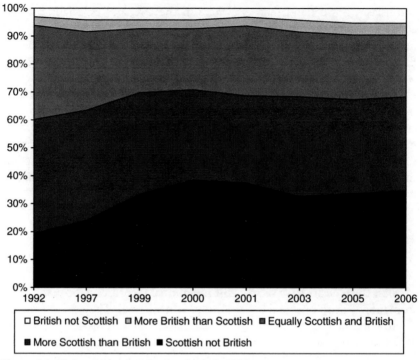

Figure 3.1 National identity, Scotland, 1992–2006

Source: Scottish Social Attitudes Survey.

a majority of Liberal Democrats and nearly half of Conservatives (SSAS 2005). Tilley and Heath (2007) show a marked decline in pride in Britain among Scots over succeeding generations, particularly so in relation to political matters such as democracy and history, as opposed to science, sports, arts, and literature. The shift is also marked in social security and in economic achievement, suggesting that newer generations do not construct their visions of economic development or social solidarity around the British nation. On the other hand, Scottishness has not displaced Britishness completely and often seems complementary rather than competitive to it, as nearly half of even SNP supporters retain some element of British identity and often take pride in the British past (Bechhofer and McCrone 2007). Only at the extremes is there a real polarization, with more than half those strongly repudiating Britain's past supporting independence against a fifth of those who were very proud, but these numbers are small and the great majority of the population take moderate positions on both questions (SSAS 2005).

Identity, however, does not impact directly on political behaviour, or else Scots would be voting massively for the nationalist party. Nor is it ever uncontested or hegemonic. Human beings have multiple identities – familial, occupational, gender, religious, and national – and these may be used and combined in different ways, only some of which are relevant to political choices. National identities themselves are complex, with most Scots able to link Britishness and Scottishness and a minority seeing these as exclusive. For some people, Scottishness is a cultural and historical identity, with no particular relevance to present-day constitutional issues. At the other extreme, some link a predominant feeling of being Scottish directly to support for independence. These identities are also linked in myriad ways to class and other identities, which may undermine or reinforce the national one.

This provides the background text upon which political entrepreneurs, both unionist and nationalist, can play to construct visions of the nation and build institutions (Reicher and Hopkins 2001). So Scotland could at one time be presented as a Protestant country, with religious and national factors reinforcing each other, a combination that underpinned unionism between the world wars. Conservative narratives of one-nation are used to combat class politics as well as Scottish separatist nationalism, with the Scottish nation inserted within the British one. On the left, a recurrent image presents Scotland as essentially egalitarian or even working class, so that class and nation inter-penetrate as mobilizing themes. The myth of progressive Scotland was one impulse behind the Home Rule movements of the late nineteenth and early twentieth centuries (Keating and Bleiman 1979). By the middle of the twentieth century, the labour movement had linked class politics and progressivism to a British discourse, portraying Scottish nationalism as divisive and reactionary. The SNP's support base in the petty bourgeoisie and small towns was used to depict them as 'Tartan Tories', while Britishness was equated with universalism and openness. These narratives have become more difficult to sustain. Protestantism no longer defines the Scottish nation, as Catholics of Irish origin have been assimilated. Across Europe, nationality movements have tended (with some notable exceptions) to move from the right to the centre and left, and cultural pluralism rather than integration is associated with progress. Scottish Labour's linking of opposition to Europe with opposition to Scottish nationalism in the 1970s exposed it as a British nationalist party rather than a universal or cosmopolitan one (Jones and Keating 1985). Class itself has been declining as a factor in political identification and choice, and New Labour has consciously recast itself as an inter-class party.

These constructions are linked to individual identities and cultural references but can never be reduced to them. Rather, they exist at the intersubjective level, in social practice and norms that give substantive meaning to notions of identity and community that might otherwise be confined to non-political realms (Keating 2008*b*). A public domain is constructed, which mediates between the level of individuals, as bearers of values, and institutions, which sustain and substantiate them. This explains why public culture may be different from individual values. There are some elements that have become dominant in Scottish public discourse, notably defence of the welfare settlement against the perceived threat from English Conservatism in the 1980s and a rebuilding of nationalism around themes of solidarity (Gall 2005; Béland and Lecours 2008). This is despite the small differences in individuals' attitudes to Thatcherism, as noted earlier. Hearn (2000) refers to the old concept of the 'moral economy', to capture a diffuse sense of what is fair, which serves to moderate the application of purely market criteria in public affairs and sustains a public domain. Stewart (2004) evokes a distinct Scottish public ethos. Even where there is disagreement about what being Scottish means, as in the contrasting images of individualist entrepreneurialism and collectivism, the fact that the question is being asked helps to define the public domain as Scottish rather than British, and to rebuild Scotland as a political community.

A similar story can be told about culture. Some stateless nationalisms have a cultural or linguistic core, and indeed, cultural distinctiveness may be part of the definition of the nation itself. It is sometimes said that culture is absent from the Scottish national debate and this is indeed true of language. Nairn (1977) argues that since the nineteenth century Scottish culture had been deformed by tartanry and the kailyard and unable to play its part in the national project. Beveridge and Turnbull (1989) asserted that Scottish culture had been inferiorized and stereotyped in a way typical of colonial societies. Yet a cultural revival in Scotland has coincided with the rise of nationalism since the 1970s and, while this does not give a unitary representation of the nation, the very argument about its meaning is evidence for a Scottish cultural sphere. Combating the old stereotypes occasionally means emptying the concept of Scottish culture of any meaning, as in the Labour-led Scottish Executive's early cultural strategy, which was so keen to de-essentialize culture and avoid giving hostages to nationalism that it was no more than a grab-bag of things happening in Scotland. More generally, however, the revival takes the form of seeing Scotland as a place of encounter of local and global cultures and of both old and modernized tradition. Scotland does not need a hegemonic culture or values to justify a national existence (McCrone 1992); the strengthening of its political and civil institutions has made the search for it less urgent, at the very time when the weakening of a previously unstated Britishness has led the UK political class to try and pin it down as a set of essentials (discussed below).

PARTY, CLASS, AND NATION

Scottish and British political parties have had to respond to these social changes, finding new formulas for accommodating changed class structures, dominant values, and the national question. The Conservatives, manifestly, have fared worst. They misread Scotland's political economy from the 1990s and failed in government to rebuild their social base. They remained a strongly British nationalist party but lost the classic unionist nuances. The nationalist rhetoric that (somewhat uncomfortably) accompanied Thatcher's attacks on the state contained echoes of imperial nostalgia, notably at the time of the Falklands War, and was backed by strong evocations of the United States and the English-speaking old dominions. Its other element, however, was drawn from the Little Englander tradition, assuming the superiority of British/English ways and historically associated with hostility to mainland Europe.

Labour was more successful in attracting the Scottish middle class vote and, with its commitment to devolution, provided a middle way in the national debate. Accepting both social change and the outcomes of Conservative policies of the 1980s and 1990s, they retained much of their electoral base while securing at least the benevolent neutrality of the business community. Yet, since devolution they have struggled to find a story of Scotland other than opposition to nationalism and the SNP. In eight years in government, they pursued, whether by choice or because they lacked a majority, a policy line rather more in tune with the Scottish moral economy than that pursued in England, with more universal social provision and less reliance on markets and competition (Keating 2005). Yet they failed to articulate this as a distinct form of Scottish social citizenship that might still be accommodated within the Union. They were unable or unwilling to follow their Catalan counterparts who have fashioned an ideology of *catalanismo*, which is distinct from both Catalan and Spanish nationalism, seeking a specific place for Catalonia within Spain and Europe.

The SNP has gained from the increased salience of Scottish themes. It has made inroads into the working class electorate, while retaining its petty bourgeois base and embracing other sections of the middle classes. The fluidity of the class system opens up further possibilities to a party without a historic class profile. Yet it remains ambivalent about the sort of Scotland it would like to see and reluctant to face up to distributive issues that might hamper its image as a catch-all party. Its support base is therefore broad but not deep. The SNP also gives the impression that it assumes that the Scottish nation is just 'there' and can simply be used both to postulate a shared national interest and to advance the self-government project. This is no doubt because national identity is indeed pervasive and little disputed. Yet, as noted earlier, the Scottish nation is always a work in progress. It is not what it was fifty years ago, and its social, economic, and political implications are by no means clear. This presents a strong contrast to similar movements elsewhere in Europe or in Quebec, which are conscious of the need to engage in continuous nation-building.

So all the main parties have had difficulty in bridging from the old politics of class and sector to the new politics of nationality and territory. The unionist parties (as they have taken to calling themselves since the SNP's electoral victory of 2007) have embraced devolution, which the Conservatives continued to resist up to 1999, but combine it with a British nationalism that fits poorly with it, and have largely failed to present devolution as a positive opportunity. The nationalists, for their part, are thirled to a rather traditional conception of what independence means and have failed to engage in the sort of nation-building, or at least a representation of the nation, on which they could base a social and economic project.

THE IDEOLOGY OF BRITISHNESS

In recent years, the British Government, supported by various intellectuals, has launched a comprehensive and ambitious plan to reassert Britishness and the value of the Union. This is aimed at two perceived threats to the nation, the multicultural and the multinational. Multiculturalism is the recognition of cultural diversity among peoples and ethnic minorities of recent immigration. Multinationalism is the recognition of the diverse nations within the United Kingdom and is of longer standing. Government's response has been to assert an ideology of Britishness that can subsume both while reducing their impact and reintegrating the British nation state.

The ideology is to be a civic one, based on common human values and open to all. Some critics have wondered how a national ideology can be based on values such as democracy and fair play that are universal, or on an open, not a closed identity. Yet this is not the main problem. Most modern states have national ideologies that combine adherence to universal values with a recognition of the nation as the place where they are realized. Indeed this was the democratic basis of the American and French revolutions at the end of the eighteenth century. A more recent version is Habermas' (1998) constitutional patriotism, in which adherence to the institutions of the state replaces blood and belonging; Colley (1999) advocates a similar construction for Britain. National narratives tend, however, to be rather thicker and more particularist. So nationalism is reconciled with universalism by the claim that this nation has a special mission, or that it discovered liberty first, or that it evinces it better than others. Its history is presented as a march of progress towards enlightenment and its symbols are given a democratic and liberal meaning, providing a normative superiority over rival national projects.

British New Labour governments have done all of these things. There has been an insistence on Britishness as a strong, albeit non-ethnic, identity, apart from and above that of the component parts. In Gordon Brown's first speech as leader to the Labour Party Conference, he mentioned Britain fifty-one times and British twenty-nine times, including British people (sixteen times) and the notorious 'British jobs for British workers'. Addressing the Fabian Society, he urged the flying of flags and, in a curious mixture of nation-building and managerialism, the need for a British mission statement (Brown 2006). This British identity is, according to a Labour minister, 'different from our English identity or Scottish identity or our Bengali or Cornish identities because it is quintessentially plural' (Wills 2008). The implication is that it is superior and broad, while the other identities are narrow and exclusive. As the Green Paper on *The Governance of Britain* (Secretary of State for Justice and Lord Chancellor 2007: 57) put it, 'There is room to celebrate multiple and different identities, but none of these identities should take precedence over the core democratic values that define what it means to be British.'

UK governments are not alone in seeking to renew a strong national identity in the face of multiculturalism and the fear of social disintegration, as similar projects are at work across Europe and North America. Yet there are two problems. The first is to subsume the different issues of multiculturalism and multinationalism under the same heading. The second is to postulate this British identity as a uniform Britishness across the whole United Kingdom, with local national identities nested below it.

Sunder Katwala (2005), General Secretary of the Fabian Society, for example, has urged that the issues of Europe, multiculturalism, and devolution should come together. Yet, while all these are about pluralism, the multicultural challenge, about the co-existence of different cultures, values, and ways of life, is not the same as the challenge of plurinationalism, which is about the boundaries of political community and the scope of the polity in which universal values will be developed.[5] Measures to tackle what the government sees as an excess of multiculturalism do not fit well with the reality of a multinational state in which the nationality bargain is being negotiated differently in different places. The constituent nations of the United Kingdom are themselves the sites of nation-building projects, based on civic and universal values and facing the challenges of multiculturalism. This is very similar to the problem that has arisen in Quebec, where Québécois of both nationalist and federalist persuasions have resisted efforts to combine the two challenges in a single logic of unity in diversity. Multiculturalism itself will therefore have to take different forms in the different parts of the United Kingdom, just as it does in Quebec and English-speaking Canada.

Lord Goldsmith's report (2008) on citizenship, commissioned by the Prime Minister, devotes a long section to citizenship education, linking this to the inculcation of Britishness in a way familiar from the France of the Third Republic; but the account refers exclusively to the English education system. There is no indication whatever of how this might work in Scotland, Wales, or Northern Ireland, or what citizenship actually means there. There is a breezy assurance that none of his recommendations will affect the recognition of national plurality within the United Kingdom, but nowhere is this plurality properly addressed. It is seen rather as a subordinate element within the overwhelming narrative of Britishness rather than a core component of that Britishness itself. A traditional unionist, on the other hand, would be aware that the meaning of Britishness itself differs from one part of the United Kingdom to another, rather than being a homogeneous identity atop diversity. Goldsmith recommends an Oath of Allegiance to the monarch and a Pledge of Allegiance to the United Kingdom by young people coming of age, with only a passing acknowledgement of how this might go down in Scotland or Northern Ireland. The new citizenship tests incorporate a knowledge of the United Kingdom but only by demanding of potential citizens a type of knowledge that most of the native-born do not possess,[6] rather than accepting diversified citizenship in the component nations. There is also the paradox that, as has been pointed out by many commentators, this kind of nation-building is essentially un-British, as is the constant evocation of citizen duties (as in Kelly and Byrne 2007).

New Labour's Britishness is relentlessly modernist. It is linked with democracy, fair play and the National Health Service and carefully detached from Empire. As Nairn (2006) has noted, it is almost completely devoid of monarchy, an important symbol of unity in the past. This gives a clue to the second problem: that UK politicians are trying to build a unitary national tradition and identity in the wrong era. Plurinational states, including Spain and Canada – having missed out building a single national identity in the nineteenth century, when it could be linked to republicanism and modernity – cannot try to build it in the different circumstances of the late twentieth or early twenty-first century. This explains the failure of Pierre Trudeau's vision of converting Canada into a mononational (albeit multicultural state), against the already-advanced project of nation-building in Quebec. New Labour similarly seeks to build a new Britain based on shared civic values, when nationalists and home rulers engaged in the same process have already stolen a lead of some twenty years in Scotland.

So the effort to promote national identities based on universal values confronts, not a Scottish identity based on exclusion and ethnicity, but a revived Scottish national identity based on exactly the same values and with a distinct European and global dimension. Evocation of the National Health Service as the embodiment of British solidarity may provide ammunition against the political right, but has no impact against Scottish (or Welsh and Irish) nationalists who are equally committed to universal provision free at the point of use. Indeed, it stumbles against the fact that the NHS is being reconstructed in different ways in the constituent parts of the United Kingdom, drawing on distinct ideas about social citizenship. While reform in England recasts the user as consumer, in Scotland and Wales the underlying image is that of citizen. Labour leaders have so far failed in weaving a narrative that links social citizenship back into a coherent nation-rebuilding project (Jeffery 2005).

While multiculturalism might better be detached from the debate on multinationalism, the same cannot easily be said about Europe, since it represents a new scale of territorial government and political community. Brown's speeches are notorious for the absence of European themes that are a staple of political discourse elsewhere in the EU. This makes it difficult for the promotion of Britishness to look other than exclusive, despite the gestures to globalization and friendly relations with Europe and the United States (which are usually given equal billing). Other European states have refashioned their national narratives to embrace the European dimension, crediting Europe for sustaining the values of the winning democracies of the Second World War. Britain's different experience, with neither defeat nor occupation, meant that it did not need such external validation for democratic and liberal values, and the arguments in favour of the European Union have been largely instrumental. The predominant image is of the EU as an arena for struggle in which ministers fight to defend the national interest against our enemies, forever drawing red lines and negotiating opt-outs. This means that Europe cannot itself provide new ways of thinking about the British Union, nor can the United Kingdom help in imagining a plurinational union on a wider scale.

History remains a battleground for rival national projects, and both New Labour and its associated intellectuals have called for a revived British history. Since the 1970s, historians have abandoned teleological or English-centric visions of the past in favour of the 'islands history' perspective (Pocock 1975; Kearney 1995; Brockliss and Eastwood 1997; Davies 1999). Some have moved further and sought to link developments here back into the broader sweep of European history (Scott 2000). New Labour, however, tends to fall back on the old Whiggish teleology, in which British history is merely a continuation of English history and represents a steady march of progress (Lee 2006). So, after referring to 2000 years of British history, Gordon Brown (2006) cites Runnymede (Magna Carta) but makes no reference whatever to non-English constitutional history. He asserts that in 1689, 'Britain [*sic*] became the first country to successfully assert the power of Parliament over the King' – this twenty-eight years before Britain came into existence. The only non-English citation is to Henry Grattan (the late eighteenth-century Irish patriot), declaring that 'We can get a Parliament from anywhere...we can only get liberty from England [*sic*].' When Jack Straw, Lord Chancellor (of England) and minister for constitutional reform, lectured in the United States on Modernising the Magna Carta, he gave a view of British constitutional history that included a list of English milestones as well as developments in the nineteenth and twentieth centuries but failed to mention the acts of union with Wales, Scotland, and Ireland; he also incorrectly told his audience that the House of Lords was currently the 'final court of appeal for the UK court system' (Straw 2008).

Much attention has been given to the teaching of British history and the need to include the good and bad of Empire, multiculturalism, and the story of the nations and regions of these islands (Colley 2003; Marsden 2005). Yet English politicians and intellectuals raising this issue address it exclusively through consideration of the 'national curriculum', which only applies in England. The same applies to citizenship education, although this is a distinctly English notion with no counterpart in the devolved nations (Andrews and Mycock 2008). It is as though the English curriculum could itself become British by being a little more pluralistic and accommodating, so allowing the same story to be told throughout the United Kingdom. Again this misses the point that the experience and meaning of Britishness themselves vary from one nation to the other and that a common history curriculum would mean a greater centralization than was ever attempted in the high days of Union. It also evades the question of whether the Union should be taught as a fundamental value, when Scottish nationalism and independence now feature in public debate as legitimate political options.

The British political elite seem to have lost their old sense of the Union and are engaged in a new form of nation-building for a new age, but one that curiously resembles the classic nation-building of the nineteenth century.

They are not alone here, since many European countries have taken up renewed national narratives in the face of immigration and cultural differentiation. In Britain, however, it cuts across the narratives of multinationalism. Ascherson (2006) claims that it is mainly the non-English elites who are making the fuss about Britishness, seeking to redeem the old unionist polity; and indeed it is they who have most to lose from the end of Union. There is in fact a debate in England, but it is a different one, in which multinationalism is brought under the rubric of multiculturalism and both are addressed within essentially English parameters.

SUPPORT FOR INDEPENDENCE AND THE UNION

Scottish national identity has been strengthening and faces a poorly-articulated concept of Britishness; but the political implications are far from obvious. Spatial rescaling is reinforcing the Scottish level of institutions, civil society and political mobilization but not effacing the British level or imposing a new set of fixed and coinciding boundaries. The old Union may be weakening, but it is not clear that a new Scotland is replacing it. In this context it is not surprising that public attitudes to constitutional change appear confused and even contradictory.

Gauging support for Scottish independence over the long run is difficult, since there is not a good time series and, as explained below, the question is not always clear. The best estimate is that it ran at about 20 per cent from the first polls in the 1960s, through the rise of the SNP in the 1970s, with a dip after the failed devolution referendum in 1979. It then started to rise during the 1980s under the Conservative Government from the mid-1980s into the 1990s, to reach around 35 per cent. This is the longest period since the arrival of democracy that Scotland has been ruled by a party for which it had not voted, putting the old unionist assumptions under considerable strain. There seems to have been a slight drop with the arrival of the Labour Government in 1997, followed by devolution, with support running just below 30 per cent (Keating 2001a). Independence appears to have become more generally accepted as a viable option and, in some ways, less polarizing. In 1979, those in favour of devolution tended to give the status quo as their second preferred option, with a strong rejection of independence. By 1997, most devolution supporters chose independence as the second option, indicating a strong rejection of the status quo and that independence was not the fearful prospect it had been twenty years earlier (Dardanelli 2005). Voters also seemed to be quite open to the idea that the United Kingdom might not last another fifty years. A YouGov poll for *The Sunday Times* in January 2007 showed 59 per cent of Scots thinking that independence was likely within the next twenty years (31% within ten years). By contrast, Surridge (2006), using election study and social survey data, finds a fall from 59 to 31 per cent of Scots thinking that independence was likely within twenty years. In 2003, 48 per cent of them would be unhappy to leave the Union, against 24 per cent who would be pleased. A YouGov poll for *The Daily Telegraph* in June 2006 showed that 70 per cent of people in Britain as a whole expected the Union to survive. Yet only 25 per cent would be unhappy if Scotland were to become independent, with 44 per cent indifferent. There is no evidence, contrary to what devolution opponents consistently argued, that devolution itself has driven up support for independence, since the increase pre-dates devolution and, if anything, support seems to have fallen away a little since. This, however, requires that we interpret the figures carefully.

Support for independence in Scotland is notoriously difficult to measure and appears to fluctuate in the short run, prompting flurries of excitement in the media, which tend to over-interpret the ups and downs. Attitudes are very sensitive to the wording of the question (as they are in other stateless nations), with 'harder' options mentioning 'separate' or 'separation' gaining less support. They are also affected by the presentation of options. For many years, a straight question about whether the respondent would vote for independence has gained substantially more support than one that compares independence with various options for devolution. Before 1999, this might be explained by some devolution voters treating independence as their second preference and opting for it rather than direct Westminster rule if those were the only choices presented. Since 1999, however, devolution has been the default option so that anyone voting against independence would in effect be voting for devolution. The anti-independence vote should thus logically be a constant. That it is not might be an example of the 'preference reversal' effect, whereby people may change their preferences between two options when a third is mentioned. This suggests that voters do not order their preferences transitively as expected by rational choice theory; this would make life extremely difficult for the political parties. Another possibility, supported by similar evidence elsewhere, is that voters do not make a clear distinction between independence and more devolution but tend in their majority to want more self-government.[7] This would lead them to favour change away from the status quo and towards more autonomist options. If independence is the only such option offered in the survey, they might be expected to gravitate towards it. It also appears that, as elsewhere, many voters like independence as a general idea but are not so sure about it as a concrete proposition, since it has to be weighed against other considerations.[8]

Even an apparently straight question asking about Yes or No to independence provokes different responses, depending on exactly how it is put. A question from ICM has asked:

> *In a referendum on independence for Scotland, how would you vote? I agree that Scotland should become an independent country. I do not agree that Scotland should become an independent country.*

Between 1998 and 2008, this has gained the support of between 40 and 56 per cent of respondents.

After the election of the SNP Government, TNS/System 3 reminded respondents of the SNP promise to hold a referendum and used the SNP's preferred question:

> *I agree that the Scottish Government should negotiate a settlement with the Government of the United Kingdom so that Scotland becomes an independent state.*

This is a harder question since it presents independence as an imminent prospect and mentions the word 'state'.[9] This question gained about 35–40 per cent support in 2007–8.

YouGov has asked an even harder question which uses the word 'separate' and reminds people that a No vote still leaves them with the Scottish Parliament:

> *If there were a referendum on whether to retain the Scottish Parliament and Executive in more or less their present form or to establish a completely separate state outside the United Kingdom, how would you vote?*

During 2007–8, this gained the support of between 25 and 27 per cent.

Taking polls as close together as possible suggests that the wording is indeed critical. ICM and YouGov polls were 16–20 points apart in their estimates of independence support in the spring of 2007. Between 1998 and 2002, ICM asked in the same survey a question about the range of constitutional options and a straight question about independence. About half of the respondents consistently supported independence in the straight choice but, when a devolutionary alternative was presented, independence support fell to around a third; this despite the fact that devolution was now the only alternative to independence.

A more consistent measure is provided by the Scottish Social Attitudes Survey (SSAS). Like other surveys, this offers a range of options: a 'hard' version of independence ('separate from the UK'); a Scottish Parliament with tax-raising powers; the present Parliament; and no Parliament:

> *Which of these statements comes closest to your view? Scotland should become independent, separate from the UK and the European Union. Scotland should*

become independent, separate from the UK but part of the European Union. Scotland should remain part of the UK, with its own elected parliament which has some taxation powers. Scotland should remain part of the UK, with its own elected parliament which has no taxation powers. Scotland should remain part of the UK without an elected parliament.

The offer of more powerful devolution again depresses independence support. Support for independence increased slowly from 29 per cent in 1999 to 34 per cent in 2005, but fell away to 23 per cent in 2007, curiously just when the SNP was winning the election (Curtice 2008). Figure 3.2 shows the trend. Evidence from other polls suggests that support for independence is fairly evenly spread throughout Scotland but is slightly higher in the Highlands and Islands and the north east.[10] It is rather evenly spread among the population but with a peak among the working class, while some polls have found higher levels among male voters and younger voters (although not always the youngest). There is therefore no evidence to suggest that Scottish nationalism is merely a displaced class, gender, or sectoral identity. It does appear to be a distinct factor not reducible to anything else.

Scottish national identity does map onto views about the constitutional future of the Union, explaining the trend towards self-government. The relationship, however, is anything but straightforward. One difficulty is that Scottish identity is so pervasive and multi-faceted that in itself it explains rather little. According to the Scottish Social Attitudes Survey, a fifth of those identifying as purely British want to have no Scottish Parliament at all, against a twentieth of those identifying as purely Scottish; this contrast is as we might

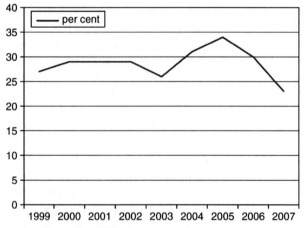

Figure 3.2 Support for independence in Scotland, 1999–2007
Source: Scottish Social Attitudes Survey.

expect. Yet it still leaves 80 per cent of the purely British as well as large majorities across all groups supporting the Parliament. Two thirds of those identifying as only or mainly Scottish think that the Scottish Executive[11] as opposed to the UK Government should have most power over how Scotland is run, but then so do half of those identifying as mainly British (SSAS 2005). Eighty per cent of those identifying as purely or mainly Scottish want the Scottish Parliament to be given more powers, but so do half of those identifying as predominantly British. In 2005, half of those identifying as only Scottish supported independence but, perhaps surprisingly, so did a fifth of those identifying as only British (although numbers here are rather low). The hardest core is the group who were purely Scottish and wanted out of both the United Kingdom and the European Union, but this amounted only to 6 per cent of respondents (SSAS 2005). So while Scottishness predicts support for constitutional change, it does not determine it. Rather, identities and their constitutional implications exist in overlapping compartments, with large room for negotiation and manoeuvre. Political parties can use this margin to construct messages and bases of support for the Union, an independent Scotland, or positions in between.

Earlier, we considered two competing hypotheses about the effect of economic conditions on support for Scottish nationalism and the Union: that bad times would encourage nationalism and good times would favour unionism; or that bad times would drive Scottish voters back to the politics of managed dependency, while in good times they would feel better able to go it alone. The historical evidence appears to point to the latter. We might, however, reformulate the hypothesis in a more subtle manner, still consistent with rational economic calculation. This is that the Scots would favour independence when they think they would be better off economically as an independent state, whether or not they are doing well in absolute terms or in relation to England. There is some evidence for this, in that those who think that the Union is not working in Scotland's interests and that Scotland is poorly treated are more likely to favour independence. According to the 2005 SSAS, just over a third of the population favour independence; the same number think that England does better than Scotland from the Union (eliminating 'don't knows'). The symmetry is misleading, however, since these are not the same people. Just over half those favouring independence think that England does better and just over half thinking that England does better are in favour of independence. This shows that those who have an economic grievance are more likely to favour independence and vice versa, but does not account for that quarter of those thinking that Scotland benefits equally who still favour independence.[12] Asking whether people think that Scotland gets less than its share of government spending also suggests a rather loose connection between the two. Just over half the population thinks that Scotland gets less than its fair share, a figure rising to a little over 60 per cent among independence supporters. Of those who think that Scotland gets less than its fair share, some 45 per cent prefer independence, marginally more than those who favour devolution. Once again, there is an overlap but it is far from perfect. Nor do we know in which direction the influence is working. There is a core of just over a fifth of electors who both believe that Scotland does badly economically and financially from the Union and support independence, but otherwise the issues are only loosely connected. Of course, the salience of the issue and the degree of information that voters have also affects attitudes. Curtice (2008), noting an increase in the 2007 SSAS in the proportion thinking that Scotland gets its fair share of spending or more, suggests that the arguments of the anti-nationalists may be beginning to register. In a larger perspective, the debate about the economics of independence and the fiscal flows has gone on so long with such weighty contributions on both sides that the two sides have probably argued each other to a standstill, their arguments cancelling each other out. In that case, voters could make the economic judgement fit their political preference rather than the other way around.

There does appear to be a consolidation of support in Scotland for self-government (Herbert 2006; Surridge 2006); support for having no Parliament at all has fallen from a steady 20 per cent before devolution to around 10 per cent in subsequent surveys. There is also a steady desire to go beyond the present settlement, but no consensus for independence in its traditional meaning. Support for independence as recorded in the SSAS is not only lower but also more polarizing than softer self-government options. In many stateless nations, there is an ambivalence about the concept of independence. Surveys in Quebec have repeatedly revealed that many electors want seemingly contradictory things, including an independent Quebec and remaining within Canada (Keating 2001*a*, *b*). Basque respondents come out in favour of having a Basque passport but remaining in Spain (Keating 2001*a*). A 1999 ICM poll in Scotland showed 82 per cent thinking that an independent Scotland should be defended by the British army, and another one in 2008 showed that 54 per cent still held that idea while 67 per cent would expect to continue paying a licence fee to the BBC (Fraser 2008). Earlier polls showed that most Scots thought that a devolved Scotland should negotiate separately in the European Union (Keating 2001*a*). It seems that electors do not draw a clear line between independence and strong forms of home rule but see self-government as a continuum. Reading the Scottish data carefully, there appears to be widespread support for more autonomy and a stronger position within the EU, but not for the classic trappings of statehood such as a separate defence force or diplomatic service. At a deeper level, this might represent a more realistic understanding of the modern polity and power than those politicians and scholars who continue to insist that sovereign statehood is still the basis for political rule.

THE END OF THE UNION?

The Union was a uniquely British form of territorial accommodation. It was less than a unitary state but more than a mere marriage of convenience. It can be understood only in relation to a distinctive British mode of governing reliant on elite management and tacit understandings, as Bulpitt (1983) notably demonstrated. This mode of governing has, if not entirely ended, been changed beyond recognition with the internal and external restructuring of the state. There have been successive phases of Union, from the sullen acceptance of the early years, through the triumphalism of the nineteenth century, to the managed dependency of the twentieth. Since the 1970s, we have seen a rebuilding of a civic Scottish nation and political space within the Union, linked in various ways to the European project. There is a process of functional change, with the rise of the new spatial economics and inter-territorial competition, putting the emphasis on self-help and decentralization. Mass opinion has shifted towards a predominantly Scottish identity, although this is by no means exclusive. There has been a change in the institutional dynamics now that the unionist parties have accepted a Scottish Parliament, ostensibly the mere creature of Westminster, which retains the power to overrule it at any time, but in reality resting upon a national consensus and a popular referendum vote. Intransigent unionists and nationalists are agreed that the institutional dynamics are leading inexorably to Scottish independence and that devolution is an unstable halfway house.

The mainstream elites, for their part, have seemingly lost the plot, and neither the Labour nor the Conservative Party has found a new mode of accommodation to suit the new conditions. The ideology of union is in crisis, tied to a particular conception of state and nation and unable to accommodate the transformation of the state and the challenges of multiculturalism and multinationalism. It has not, however, given way to an alternative hegemonic ideology or practice based on the component nations. Scottish, let alone Welsh or Irish, nationalism is not the state-building movement familiar to historians of the nineteenth and twentieth centuries. Support for an independent Scottish nation state is limited, even when this is placed within the context of the overarching European Union. There is, rather, an inchoate yearning for a renegotiated form of polity, recognizing the limitations of sovereign authority in the modern world. One party, the SNP, proposes the resumption of Scottish independence, so that the nation can make its own choices about how it fits into the emerging international order. The unionist parties, for their part, talk about reforming the Union from within. The following chapters consider these options in more detail.

4

Becoming Independent

CAN SCOTLAND SECEDE?

Scottish independence in the traditional sense implies secession from the United Kingdom and the establishment of a separate state, sovereign in international law and a member of the United Nations and other international institutions; this, essentially, is the policy of the Scottish National Party (SNP). The question of whether secession is permissible has two aspects: that of ethics or morality; and that of law and constitutional propriety.

Almost everybody would concede that a separation mutually agreed between two parts of a state is morally permissible. The problem arises when one part wishes to secede unilaterally. For nationalists, there is no problem, since nations have the right to self-government and if these do not correspond to the state, then they are justified in setting up their own. Unfortunately, this does not take us very far, since the concept of nationality is itself subjective and contested. Indeed, the claim and right to self-determination are among the elements that define groups as nations, rendering the argument rather circular. Nationalists are, further, caught in a scholastic trap by their opponents. If they are not culturally or 'ethnically' distinct in some way, they are dismissed as not a real community; but if they are distinct, they are told that they are particularists who represent an obstacle to universal human equality. They can, and do, ask by what criterion the existing states have a right to self-determination or separate existence. Defenders of the existing states in turn contend that the state depends on a higher, civic principle that transcends ethnic or cultural particularism and constitutes a space for the realization of universal values. As we have seen, this is part of the argument underpinning the new Britishness agenda. In yet a further twist, however, minority nationalists now argue that theirs too is a civic nationality based on liberal and universal values and has nothing to do with ethnic particularism. The ethical status of the two claims, for the state and the stateless nation, are thus morally equivalent. This, as I have argued elsewhere, is a particularly powerful form of nationalism, since it predicates the clash of two projects occupying the same moral ground (Keating 2001a, 2001b).

Permissive secession theorists dispense with the nationality principle altogether and argue that the fundamentals of democracy require that any group of people be allowed to constitute themselves into an independent state (Beran 1998). This position has been criticized as destabilizing, since it provides an invitation for people to manipulate state boundaries to suit their short-term convenience and leave the remaining population of the state to cope with the consequences. Rich areas could abandon poor regions, and the moral obligations underpinning statehood would be violated. Most political theorists take the more restrictive position that secession is permissible only when the rights of a people have been violated or manifest oppression has taken place (Buchanan 2004). This in turn has been criticized as unduly limiting (Moore 2001), since it assumes that existing state boundaries are morally neutral and that the burden of proof must rest on those proposing to change them. It could also be an incentive to militants to provoke conflict and repression, so as to create the requisite grievance. Some theorists make an exception for groups and territories that have been self-governing in the past and came into a more or less voluntary union with another state, without surrendering their original rights. This is the argument made by the secessionist states of the United States in the 1860s and by Quebec, Scottish, and other nationalists; but as a general argument it is very difficult to operationalize, since the past is subject to so much argument and interpretation that the debate about what happened in the past becomes just another way of arguing about the present, rather than a way of resolving the issue. Miller (2001) takes the argument the other way and argues in the case of Scotland that it owes a moral obligation from the way it has benefited from the Union over time and cannot unilaterally repudiate this. Moreover, there is an overarching British community in whose survival the English have a legitimate stake.

Contextual approaches argue that we cannot resolve specific questions by appealing to universal principles but must appraise the ethical, historical, and political issues at stake in each case (Coppieters and Sakwa 2003; Keating 2008c). Rather than a reductionist attitude towards self-government claims – in which it all comes down to a single principle (which is inevitably contested) – we can take a summative approach, which asks of individual cases what claims and counterclaims are being made. Secessionist movements do not generally spring up for purely opportunistic reasons or to secure short-term economic advantages, as mobilizing for secession is a difficult and costly business. Nationality may be a slippery term and nations very difficult to identify using objective criteria; but there is a sociological difference between communities that have developed strong forms of collective political identity and a historic narrative to underpin it and mere communities of convenience. The distinction is clearer in some contexts than in others, but it is not difficult to distinguish between Scotland and the 'nation' of Padania, invented by the Italian Lega Nord as purportedly 'the oldest community in Europe' (Oneto 1997). Similarly, historic understandings of self-government and rights are stronger in some places than in others. Secessionist movements may be more ethnically exclusive or more civic and inclusive in determining who belongs to the nation and the moral status of their claims differs accordingly. So, for example, analogies between Scotland and Republika Srpska within Bosnia do not survive a moment's scrutiny (Keating 2008c).

As we have seen, the United Kingdom has evolved as a community of nations, whose boundaries and constitution have been contested but in which the claims of an encompassing British nationality have never been able to trump those of the constituent parts. Scotland is not an ethnic fragment but a national and civic community in which the boundaries of the national community have been built and rebuilt to coincide with the territorial unit. This means that one classic problem of secession, that of minorities trapped within the new borders, does not arise. A Scottish right of self-determination, implicit in the concept of union, has remained at least implicitly in all discussions about the constitution. The consequence is that the ethical questions about the right of self-determination that bedevil debates around secession in other states have hardly arisen in the Scottish case. Even the most unionist of politicians accept the legitimacy of Scottish independence, on condition only that this is the will of the Scottish people. So John Major (1993) declared that no nation could be kept in a union against its will, while even Margaret Thatcher (1993: 624) conceded that 'As a nation, they (the Scots) have an undoubted right to national self-determination; thus far they have exercised that right by joining and remaining in the Union. Should they determine on independence no English party or politician would stand in their way, however much we might regret their departure.' Labour politicians have been less explicit; but in recent years no senior representative of the party has denied Scotland's right to independence in principle. Former First Minister Donald Dewar effectively conceded it in 1994 (Murkens 2002), and Scottish leader Wendy Alexander even called for an independence referendum in 2008; she was called to order by the UK leadership, but on the timing of the demand rather than the principle of self-determination.

The legal and constitutional arguments about secession are complex. International law upholds the principle of self-determination but is far from clear on what this means in practice. The United Nations Charter refers to it as the basis for friendly relations among nations, and the International Covenants on Civil and Political Rights and on Economic, Social and Cultural Rights of 1966 recognize the right of 'peoples' to 'self-determination'; but in practice this has been interpreted to refer to the right of existing states to their territorial integrity, with secession permissible only in the case of colonial possessions – the so-called 'salt water doctrine'. Self-determination in existing states is interpreted effectively as democracy and, while some Scottish home rulers wanted to invoke this in the 1980s on the grounds that Scotland was being denied it by being outvoted by England, this made no progress as a matter of international law. The Supreme Court of Canada (1998), in its famous judgment on the right of Quebec to secede, found no grounds in international law, or in the Canadian Constitution; although it did rule that, should a province wish to secede, the Canadian Government would be bound to negotiate with it on the principle of respecting the democratic will. The Spanish Constitution, by contrast, explicitly rules out secession by stipulating the indissoluble unity of the Spanish nation.

The British Constitution is silent on the matter, both in written provisions and in unwritten convention; but there is a precedent in the secession of most of Ireland and the permissive clause in the Northern Ireland Act of 1998 providing for Irish unity by consent. Paradoxically, the most ardent unionists, by insisting on the absolute sovereignty of Westminster, have to allow the legality of at least an agreed secession since the will of Parliament is subject to no higher appeal. It was this snare that trapped Dicey in the early twentieth century when he tried to argue that both Westminster was supreme and that an act giving home rule to Ireland would be unconstitutional. This would surely be the decisive argument and, given that the Westminster parties and English public opinion agree that a Scottish desire for independence would have to be respected, there seems no constitutional obstacle. The difficulty, rather, would lie in the procedure.

NEGOTIATING INDEPENDENCE

For many years, the SNP position was that winning a majority of Scottish seats at Westminster would provide a mandate to negotiate independence. This stance, which followed the Irish precedent, was rejected by the unionist parties, not because of the principle of secession but on democratic grounds. After 1999 the SNP changed their position so that the trigger was to be a pro-independence majority in the Scottish Parliament, with the eventual constitution subject to a referendum. As proportional representation reduced the prospects of gaining the requisite majority, more emphasis was put on the referendum, and by 2003 the party was promising an independence referendum during the first mandate of an SNP administration. The minority government formed in 2007 duly proceeded on these lines, with a 'national conversation' leading to a referendum scheduled for 2010. The unionist parties denounced the referendum strategy as unwanted, and the Liberal Democrats made this the breaking point in coalition negotiations with the SNP. Yet, while the unionists used their majority in the Scottish Parliament to launch their own counterproposals, they at no point claimed that the referendum itself was illegitimate. Indeed in the course of a very confusing week, Labour even seemed to endorse it, while promising to campaign for a No vote. Opinion on the legality of an independence referendum has been rather confused. Clearly, negotiating independence is outwith the competence of the Scottish Government and Parliament, since the 1998 Act reserves the matter of the union to Westminster. On the other hand, there seems little to stop the Scottish Parliament holding a consultative referendum on the principle. This was the device used by the Basque Government in 2008 to advance its agenda, by calling a popular 'consultation' rather than using the word 'referendum'. In that case, the Spanish parties insisted that the procedure was still unconstitutional and had the initiative struck down by the Constitutional Court. In the Scottish case, the unionists seem to have decided that resisting on this point would be counterproductive. The nationalists thus won an important point of principle; the mechanics are another matter.

Since the 1970s the referendum has become the accepted British way of dealing with constitutional matters but without consistent rules. There was a referendum on the European Community in 1975 and the 1997 Labour Government promised referendums on both the EU constitutional treaty and entry into the Euro, although neither happened. Referendums have been used on devolution matters, in 1979 and 1997 for Scotland and Wales, in 1998 for Northern Ireland, in 1997 for the government of Greater London, and in 2004 for English regional devolution. Referendums are provided for in the Northern Ireland Act (for unity with the Irish Republic) and the Government of Wales Act (2006) (for extending the legislative powers of the National Assembly for Wales).

The normal rule in referendums is that a majority of those voting will carry the day, although some constitutions have special arrangements requiring super-majorities. The 'fast track' to regional autonomy in Spain required majorities of the entire electorate (and not just those voting) in an effort to limit the process to the historic nationalities.[1] Italian referendums to repeal legislation are valid only if more than 50 per cent of the electorate turns out. The 1979 referendums in Scotland and Wales were saddled with a provision that required a positive vote on the part of 40 per cent of the entire electorate – a difficult threshold that sabotaged Scottish devolution although the majority of those voting had supported it. This left a bitter legacy in Scotland and no other UK referendum rule has required anything other than a simple majority, so allowing Welsh devolution to go ahead with a bare majority amounting to only a quarter of the electorate.

It is widely argued that, secession being such a serious and irreversible matter, independence referendums should be subject to a super-majority. In practice, most independence referendums, whether in the former Soviet Union, former Jugoslavia, East Timor or, earlier, in Norway, have followed such powerful mobilization that they have carried by huge majorities, putting the popular will beyond doubt. The case of Quebec is more difficult. In 1995, a referendum on a rather ambivalent question asking whether Quebec should become sovereign after having made an offer of partnership with Canada was defeated by less than 1 per cent of the popular vote, on a turnout of 93 per cent. After taking the advice of the Supreme Court (see earlier), the Parliament of Canada declared (in the 1999 Clarity Bill) that such a referendum should be respected only if based on a clear question and passed by a clear majority. The difficulty lies in defining these terms. The Canadian Parliament clearly had in mind a majority of more than 50 per cent plus one of those voting, although this is not specified in law. A 'clear question' is even more difficult, given the slippery nature of the issue. As noted earlier (Chapter 3), very different levels of support can be generated for independence in Scotland depending on exactly how the question is framed. Some commentators have raised a further barrier in the form of a second referendum, although Murkens (2002) has suggested that this might remove the need for a qualified majority.

This issue has barely been broached in the Scottish debate, while the reluctance of the unionist parties to talk about a referendum at all has allowed the nationalists to make the running on three key issues: the threshold required for the referendum to pass; the need for one or two referendums; and the question to be asked. The discussion paper *Choosing Scotland's Future* produced by the Scottish Government (2007) expressed a strong preference for a simple majority of those voting. It mentioned the possibility of two referendums, one on the principle of independence and another one to ratify the agreed settlement, but was sceptical on this. The question proposed in the discussion paper was a clear one, a great deal clearer indeed than the Quebec proposal of 1995. It was:

> I AGREE that the Scottish Government should negotiate a settlement with the Government of the United Kingdom so that Scotland becomes an independent state.

Were such a question to be put successfully to Scottish voters, the Scottish Government would take it as a mandate for independence, but it would then have to open negotiations. The response of the UK Government and of English opinion could take three forms. First, they could resist, claiming that the unity of the United Kingdom could not be violated or disputing the size of the majority or the terms of the question. Since they have largely conceded the right of Scottish self-determination, it is likely that the argument would be on the latter grounds and could be protracted. Second, they could accept Scottish secession but pose tough conditions, again leading to protracted negotiations. Third, they could welcome Scottish secession, if this had come after a period of conflict, and the issue of Scottish (over)representation in Parliament and government had generated a grievance in England. What we know about attitudes in England suggests that this is not unlikely, but that does not mean that negotiations would be easy.

Let us assume that an independence-minded Scottish Government had gained consent to the independence question and that the size of the majority was not questioned. A combination of 'pull' in Scotland and 'push' from England had made independence the agreed option. There would then follow a period of negotiation to define the issues in detail. We cannot predict what the response in England would be, but evidence so far suggests less concern with the principle of Scottish independence than with a perceived Scottish advantage within the Union. A period of tension between Edinburgh and London followed by a referendum campaign would, moreover, create their own political facts and legacies, which would in turn colour the negotiations. Again, there are three possibilities. Perhaps the least likely is a continued friendship and good-natured negotiation and the search for a form of separation that would maximize the common interests of both sides. A second is a resentful hostility, combined with a realistic appreciation that there are still common interests at stake and that both sides have much to gain from a constructive approach. A third is a dog-in-the-manger hostility in which the United Kingdom seeks to punish Scotland, even at the cost of its own long-term interests. All three attitudes were visible in the rest of Canada in the run-up to the Quebec referendum of 1995. Young's survey (1995) of peaceful secessions suggests, however, that the second is the most likely scenario. The two sides tend to move rapidly to minimize disruption and safeguard their essential interests, the issues in dispute are narrowed down, and agreement is reached.

Young also notes a tendency for the seceding and host state to forge internal unity, with broad-based governments and a mobilization of opinion, even if there was not full consensus in advance of the process. This is more difficult to imagine in the Scottish case, since it is unlikely that a single party will ever gain a majority in the Scottish Parliament and the parties are themselves divided on the constitutional issue. After 2007, there was division between the minority government, committed to independence, and the Parliament, where a unionist majority launched its own process in alliance with the UK

Government. The unionist parties, particularly the Labour Party, have a great deal to lose from Scottish independence and little to gain from presenting a common front with the SNP. Moreover, the UK negotiators, depending on which party is in power at the time, may include Scottish MPs in senior positions. The principal issues for negotiation include the new state borders, the division of assets and liabilities, new institutions for cooperation, and citizenship rules.

DIVIDING THE ASSETS AND LIABILITIES

The land border between Scotland and England is not in dispute, since it has been stable since 1237, apart from the occasional question about Berwick-on-Tweed. During the 1970s, there were home rule movements in Orkney and Shetland, opportunistically encouraged by anti-devolutionists from the south; but it is no longer disputed that they form part of Scotland. Their supposed ethnic differentiation is hardly relevant to modern conditions, and there is no longer a significant difference in their degree of support for the various measures of self-determination. So the possibility of parts of Scotland opting back into the United Kingdom, a big issue in the Quebec case, does not arise. The sea border would be more contentious, since it affects the ownership of oil and gas fields. There is at present a boundary, determining the application of Scottish or English law to offshore installations, but this has no international standing. International law itself is not clear, consisting of a series of conventions, agreements, and arbitration rulings; but the most consistent criterion appears to be the equidistance principle, simple in theory but very complicated in practice, as it involves determining the lie of coastlines and islands (Murkens 2002). It is likely that a ruling would have to be obtained from the International Court of Justice or from an agreed arbiter.

Assets include infrastructure and buildings, movable property, equity holdings, and intellectual property rights. Liabilities consist of public debt together with responsibility for future payments, such as pensions. It is likely that all UK fixed assets in Scotland would become the property of the Scottish Government, except for those used in continuing joint activities (including possibly defence). Movable property would have to be negotiated although it is likely that some formula would be found. Other assets could be divided on a population basis, a rough but simple formula. More difficult would be the valuation of the assets, questions of compensation, and the division of liabilities, including public sector pensions and debt. Radically different claims are likely to be made. Scotland could argue that assets belong to

Scotland and should be transferred without compensation, and that debt was run up by the UK Government without regard to Scotland. They might add that Scotland has historically suffered from getting less than its fair share and stake a claim to infrastructure and buildings in London to which Scottish taxpayers have contributed. The United Kingdom could counter that assets were acquired with UK money and that Scotland has a historic debt from the decades in which its levels of public spending exceeded the taxes raised there. In turn, the SNP has argued that, through oil revenues, Scotland has already paid for its own infrastructure and should owe nothing. Similar contrasting arguments could be made about public sector pensions. There could be a commission to examine the details of these claims, value assets, and calculate levels of historic debt, but this would be unlikely to generate consensus. These are essentially political claims and it is likely that a simple formula would be used, assigning assets to the territory where they are located and combining territory and population to divide the debt. This has been the practice elsewhere (Young 1995). Depending on what common services are retained, whether in defence, security, or regulatory institutions, there would also need to be a calculation of contributions. Again both sides could proffer their own criteria, based variously on population, wealth, location, or use. Given the impossibility of reaching a consensus on these, it is likely that a simpler population-based formula would prevail.

CITIZENSHIP

Resolving the citizenship problem would be difficult, since British citizenship is itself so complicated. A new Scottish citizenship, in line with international norms, would be open to all UK citizens residing in Scotland and to those living abroad born in Scotland or with a Scottish parent. Applying the same principle, it would be possible for people living in Scotland but born, or with a parent born, in the rest of the United Kingdom, to retain British citizenship. This would, however, mean that many Scots-born people who voted No to independence would have their citizenship altered by the vote of the majority of their compatriots, and there would be demands to retain British citizenship more widely or for dual citizenship. Dual citizenship is not prohibited in British law and is widely practised; but it seems unlikely that either side would wish to extend British citizenship to the whole Scottish nation, still less to extend Scottish citizenship reciprocally to everyone in the rest of the United Kingdom. Another possibility would be to allow anyone the option to retain British citizenship, but this would be meaningful only if dual citizenship were not allowed – otherwise we would be back to universal dual citizenship. The Irish precedent is not helpful here. After 1922, Irish people remained British subjects because Ireland was still in the Commonwealth, giving them much the same rights as British-born subjects. When Ireland withdrew from the Commonwealth in 1949, however, these rights lapsed and the Irish lost their citizenship and rights to a British passport, unless they could demonstrate a 'substantial connection' with the United Kingdom.

Citizenship rights can be more or less inclusive both in relation to the range of entitlements that they carry and in the extent of the group having these rights. British citizenship is the product of successive revisions of the law and is remarkably varied on both dimensions. The dissolution of the Anglo–Irish Union and, later, of the British Empire left a legacy of entitlements and provisions so that, for example, Irish and Commonwealth citizens retain the right to vote at British elections. Lord Goldsmith's report (2008) on citizenship, aimed at producing a new British national identity, proposed to abolish this right, thus going directly against the concept of an evolving set of unions that might underpin a new settlement in Scotland. Indeed Goldsmith seemed unaware that the right of Irish citizens to vote in the United Kingdom had been made reciprocal in the 1980s and confirmed in the Northern Ireland peace agreement, precisely in order to bring the British and the Irish, and the two communities in Northern Ireland, closer together without putting in question the principle of the sovereignty of the two states. Rather than extending dual citizenship indefinitely after independence, it is likely that rights will be further unpacked so that Scots, English, Welsh, and Northern Irish will enjoy various reciprocal privileges. There might be mutual rights to vote and stand in elections for UK and Scottish citizens resident on each other's territory, going beyond the municipal and European electoral rights enshrined in the EU law.

Social citizenship (Marshall 1992) refers to entitlements to public services and support. While this used to be linked straightforwardly to the nation state, European welfare systems have become more complex as they have been differentiated territorially, while subject to competitive pressures and the rules of the single market, creating intricate patterns of rights within and across states and regions (Ferrera 2006). Independence would mean the fragmentation of a unified social security system, based on common nationality; but there might be demands for various forms of reciprocity, since integration of social security allows very free movement of people among the parts of the United Kingdom. Assuming that governments on both sides of the border favoured maintaining the common labour market, there might therefore be a strong case for transferability and mutual recognition of entitlements in matters such as health care, pensions, and unemployment benefits. On the other hand, a Scotland with open borders to England would potentially be open to 'welfare migration', as individuals sought out the highest welfare standards, suggesting that more restrictive rules might be necessary. The provision whereby Scotland is allowed to charge university fees to English students while exempting its own would no longer be legal under European law,[2] raising issues that might be addressed as part of a broader bilateral settlement. This might give substance to the otherwise vague concept of a 'social union', recognizing the interdependence of labour markets within Britain and providing for a deeper union than that provided by the European *acquis*.

THE CONSTITUTION OF SCOTLAND

The immediate effect of Scottish independence would be to transfer to the Scottish Parliament all powers currently held at Westminster; but Scotland would presumably want its own written constitution. The doctrine of the absolute sovereignty of the Crown-in-Parliament has been subject to consistent criticism in Scotland, and there would doubtless be a statement vesting sovereignty in the Scottish people. Beyond this, the process of framing a constitution would allow a debate about common values and nationhood following a probably divisive referendum campaign. It could reaffirm the civic and inclusive nature of the Scottish nation and citizenship by specifying these in legal rather than ethnic or ancestral terms. In this way, self-government could be anchored in democracy and liberalism and a commitment to universal values.

The decision as to whether to retain the monarchy would be deferred to a referendum, but if a republic were chosen, nobody has suggested other than an honorary president, with executive power vested in the government responsible to the Parliament. Scotland would be unlikely to follow the British practice in which ministers exercise wide prerogative powers derived from the monarch, and would give a statutory and parliamentary basis to ministerial powers – a reform also foreshadowed in the British White Paper on constitutional reform (Secretary of State for Justice and Lord Chancellor 2007). The European Convention for the Protection of Human Rights and Fundamental Freedoms (ECHR) could be included within the constitution, and thus entrenched more strongly than at Westminster. There may be a case for a Scottish Charter of Rights, although it is not clear what this would add to the European one. Some constitutions also contain lists of social and economic rights, but these are often of no more than declaratory importance, since they imply a claim on public or private resources that is difficult to translate into practice.

Scotland's membership of the European Union (EU) could also be included in the constitution, to give coherence to the body of constitutional and supranational law. There might be a guarantee of the right of local self-government, as exists in several European constitutions, without specifying the precise form that the local government should take. A supreme court could then be responsible for ruling on constitutional matters, including the legality of acts of Parliament and ministerial actions, and their conformity with the EU and ECHR provisions. Above this, for European matters, the European Court of Justice, which rules on the EU, and the European Court of Human Rights, responsible for the application of the ECHR, would remain.

THE EUROPEAN DIMENSION

Continued membership of the EU has become a central and essential element in the independence prospectus, but there has been some debate over whether Scotland would automatically become a member of the EU, whether it would have to apply for membership, and whether in that case it would be accepted. As with other matters, there is no law, since the situation was not anticipated and there have been no precedents. Greenland left the EU when it gained home rule in 1979, and eastern Germany automatically entered when Germany reunited in 1990; but neither of these fits the case. Nationalists argue that Scotland will gain membership automatically since there is no ground or precedent for the EU expelling a constituent part of its territory – although the paper *Choosing Scotland's Future* (Scottish Government 2007: 23) adds the qualification 'following negotiations on the detailed terms of membership'. Murkens (2002) argues that the rest of the United Kingdom would be the successor state, taking the seat in the EU, while Scotland would be obliged to apply for membership. In that case, the argument becomes as much political as legal. On the one hand, Scotland meets the requirements of the *acquis communautaire*, which means that the EU could not properly refuse it. Other member states, including the remaining United Kingdom, would have an interest in minimizing disruption and maximizing stability, as would the business community and the United States. The EU has more difficult supplicants to worry about, including Turkey and the Balkans, and would hardly want to create problems in an otherwise peaceful and stable part of the continent. On the other hand, some states, notably Spain, would see Scottish independence as a dangerous precedent for their own minority nations; states with secessionist movements or centralizing governments were not prepared to recognize Kosovo in 2008 despite the special arguments made for it as the last episode in the disintegration of Jugoslavia. The Spanish and other governments might, if they could not stop Scottish membership altogether, make its terms as difficult as possible as a deterrent to others. This could affect matters such as budgetary contributions, representation in the European Parliament, and sectoral matters such as agriculture and fisheries (the last would cause particular problems with Spain).

If Scotland were obliged to join the EU as a new member, it could not formally enjoy the opt-outs enjoyed by the United Kingdom, since these were negotiated by an existing member state at the time of the relevant treaties. Scotland would thus be in the same position as the countries of central and eastern Europe, who have had to adopt the entire *acquis communautaire* as it was at the time of accession. It would have to accept the Charter of Rights,[3] policies on justice and home affairs and immigration from which the United Kingdom has opted out, and the Euro (discussed in Chapter 5) and the Common Fisheries Policy from which the SNP wishes to opt out.

Beyond the principle of EU membership, there is the question of what type of EU Scotland will support and of its role within it. There are two dimensions here. The first concerns the constitution of the EU, whether as a body of sovereign states (the intergovernmental vision) or as a political union (the supranational or federal vision). Supranationalists prefer qualified majority voting in the Council of Ministers, which has been steadily extended since the 1980s, while intergovernmentalists defend the national veto. Supranationalists would give more power to the European Parliament, while intergovernmentalists would redress the 'democratic deficit' by strengthening the role of member state parliaments. Supranationalists are also inclined to a larger role for the Commission, representing a general European perspective and in general like the 'Community method', the complex process in which national, sectoral, and European interests are negotiated at multiple levels, with the Commission retaining the initiative and bringing in allies along the way.

British policy towards the EU has been of cautious support, embracing the single market and enlargement of the Union but opposing both supranationalism and the extension of its policy fields. When competences have been extended, the United Kingdom has frequently opted out. It supported majority voting in order to get the single market programme through, but opposed its extension to other matters. The French line, by contrast, has been to welcome the extension of competences but to prefer the intergovernmental model of decision-making. Germany has historically been happy with political integration and the federal vision, but has sometimes been cautious about extending the competences. Spain, Italy (at least until the arrival of the

Berlusconi Government), and the Benelux countries have historically supported both stronger central institutions and wider powers (although here,
too, there are changes with the Dutch rejection of the draft constitutional
treaty).

The second dimension concerns the scope of the Union, whether it is to be
confined to market integration or take in other policy dimensions. British
social and economic policies have emphasized a model based on deregulated
labour markets, competition, and relatively weak social provision, against a
more social and welfarist conception in the core countries of the EU. The
concept of social Europe was elaborated in the 1980s by Commission President Jacques Delors, who argued that deepening of the market should be
accompanied by provision for those who lose out and protection of labour
standards. It was strongly opposed by the government of Margaret Thatcher
who, in her famous Bruges speech, declared that she had not rolled back the
frontiers of the state in Britain only to see them pushed forward again by
Europe. In practice, there was never any prospect of a welfare state developing
in Europe; the social Europe agenda came down to some labour market
regulation and a commitment to protect a vaguely defined European social
model, given expression in the Social Chapter of the Maastricht Treaty of
1992. Delors' concept of social Europe was a critical factor in converting the
trade unions and the Labour Party to support for Europe in these years and,
when Labour returned to power in 1997, it promptly signed up to the Social
Chapter, from which the Conservatives had secured an opt-out. A few years
later, however, the Labour Government had reverted to the British type and
refused to sign on to the Charter of Rights contained in the draft constitutional treaty and the Lisbon Treaty, seeing it as a threat to the British
deregulated labour market. British governments have also opposed greater
integration of justice and home affairs and immigration policies as well as
French proposals for an 'economic government' for Europe, which could
engage in more interventionist policies and harmonize taxation rates in
order to prevent competitive tax-cutting and the consequent undermining
of welfare services.

The Schengen agreement on passport-free travel, which allows people to
move across the space of the Union without encountering borders, has been
part of the *acquis communautaire* since the Amsterdam Treaty in 1999, so that
technically Scotland would be obliged to join it. Unionist taunts that independence would mean border posts on the Tweed are unfair since these would
result from British refusal to join Schengen and its retention of border posts
with all its EU partners; but border controls there would be. In practice, it
might be able to negotiate an opt-out, arguing that it is in the same position as
Ireland, which had to remain out when the United Kingdom did, in order to

maintain the free travel area. In this case, Scotland would have to maintain controls with the rest of the EU. As the UK Government has been strengthening its border controls, Scotland would be obliged to follow suit, taking its policy line from the south. Immigration policy would be the responsibility of the Scottish Government, and there has been a broad consensus in Scottish politics that immigration should be encouraged to address the demographic deficit. An independent Scotland, responsible for financing its own pensions, would have an even greater incentive to encourage immigration but, with a common travel area with England, it would be very difficult to prevent people from then moving south. Such migrants (except for citizens of the EU and European Economic Area, which are another matter) would not have the right to work in England or Wales but could easily join the undocumented labour force, increasing the cost of enforcement for the authorities there. The result could be pressure for a standardized and uniform immigration regime across the former United Kingdom, or checks at the borders. In the latter case, Scotland might as well join the Schengen area and enjoy free travel with the rest of Europe.

The SNP's vision of Europe has never been very clear. It has promised to use independence to cut corporate (and possibly personal) tax rates to imitate the Irish success in attracting inward investment, and so opposes tax harmonization. Yet it can be very plausibly argued that an economic government and tax harmonization would be in the interest of a small nation like Scotland, since a free-for-all competition for investment could see it losing out to other countries with poorer social standards and less compunction about minimizing business taxation (see Chapter 5). The SNP also envisages an intergovernmental EU rather than one moving towards federation. Such might seem the best way to enhance Scottish independence, but this is by no means obvious. National vetoes in the Council of Ministers give the small states the same clout as the larger ones, and at one time smaller states were inclined to favour retaining them, fearing that they would be dominated by their big partners. In practice, however, it is hard for them to use the veto, since they would come under immense pressure and need to build up goodwill in a way that is less important for large states. Majority voting, on the other hand, allows them to forge winning coalitions with other states, bargain for influence, and reduce bullying by the big players. Over the years they have come to realize that their best chance lies in a stronger and more supranational Union, with a powerful Commission and a stress on the 'Community method', which is a decision-making process rooted in deeper forms of integration (Magnette and Nicolaïdes 2005). Moreover, when the Council does proceed by majority voting, small nations are more inclined to side with the majority, suggesting that they realize that this is the best way to maximize their impact (Mattila and Lane 2001; Mattila 2004). SNP policy is to opt out of the Common Fisheries Policy (CFP), and its leaders suggested that this would be a make-or-break issue in the draft constitutional treaty and then the Lisbon Treaty. Indeed the line on the Lisbon Treaty was that an independent Scotland would hold a referendum and, if the Treaty were not amended to exclude the CFP, the SNP would call for a No vote. Such a strategy of threatening to hold up the entire constitutional reform in defence of one sector in one small member state[4] is the very opposite of the Community method, which involves linking sectors, bargaining across the range of issues, and not making aggressive threats.

SNP thinking also suggests that it might seek an *à la carte* form of membership, picking and choosing among policies and retaining the maximum of independence. This is not as easy as it seems. Denmark (within the EU) and Norway (outside it) have chosen a strategy of distance, but in practice have to accept policies that they have had no influence in shaping. Norway has to accept most of the *acquis communautaire* as the price of access to EU markets under the European Economic Area, while the Danish currency is tied to the Euro, subjecting Denmark to the policies of the European Central Bank. Danish opt-outs on citizenship and justice and home affairs have proved similarly illusory since the Danes have felt obliged to adopt most of the policies involved (Hansen 2002), while their opt-out of European defence is meaningless since they are full members of NATO. So once again, we find that independence is not what it seems.

THE SECURITY DIMENSION

There is little doubt that the more secure international environment within western Europe is one factor that has encouraged the expression of Scottish and other nationalisms, and in the debate on independence the security issue has been remarkable for its low profile. No party imagines that Scotland could effectively defend itself against the sort of aggression that marked Europe in the 1930s, and even the 'armed neutrality' espoused by Sweden during the Cold War is contemplated by few. The options therefore lie between having no defence policy at all, and having a collective security system with other states, including the rest of the United Kingdom. The former is not totally unrealistic. In the modern world, an independent Scotland would have few armed enemies in the traditional sense and, even if it were to make no defence effort at all, its European neighbours and the United States would have an interest in preventing hostile powers gaining a foothold there. It could therefore 'free-ride' in defence matters, declaring itself neutral and dedicating itself to peacemaking around the world. With only slight exaggeration, this is the stance of the Republic of Ireland.

SNP policy, however, leans to the collective security option and envisages Scotland as a member of bodies, including the Organization for Security and Cooperation in Europe and the Western European Union (Scottish Government 2008). It opposes Scottish membership of NATO, however, a long-standing policy connected with Cold War and anti-nuclear politics. A review of this policy was promised but abandoned with the outbreak of the 2003 Iraq war, which renewed hostility to the Anglo–American alliance. In principle, a strategy of collective European security might make sense, as part of a wider commitment to Europe and a less Atlanticist orientation to policy than that which has characterized successive UK governments. The problem is that this distinct European defence strategy has never quite materialized. A Common Foreign and Security Policy is one pillar of the EU, and the Lisbon Treaty promised to strengthen it with a 'foreign minister' sitting both in the Commission and in the Council of Ministers. The Western European Union (WEU), established in 1948 for collective security but subordinated to NATO during the Cold War, has been revived since the 1990s and brought into the EU orbit. Not all EU members, however, are in the WEU, with the neutral states of Ireland, Sweden, and Finland remaining out, together with Denmark. A European Rapid Reaction Force has been established to intervene in trouble spots and various tasks, such as the international military presence in Bosnia, have been contracted to the EU. Despite all this, however, the European military operations remain dependent on NATO logistical support and must be seen as a sphere of operations within the wider North Atlantic security system. All WEU members are in NATO, and it would make little sense for Scotland to play its part in it while keeping out of NATO.

An independent Scotland would have its own armed forces, drawn presumably from the Scottish elements of the British army; but these would be small and unable to cover the complete range of military tasks. As part of NATO, including the joint military command, and as part of the EU military effort, they could assume specialized roles, in cooperation, among others, with the forces of the rest of the United Kingdom. This does represent a reduction in Scottish independence, and one that might become more significant as NATO tasks and spheres of action expand. No longer confined to protecting western Europe in the event of war with the Soviet Union, NATO has assumed responsibilities in Afghanistan, in Kosovo and, potentially, elsewhere, as the military arm of the western powers. Countries are not obliged to commit troops to NATO operations outside Europe, but they are politically implicated in the decision to intervene.

Security policy has in recent years expanded beyond the traditional task of defending the borders, into the new security agenda in which the domestic and foreign arenas merge, notably in relation to terrorism. An independent Scotland would need to commit to common European policies in this field and to cooperate closely with the rest of the United Kingdom, especially if it opted to remain out of Schengen and in the British–Irish travel area.

OTHER UNIONS

A Scotland withdrawing from the United Kingdom would thus remain a member of the European Union and the North Atlantic security area, although subject to competing pulls. There are other unions, too, which are relevant (MacCormick 2005). The independence proposals of the Scottish Government (2007) insisted that the Union of the Crowns of 1603 would remain in force, although this seems to mean no more than that the British monarch would remain head of state, as in several Commonwealth countries. In this case, the monarch would act in Scotland only on the proposal of Scottish ministers, including in foreign affairs – which was not always the case between 1603 and 1707 (Sutherland 1976). Scotland would also remain a member of the Commonwealth itself and, although the political significance of this is much diminished, it would provide a platform for participation in global debates.

Nationalists are prone to stress that, after independence, the 'social union' would continue. It is by no means clear what this means, beyond the socio-logical observation that families and friendships will continue to straddle the border and that Scots and English will still have much in common. Much the same has been true of Britain and Ireland since 1922. If the 'social union' refers to institutions or public policies, however, matters get very compli-cated. In the debates on Quebec independence, there has been a division between those who think that existing international institutions, including the North American Free Trade Agreement (NAFTA), would provide an adequate external support system, or whether something extra would be desirable. The failure of the respective protagonists, Jacques Parizeau and Lucien Bouchard, to resolve this led to the convoluted question in the referendum of 1995 in which voters were asked to support a declaration of sovereignty, after *offering* a partnership agreement to the rest of Canada. The question is less acute in the Scottish case, since the EU takes care of a lot more of the externalities than does NAFTA; but there may still be a case for a tighter agreement. Nationalists have from time to time talked of a common area formed by the (British) Isles and dreamed of something like the Nordic Council, created after the Second World War as a form of mutual cooperation. This is an organization with both a parliamentary body and a ministerial meeting (the Nordic Council of Ministers) and including the states of Sweden, Denmark, Norway, Iceland, and Finland with the self-governing territories of Greenland, Faroe, and the Åland Islands (Qvortrup 2001). It meets at regular intervals and works by consensus, adopting policies on matters of common interest. With free trade in Europe, through the EU and the European Economic Area and free movement in the Schengen area, some of the functions of the Nordic Council have been superseded; while the non-membership in the EU of Norway and, before 1995, of Sweden and Finland has divided the members. There is no element of supranationalism in its workings since, although policies adopted are binding on members, they have to be agreed by unanimity in the first place.

The concept of a union of the Isles first came into British law in the Northern Ireland Act of 1998, which proposed the British–Irish Council (sometimes known as the Council of the Isles), which brings together the United Kingdom Government, Scotland, Wales, Northern Ireland, the Republic of Ireland, the Channel Islands, and the Isle of Man. The origins of this have everything to do with the Northern Ireland conflict – to satisfy the demands of Irish nationalists for a broader forum, while not upsetting unionists – and little to do with a new vision of the islands as a political or social union. It has, however, been taken up by Scottish nationalists as a way of softening the impact of independence and promising a broader framework based on historical linkages. In the event of Scottish independence, it might be developed further as a forum for intergovernmental cooperation. It could help diffuse policy ideas and good practice and allow the exchange and secondment of officials. Around its meetings, new networks could develop and alliances form, with a view to cooperation in European forums. There could be agreements on mobility, recognition of qualifications, and transferability of social entitlements, going further than those provided for by the European Union, as happens in the Nordic zone. Joint programmes might be developed in education and research. These could all help address the costs of independence and reduce the risk of isolation. They would not, however, fundamentally alter power relationships since such a union would be dominated by the United Kingdom, which would never allow itself to be outvoted or subordinated to the preferences of its smaller partners. The Nordic Council, in contrast, is more balanced, with no country comprising anything like a majority of population. Even an effort by Sweden to increase its influence in proportion to its 40 per cent financial contribution was firmly rejected by the others teaming up against it (Qvortrup 2001).

An economic union between Scotland and England would be assured by the EU, but existing economic linkages go deeper than the rules of the European single market. The SNP has abandoned its support for a separate currency and now accepts that Scotland would need to be part of a currency union, whether of the Pound or of the Euro. The idea is that, initially, the Pound will be retained, with a later decision on whether to switch to the Euro. As the research done on the prospect of Quebec independence showed, there is nothing to stop a seceding state using the currency of its former partner even without permission (Fortin 1992; Gendron and Desjardins 1992). There is also the precedent of Ireland, whose currency was tied to Sterling for fifty years after independence. The various forms of monetary union with Sterling would, however, tightly constrain Scotland's room for manoeuvre and leave it dependent on decisions taken in London, as discussed in Chapter 5.

The economic union will also continue in the form of cross-border trade flows, which at present dwarf flows between Scotland and the rest of the world and make Scotland vulnerable to changes in market conditions in England. Recession in the south would spill over into Scotland in the form of reduced demands for Scottish products. Housing markets would also be linked, with a spillover of the price fluctuations that have become an important influence on general economic conditions. Ownership of firms and investment are also more integrated within the UK single market than across Europe as a whole. Banks and financial services would operate across the whole of the former United Kingdom. Hints have been dropped by SNP leaders that an independent Scotland could continue within a single regulatory framework for financial services – a proposal that takes us towards the kinds of sovereignty-association discussed in Chapter 6. The banking crisis of 2008 has thrown this issue into sharp relief, reminding us of the extent to which internationalized banks and finance houses have relied on national regulatory systems and implicit (now explicit) government guarantees of their solvency. Small countries with large financial service sectors, like Ireland and Iceland, have been hard hit; and an independent Scotland might prefer a supranational regulatory and guarantee system, so retaining another element of the economic union. This economic union would represent the starting point for an independent Scotland as it did for Ireland in 1922. Over time, matters could change, depending on the decisions taken by Scottish policy-makers, a matter pursued in the next chapter.

Unions also exist in civil society. Business representative groups and trade unions are overwhelmingly organized on a British or UK basis (Keating 2005), albeit with arrangements for dealing with Scottish business. There is no reason to think that this would change radically after independence. The Irish trade union movement still includes British unions, as well as all-Ireland ones, and some confined to the territory of the Republic. Canadian trade unions are sometimes affiliates of US-based unions, although there has been a tendency since the 1960s for the Canadian elements to become independent. British industrial relations, for reasons that have nothing to do with Scottish nationalism, have been increasingly decentralized since the 1980s, with fewer national-level bargains. This would remove one element of uniformity that would have existed were Scotland to have become independent in an earlier era, as noted in the 1970s by McCrone (1975). There still remains, however, a UK framework for industrial relations, which would not itself be broken by independence. This could mean that governments on both sides of the border would be faced with many similar issues and demands, giving them a common policy agenda. Of course, Scotland would be free to respond in its own way, but this response would be tightly constrained by the group pressures and conditions. It would also be under pressure from the United Kingdom not to take decisions that would have negative spillovers south of the border. Independence would increase the margin of discretion in policy-making, but subject to domestic and international constraints.

CHOOSING UNIONS

Politicians of all stripes in Scotland have come to realize that independence and statehood in the old form is no longer viable. Unionists have rediscovered the language of union, as a flexible form of political accommodation among nations and regions, now nested within a broader European Union, which they support with varying degrees of enthusiasm. Nationalists for their part have also embraced the language of union, partly as a form of reassurance against accusations of separatism, but also to place their project in a broader context – hence their talk of the social union and embrace of the European Union. The choice is now less between union and separation than among different types and levels of union. Independence in an obvious way is a blow to the British Union, but its effects will by no means disappear.

At a broader, geo-strategic level, Scotland would be caught between competing Anglo–American (or Atlanticist) and European poles, with implications for social and economic as well as foreign and security policy. One scenario for an independent Scotland is to cling to existing forms as an external support system, and to minimize disruption. Such would be the rationale for keeping the Pound Sterling as the currency, to preserve as much as possible of the UK internal market, to cleave to the Anglo–British model of economic management with its emphasis on markets, deregulation, and tax competition, and to remain outside the Schengen area. If it remains within the British sphere, it will become in many respects a policy-taker, being obliged to follow the lines of British policy over a range of labour market and economic policies. Another scenario would see Scotland move out of the British orbit and into the European one, embracing the full range of EU policies and entering the core of European institutions. States that are opted into the maximum of issue areas have a presence across the policy field and gain experience in influence. EU policy-making is a highly complex matter, conducted in the Council of Ministers, in sectoral and intergovernmental committees (known collectively as comitology), and through lobbies and networks. The more deeply a country is implicated in this, the greater its potential influence. In the longer run, it is very possible that the future of Europe will be of a two-tier or variable-geometry union, with some countries forming a core or opting into more common policies, whether within the formal structures of the Union or not. Scotland would then face the choice of joining the core or of staying with its neighbours at a distance. It is arguable that its real autonomy and influence would be best served by tighter integration into the core, which in turn would pull it away from the Anglo–Atlantic pole. This, however, would imply a considerable shift in economic orientation (discussed in Chapter 5).

It also implies adopting the Euro, entering the Schengen area, and embracing the European Charter of Rights and the European social model (for a social democratic Scotland) in its various manifestations. This would require not merely a political restructuring, with the assumption of formal independence, but a profound change in social and economic structures and policies. Such a transformation took a long time to occur in Ireland, where the immediate effect of independence was to reinforce existing, conservative forces and retard social modernization (Garvin 2004). In the Scottish case, it raises profound questions about the political economy of the new state.

5

The Political Economy of Independence: Large States and Small Nations

National independence has traditionally been a constitutional matter, raising the questions about self-determination, legitimacy, and recognition discussed in the last chapter. In a wider sense, however, independence is about the ability of a nation to mount its own economic and social development project. For most of the nineteenth and twentieth centuries, this usually pointed towards statehood, taking control of the levers of change, in the form of macroeconomic policies, monetary policy, control of investment and sometimes nationalization. Large states, with big domestic markets and raw materials (or access to these through imperial conquest) had the advantage. Yet in a longer historical perspective, the optimum economic size of political units has varied according to the prevailing conditions. Before the Napoleonic era, city-states astride trading routes could flourish (Spruyt 1994; Tilly 1994). Changing technologies of war then made the city-state vulnerable, while the nineteenth century saw the consolidation of large states over much of Europe and the removal of internal trade barriers. While the motives were largely geo-political, the result was the creation of large internal markets and the expansion of national capitalism. Yet the newly unified states were by no means always optimal trading areas. Indeed much of territorial tension in European states in the late nineteenth century resulted from the imposition of new external economic barriers, changing the terms of trade, and making former centres into peripheries and vice versa (Keating 1998). Scotland fitted into the British imperial economy in the nineteenth century as an important industrial centre, oriented to free trade. After the First World War it re-emerged as a dependent branch of a less globalized British national economy, its politics focused more on seeking protection and resource transfers from the centre. This dependence was a decisive objection to Scottish independence between the wars, a time of national protectionism and collapse of the international trading system. During the first fifty years after the Second World War, few people questioned the argument that larger units, exploiting economies of scale, were more efficient and represented the future.

By the late twentieth century, however, the argument had turned again, and much recent economic thinking challenges the assumption that large states have inherent advantages. International free trade, the World Trade Organization and especially the European Union have helped guarantee access to wider markets for the smallest of states. European monetary union enables small countries to preserve independence without the burden of a national currency and the vulnerability to speculators that it entails. On the other hand, even large states find their freedom to set their own macroeconomic policies highly constrained by global interdependencies, while European rules on deficits and debt restrict the practices of Keynesian anti-cyclical policy.

Alesina and Spolaore (2003) argue that the need for large states has disappeared and that small states are equally viable. Indeed they may be preferable on two grounds: because they perform better economically according to statistical calculations; and because they are more homogeneous, so that the population is likely to share policy preferences. The argument has many weaknesses, starting with the idea of homogeneity. If this means ethnically homogeneous, the argument is ethically dubious and empirically wrong; indeed the whole idea of ethnic homogeneity is elusive. If, on the other hand, it just means that fewer people need to agree, this would imply extremely small units indeed, since a population of 5 million is not much more likely to have unanimous views than one of 50 million. Following Alesina and Spolaore's logic, Aberdeen might have more of a case for independence than would Scotland. Their argument derives from public choice assumptions about the individual seeking his or her own personal utility and cooperating with others only where necessary to achieve it. This ignores the fact that claims for self-government are made, not in the name of preference-seeking individuals but, rather, in the name of nations, which are forged through historical experience and moulded by institutions. Indeed, Alesina and Spolaore use the term 'nation' as a synonym for states, preventing them from problematizing the relationship between the two. The state system of Europe was not constructed on the basis of optimal economic units, and it is not going to fragment just because the economic calculations have changed. Alesina and Spolaore neglect the role of politics and institutions almost completely, although these provide the settings within which people make collective choices. Much the same can be said of other public choice efforts to calculate the optimum size of polities, such as Frey and Eichenberger's proposal (1999) that different forms of organization can be used for different public tasks. Political order is never the product of purely functional logic.

While incomplete and politically rather naïve, however, these contributions do show that smaller units can be viable in certain conditions and under specific external security and economic regimes, in the past as in the future.

Globalization does not bring new nations into existence but, where they have been created in the past or present, it enlarges the options they have for their full realization. This transforms the economic calculations as to Scottish independence that have, for over a hundred years, been a pillar of the Union. Now it is possible to argue that Scotland could make its own way in European and global markets, breaking out of the managed dependency of the twentieth-century Union. How well it would do and what institutions and policies it would have to adopt are another and more complicated matter.

WINNERS AND LOSERS

Calculations of whether Scotland would gain or lose from independence are inevitably controversial and often depend on contestable claims about how well it has done under the Union. Both nationalists and unionists are on a cleft stick here. Unionists want to argue that Scotland is thriving under the Union but point to its supposedly low growth rate to claim that it could not afford independence. Nationalists want to show that it is doing badly under the Union but that it already has a viable economy. As noted earlier, the time-series data on the performance of the Scottish economy over the long term are varied in quality and their interpretation very politicized. After devolution, there was a lively debate in which unionists and nationalists seemed to agree that Scotland had done badly compared with the rest of the United Kingdom while drawing contrasting lessons. Alarmists warned that this gap had marked the entire twentieth century and represented a damning indictment of Scottish economic capacity. Similar claims have been made at regular intervals (e.g. Danson 1990). Labour politician Wendy Alexander (2003) warned that the situation might be so dire as to require the subordination of all other objectives to the needs of growth. After the elections of 2007, First Minister Alex Salmond declared that 'Scotland's economy has suffered from decades of mediocrity. Over the last 30 years, Scotland's growth has averaged just 1.8 per cent – around a half of the average rate of growth for small European countries. And over the last 25 years, this same figure can be compared to the UK's growth rate of 2.3 per cent' (http://www.scotland.gov.uk/News/Releases/2007/11/13122603).

There was always something suspicious about these claims since if decline was that well entrenched, then Scottish living standards would have been a fraction of England's, not almost the same. About half of the discrepancy might be accounted for by changing population relativities, which mean that England needs a higher rate of growth to maintain the *per capita* equivalent.

Figures on Scottish GDP (or its equivalents) *per capita* in relation to other parts of the UK shown in Figure 2.1 (p. 33) indicate that it has fluctuated since 1924 between the upper 80s and just over 100 per cent. It touched a high in the mid-1990s with the benefits of oil, surpassing the UK average, but since devolution has been around 95 per cent, rather good by historical standards. Another problem is the comparison with a UK average that is largely determined by London and the South-East. In comparison with Wales, Northern Ireland and the regions of England, Scotland usually performs above the average. Among the twelve UK standard regions (Scotland, Wales, Northern Ireland and the regions of England), Scotland came joint third in 2006 (*Regional Trends* 2008). There is also increasing evidence that Scotland's performance might just not have been calculated correctly: since the quality of the data is poor, it is difficult to break down the territorial components of a single economic area, and different measures give different results (McLaren and Harris 2007). Finally, it may be that Scotland has kept up with England because its poor economic performance has been offset by favourable treatment in public expenditure and transfers from the south, which have favourable multiplier effects.[1]

This is the strongest unionist claim, since it implies that an independent Scotland would be worse off. It is also difficult to test, as, not surprisingly, there have been wide discrepancies in the calculations of the fiscal imbalance, the difference between what is raised in Scotland from taxes and charges and total government spending there. Neither is easy to estimate. Personal taxes might be calculated by place of residence or place of work; in the various calculations, residence is used. Business taxation in principle is credited to the place in which the activity takes place, but the production process may be spread across several places, with headquarters activities raising further difficulties. Spending might be attributed to the place in which the spending takes place, but the normal procedure is to attribute it to the place where the beneficiaries are located. This makes a difference since it means that various central government activities carried out in London might be taken to benefit the United Kingdom as a whole, although the local multiplier effects would be biased to South-East England.

Matters are not made simpler by the fact that there has never been a consistent formula determining the balance of spending among the regions and nations of the United Kingdom. In the nineteenth century, various government grants were attributed to Scotland on a basis derived from its percentage contribution to probate duties in 1886 (Heald and McLeod 2002*a*, *b*). This 'Goschen Formula' gave Scotland 11/80 of any general increase, roughly in line with its share of population. It was extended to some other services during the early twentieth century but never formed a comprehensive basis for allocating spending (Mitchell 2003). As Scotland's share of the UK population fell during the twentieth century, the Goschen Formula gradually produced higher spending *per capita*. After the Second World War, it gradually fell into disuse, although it was used in educational funding as late as 1959. Thereafter, changes in Scottish Office spending were negotiated, like that of other departments, with the Treasury. Yet shades of the old formula remained, as the Scottish Office negotiating position was to take the Goschen share of expenditure increases as a minimum, and then make a case for additional spending on individual items wherever it could (McLean and McMillan 2005). It then had a certain margin of discretion in reallocating the money according to its own priorities (Haddow 1969). There are endless arguments about exactly how much Scotland gets and whether this is 'fair' in relation to its needs or its tax contribution, but the system did secure higher levels of spending in Scotland than in England and Wales during the 1960s and 1970s (Short 1982; Heald 1983, 1992).

From the late 1970s, allocations were governed by the Barnett Formula[2] under which most expenditure incurred by the Scottish Office (and later the Scottish Executive/Government) was concentrated into a single block, within which Scottish ministers had discretion. The size of this block is calculated by historic spending and a population-related share of the increase or decrease in English expenditure on equivalent functions. This now accounts for about 60 per cent of all government expenditure in Scotland. The remainder is expenditure on UK government functions, notably social security, pensions, and defence, which are not allocated territorially. They do, however, feature in the calculations of how well Scotland does from government spending, with pensions and social security being calculated according to the location of claimants while defence expenditure is assumed to benefit everyone equally. If Barnett were applied consistently, then Scotland's expenditure advantages should diminish over time, as the population-based element became more important and the historic levels less. In practice, this did not happen for nearly thirty years, as successive Labour and Conservative governments found ways of mitigating its impact, following on the time-honoured territorial management expedient of using material compensation for the denial of self-government (Keating 2005). After devolution, the 'Barnett squeeze' began to be felt, with Scottish relative expenditure levels coming down towards those in England; but then Scotland's share of total government spending went back to historic levels, for reasons that are not entirely clear but include an increase in social security payments, outwith the block (McCrone 2007).

Barnett is consistently misinterpreted by commentators in England as a mechanism for giving Scotland extra spending, although it is in fact the opposite, a mechanism for convergence – rather than calling for the end of Barnett, they should logically be calling for its more stringent application. Labour ministers have misleadingly insisted that expenditure is allocated on the basis of need, although no such criteria have ever been formulated.[3] The Treasury's 1978 Needs Assessment Study, commissioned in anticipation of devolution but never used, claimed that Scotland's higher spending levels could be justified only partially by greater needs. Be that as it may, if Barnett does result in convergence over time this would undermine a pillar of the unionist argument, that Scotland's generous welfare state is only possible thanks to English taxpayers. For supporters of Scottish independence, however, it is irrelevant, since an independent Scotland would have to raise all its own revenues. The argument then shifts from expenditure to revenues, and whether Scotland's existing levels of spending are covered by taxes levied there. Not surprisingly, there is no more consensus here.

McCrone (1969) calculated that Scotland had a notional budget deficit in 1967 when the UK budget was in surplus. Short (1982) and Heald (1983, 1992), while not systematically calculating tax returns, suggest that Scotland was a net expenditure beneficiary. Since 1992, the Scottish Office, then the Scottish Government has produced *Government Expenditure and Revenues in Scotland* (GERS), which estimates both sides of the balance. Under Conservative and Labour governments, it consistently has long shown that Scotland raises less than it spends, the report for 2004–5 suggesting a fiscal deficit of 12.6 per cent of GDP – this was presented as unsustainable, although, ironically, the UK deficit was to hit this level in 2009. Even in 2000–1, when the UK budget as a whole was in surplus, Scotland was shown with a deficit of 6.9 per cent of GDP. In the longer run, the GERS figures showed Scotland with an average fiscal deficit of just over 10 per cent of GDP since 1980, compared with 3.5 per cent for the United Kingdom (Scottish Executive 2006).

Critics, however, have taken issue with many of the assumptions of the GERS (Cuthbert and Cuthbert 2007). There may be a bias in the calculation of corporation tax, often attributed to the London headquarters of firms even though actual production may be more dispersed. The overall figure for spending is made up of 'identifiable' expenditures, which can be attributed to a territory, together with 'non-identifiable' expenditures (such as foreign affairs and defence) that are then assigned to the different parts of the United Kingdom on the basis of population. Defence expenditure is assumed to benefit all parts of the United Kingdom equally, but there are economic benefits to the places where it is incurred. There are asymmetries in the calculations, so that all expenditure of the Scottish Government is considered to be for the benefit of the population of Scotland, while similar items in the budgets of Whitehall departments may be labelled as UK rather than English. Spending on the 2012 London Olympic Games is considered to benefit all of the UK and does not generate Barnett consequentials, while Scotland has (at the time of writing) received no similar credit for the 2014 Commonwealth Games in Glasgow. Whitehall departments have sometimes attributed parts of their spending to Scotland on a population basis, even when the corresponding function is devolved in Scotland. GERS was originally intended to give the Conservative Government ammunition against SNP claims of neglect and to show that the Scottish Office was working well, although the Secretary of State was criticized for risking an English backlash. Since then, however, the statisticians in Edinburgh have worked to refine the methodology, taking into account many of the criticisms, as acknowledged by some of the critics themselves (Cuthbert and Cuthbert 2008). The net effect of these refinements has been gradually to reduce Scotland's notional budget deficit, since the errors have nearly all pointed in the same direction.[4]

The figures, moreover, look very different if North Sea oil is taken into account. Traditionally, this has been allocated to a statistical region known as Extra-Regio and excluded from Scottish accounts. If Scotland were to become independent, part of this region would be within its territorial waters, although there have long been arguments about just how much. The sea might be allocated by dividing it along the line of latitude, favouring Scotland, or by projecting the border in a straight line, favouring England. There are already sea borders for determining the application of Scottish law (the line of latitude) and for fisheries, which follows the median point principle, but it is not clear how relevant these would be in the case of independence. More recently, a consensus has been forming that the most reasonable procedure would be to follow the median point, as in the calculations made by Kemp and Stephen (2008). This shows that over time between 80 per cent and 90 per cent of oil and gas revenues could be attributed to Scotland with the figure projected at the higher end of the range up to 2013.

If oil revenues are credited to Scotland, then the income side looks a lot better, although the effect on the surplus or deficit as a percentage of GDP is less dramatic, since the GDP needs also to be increased to take in the oil economy. Figure 5.1 gives North Sea revenues (attributing 85% to Scotland) compared with Scottish non-oil GDP. It shows dramatic fluctuations in the impact, with oil revenues at one point exceeding half of the entire non-oil economy. In 1997, by selecting the base years carefully, a Scottish nationalist MP extracted from the Treasury the admission that, on the assumption that 90 per cent of the oil revenues were attributed to Scotland, then in the period 1978–95 Scotland had contributed a net £27 billion to the Exchequer (Taylor

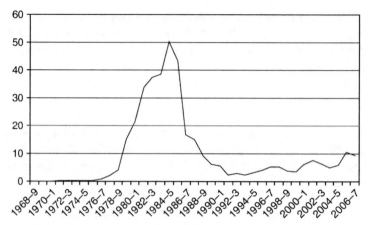

Figure 5.1 Eighty-five per cent North Sea oil revenue as percentage of Scottish non-oil GDP

Source: HM Treasury.

2002). Jones (2002) concurs that, if the oil revenues are attributed to Scotland, it would have enjoyed substantial budgetary surpluses in the 1980s. This is of historic significance, as it was a time of severe recession, caused by a combination of global circumstances and restrictive UK government policy, when an independent Scotland could have made very different policy choices. During the 1990s, because of changes in oil taxation, prices, and production levels, the notional Scottish surplus disappeared. Still taking oil into account (but without the later GERS methodological refinements), Midwinter (2007) showed an average deficit between 1993–4 and 2000–1 of £4.1 billion. This is around 5 per cent of GDP, well outside the Maastricht criteria limiting deficits for countries in the Euro-zone. GERS now produces estimates as to Scotland's notional fiscal deficit with different scenarios crediting Scotland with more or less of the oil. The most recent ones attribute none of the oil to Scotland; a population-based share; and a geographical share based on the Kemp and Stephen calculations. These show a similar picture, with oil revenues reaching a high point in 1984–6 and a low point in 1994–5 (Scottish Government 2008). Figure 5.2 compares the notional Scottish and UK budget deficits over the years, although these numbers need to be taken with caution, as they are constantly being corrected and recalculated and the earlier numbers have not been revised to take into account the improved GERS methodology.

If we take the rectifications in the GERS calculations together with the oil revenues, then Scotland's fiscal position in the 2000s looks a great deal better

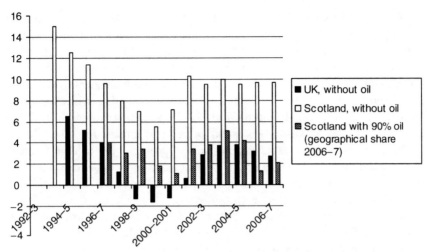

Figure 5.2 UK and Scottish fiscal deficits, 1992–2006 (% GDP)
Source: GERS.

than in the earlier calculations. In 2006–7, Scotland would have a fiscal deficit of 9.7 per cent of GDP without oil but of only 2.1 per cent with its geographical share, a smaller deficit than the UK Government had at that time (2.3%) (Scottish Government 2008). Rising oil prices would only improve matters. Calculations by *The Economist* (26 July 2008) based on the most recent statistical revisions and the Kemp/Stephen criterion show that, without oil, Scotland was in deficit by about 5 per cent during the 1980s and around 2000, and in serious deficit in the mid-1990s and late 2000s. With oil, it was in massive surplus during the 1980s but ran a big deficit in the mid-1990s. By the late 2000s, there was a big difference between the figures without oil (a deficit of over 10%) and with oil (a small surplus).

Needless to say, SNP calculations of Scotland's putative deficit differ even more radically from those of unionists. It has often argued that an independent Scotland should not take any responsibility for the UK debt, since oil revenues have long ago paid off its share (SNP 1999, 2000, 2006). At other times, SNP calculations appear to leave out defence spending (e.g. SNP 2006). The detailed SNP calculations for 2005–6 cannot be compared directly with GERS. However, we can note that for 2000–1, when GERS showed Scotland in deficit of £5.9 billion (or £1.1 billion with oil), the SNP had it in surplus to the tune of £2.5 billion or £5.2 billion without a share of debt. The following year, GERS showed a deficit of £8.8 billion (£2.9 billion with oil) while the SNP had a surplus of £4.9 billion, or £7.0 billion without debt.

In 2003–4, GERS showed a Scottish deficit of 12.9 per cent of GDP (6.2% with oil) while the SNP had it in balance taking a share of debt, and in surplus without. With the arrival of the SNP in government in 2007 the issue might have become very contentious, but serendipitously high oil prices showed Scotland in a favourable position even within GERS; then UK public finances collapsed.

So, while there are discrepancies in the various calculations, oil revenues make a big difference, although GERS figures suggest that they would not always fill the gap. Moreover, as oil prices and extraction rates change rapidly, revenues fluctuate, which is less a problem for a large country with a diversified revenue base than for a small country dependent on oil. It would be necessary, at times of high oil revenues, to run a fiscal surplus as in Norway, where in 2008 it amounted to 17 per cent of GDP. Social security expenditures similarly fluctuate, rising rapidly in times of recession. In a large country, the costs can be spread widely, which is particularly important in the case of asymmetric shocks in the form of an economic downturn affecting one part of the country more than another. They can also be spread over time, with surpluses accumulating in good times allowing higher social security spending later. In a small country, these automatic stabilizers are not so easily available. Currently social security is paid from the UK Government outwith the Barnett Formula, and the need to keep it so is one of the strongest arguments made against Scottish independence.

An independent Scotland could address this problem by putting aside oil revenues at times of high prices and production into a special fund, as is indeed the policy of the SNP. Such a fund could contribute to domestic investment, but much of it would have to be placed overseas to escape inflationary consequences. Such is the practice in Norway, where the fund had, as of 2008, $375 billion in assets, of which 50 per cent can be placed in the international stock market. An independent Scotland might also be wise to increase oil taxation and royalty levels to get the most out of the asset. This would reduce the rate of extraction, but that in turn would be to the advantage of a small country like Scotland that could not absorb all the revenues in the short run but might safeguard the asset for future generations. This does not appear to form part of the strategy of the SNP, which has regularly criticized high levels of taxation on oil companies and worried about the consequent slowdown of extraction rates. A policy of higher taxes, slower extraction and building up a capital fund would also reduce starkly the amount of oil revenue available to bridge any fiscal deficit arising from independence. Oil, then, would make a big contribution to the economic viability of an independent Scotland, but it is not a panacea.

MACROECONOMIC POLICY

A long-standing nationalist argument is that UK macroeconomic policy has been driven by the Treasury and the Bank of England concerned with controlling inflationary pressures in the south, and looking after the interests of the financial sector in the City of London. The Pound Sterling has been overvalued, both under the fixed parity regime of Bretton Woods and since, under floating rates. Concern with budgetary and trade deficits produced an anti-growth bias in policy, blamed more generally for the neglect of manufacturing industry and the collapse of the old industrial centres around the UK periphery. There is certainly something to be said for this critique as applied in the past, but it is of diminishing validity nowadays. Governments during the late 1990s and 2000s abandoned all concern with trade flows, while balance-of-payments deficits much worse than those that provoked regular crises in the 1960s and 1970s are just ignored. Consumer debt was allowed to spiral, as was government borrowing. This model of economic management may have been unsustainable, but it cannot be said that it was excessively deflationary. Scotland, moreover, disproportionately participated in the over-expansion of the financial services sector since the 1980s. It is no longer clear, therefore, that an independent Scotland would be free to pursue a more expansive macroeconomic strategy than that which it has experienced as part of the United Kingdom; Ireland now shows the dangers of trying.

It has long been argued by nationalists that North Sea oil would make Scots among the wealthiest people in the world but this, like the argument on the fiscal dividend of oil, is more complicated in practice. Taking oil into account can make Scotland's GDP look up to 20 per cent bigger, but this is a notional figure as most of this money does not flow into Scottish hands and would not after independence. More important is the multiplier effect, as oil spending spills over into other sectors. These direct and indirect effects (leaving aside government revenues discussed above) would not be changed by independence, unless it were decided to increase the rate of oil extraction. Such an expansionary, oil-based policy could add to inflationary pressures unless the labour supply were increased, either through increased immigration or by mobilizing a larger share of the population in those localities and sections where participation is still low, implying an activist policy of the sort discussed below. More broadly, in any case, an independent Scotland would be severely curtailed in its freedom to pursue an autonomous macroeconomic policy by international forces.

During the 1970s, the SNP promised a separate Scottish currency and would boast of how high it might rise on the foreign exchanges, fortified with oil. An inflated petro-currency, however, could devastate the country's export base (as indeed happened with the Pound in the 1980s), and a Scottish currency would be open to speculative flows and attacks. Others have argued that Scotland could sustain a low exchange rate to improve its competitiveness (MacLeod and Russell 2006). In practice, small countries have little control over their exchange rates given the mass of speculative flows, and EU rules require central banks to be independent, depriving governments of the main instrument they might use for the purpose, the power to set interest rates. In recognition of all this, it is no longer the policy of the SNP to have an independent currency; instead there would be a choice between the Pound Sterling and the Euro. Both would entail major restrictions on economic independence, since monetary policy and, with it, much of fiscal policy would be determined elsewhere.

Retaining the Pound could in practice take several forms. Scotland could adopt its own currency but manage it so as to keep parity with the Pound, as Denmark does in relation to the Euro. This could be costly and risk a run on the currency if markets lost confidence and the Scottish authorities could not hold the line. Another device is a currency board, used by several countries to peg their currencies to the US Dollar or the Euro. This is more restrictive since the currency board is not allowed to create money and can issue only against holdings of the target currency, in this case the Pound. Interest rates are largely harmonized through arbitrage, as investors switch funds to take advantage of any differences. Scotland would thus lack the ability to set its own monetary policy. An even tighter link is provided by 'dollarization',[5] in which Scotland would simply use the Pound as its currency. This might be done by consent with the UK, leaving the entire system of banking regulation with the authorities in London (Bank of England and Financial Services Authority). It could even be done unilaterally, as Quebec proposed in 1995, but in this case the London authorities would have no responsibility in, or concern for, the Scottish financial system. To date, dollarization has been used only by very small and peripheral countries and semi-independent territories. Although Argentina contemplated it at one time, they did not get much encouragement from the United States.

If Scotland were to join the Euro, it would have some influence over policy, as a member of the Council of Finance Ministers (EcoFin), and have a say in the appointment of the board of the European Central Bank. Scotland would, like other member states, be subject to the restrictions imposed by the Stability Pact on debt and budgetary deficits, and be in a weaker position than the large member states to ignore these. Joining the Euro would mean aligning its economic cycle with that of the other Euro-zone members (although these have not completely succeeded in this), implying a major change from its present synchronization with England and its pattern of trade. At present, just 52 per cent of Scottish exports and 36 per cent of Scottish imports are to/from the EU, compared with 62 per cent and 54 per cent respectively for the United Kingdom (Office for National Statistics 2008), suggesting that it has a long way to go. In the Irish case, the reorientation of trade has been considerable, breaking the former dependence on the UK market. The adjustment in Scotland would not, however, be automatic and would require a programme for convergence and major internal restructuring.

All of this suggests that Scotland could be an economic success story, a conclusion reached in the mid-1970s by McCrone (1975) with his secret warnings to the Labour Government that the SNP had a credible case. This would, however, depend on an independent Scotland pursuing the right policies and exercising firm control. This in turn points to a further difficulty with all these calculations. Like most economic scenarios, they rely on assumptions from economic theory or about the likely behaviour of actors; and the data on which they rely are at best estimates and often controversial. Differences in Scotland's notional fiscal deficit thus vary enormously. The calculations and the assumptions are so contested that the arguments seem to cancel each other out, leaving electors to decide the issue on other grounds. More seriously still, they are based on estimating the effects of one change at a time, assuming that other things would remain the same. This is known as static analysis, and is the only way in which we can study the impact of single factors on outcomes. It is, however, a poor way of predicting the future, when many things may be changing at the same time. An independent Scotland would not by definition be the same as present Scotland but would have to find its own niche in global and European markets so as best to exploit its resources and advantages.

THE COMPETITION STATE

Many of the traditional economic arguments against independence have focused on the inability of an independent Scotland to run its own separate macroeconomic policies using fiscal and monetary instruments. It is true that an independent Scotland's macroeconomic options would be highly constrained, but this is nowadays true of large states as well. Monetary policy has been taken out of the hands of politicians (both in the United Kingdom and in the Euro-zone) and moved, horizontally, to independent central banks. Within the Euro-zone, it has further moved, vertically, up to the European Central Bank. Fiscal policy is closely restricted by the Stability Pact, which limits budgetary deficits and debt. The emphasis in growth policies has shifted from macroeconomic regulation and national independence towards facing and adapting to the demands of global markets. A new conception has emerged, the competition state, which accepts the global division of labour and seeks a place in it. Economic independence has gone, and nations seek to retain political autonomy, not by resisting, but by managing their adaptation to external forces. Growth theory now places less emphasis on traditional factor endowments such as raw materials or proximity to markets and more on innovation, adaptability to changing conditions of production, skills, research and development, and favourable public policies.

There is no single recipe, and countries have taken different routes. Nor has social science been very good at looking at cases comparatively to work out why some have succeeded more than others. Too often, single cases are explained in an *ad hoc* manner, or the author reads into the case whatever model he or she is pushing at the time. Ireland's economic miracle in the 1990s and 2000s has been subject to multiple interpretations, none of which really seems convincing when we compare it with less successful cases (Keating 2006*a*). What all the models have in common, however, is a way of responding to changed external conditions and shocks that does not rely on the buffering effects of a large state or risks pooled with a large number of fellow citizens. Two ideal types of competition state identified in the literature allow us to explore the choices open to a small independent trading nation.

One school of thought argues that independent small nations must compete in world markets by attracting inward investment and stimulating local entrepreneurship through uncompromising free-market policies. There is an emphasis on low personal and, especially, corporate taxes. Flexible labour markets are needed, it is argued, to allow rapid wage adjustment to changed external conditions. Business regulation should be cut to the minimum, and environmental policies tailored to the interests of producers. An extreme version of this vision is presented by Ohmae (1995), who praises 'regional states', small jurisdictions with minimum government, no welfare state and dedicated single-mindedly to the pursuit of growth.[6] In a less drastic version, the cost-cutting and low tax model has been advocated in Scotland by George Kerevan (2006, 2007), Thomson, Mawdsley, and Payne (2008),[7] and a neo-liberal tendency within Scottish nationalism, often inspired by the case of Ireland and exemplified by MacLeod and Russell (2006). Tax cuts would be matched by reductions in public spending and a general rolling back of the state.

It is not clear, however, that low corporate taxes would be an economic panacea (Krugman 2003). They may be effective in attracting inward investment in a newly-industrializing country catching up with its neighbours; this may be a lesson from Ireland. In a mature industrial or post-industrial economy, the tax cuts mostly provide a free gift to existing enterprises that do not need the incentives. The manufacturing industries at which they have been aimed are now migrating to even lower-cost jurisdictions in central and eastern Europe, Asia, and elsewhere. Multinational firms use low-tax jurisdictions to declare their profits by complex transfer-pricing ruses, and the repatriated profits sharply reduce the advantage to national income. One country's tax cuts then stimulate competitive tax-cutting by others, provoking a 'race to the bottom' in which social spending is progressively cut back.

A sector of opinion argues that this would be no bad thing, as the public sector in Scotland, at around 50 per cent of GDP,[8] is 'crowding out' private investment and growth (Mackay and Bell 2006).[9] There are several versions of this argument, one of which is that taxation for public services is squeezing out consumer spending, hardly a plausible argument during the consumer boom of the late 1990s and into the 2000s. Another is that it is creating a shortage of investment capital, since interest rates are bid up. This argument does not hold when Scotland is in a monetary union in which interest rates are set externally, whether within the Pound or the Euro-zone (Allan, Ashcroft, and Plotnikova 2007). Then there is the argument that the public sector is absorbing too much of the labour force. Yet what surely matters is what these people are doing, not whether they are employed in the public or the private sector (Birch and Cumbers 2007). One might argue that the very weakness of the private sector in Scotland means that the public sector must be both strong and efficient. For example, the poor role of the private sector in research and development is partly offset by the relatively good performance of universities. Scotland's poor health conditions are an economic as well as a social problem and require a large investment in both preventative and curative care, which will come only from the public sector. There seems little empirical evidence that the public sector is presently crowding out growth (Allan, Ashcroft, and Plotnikova 2007), and there are examples of prosperous independent countries with both large and small public sectors.

The policy of the SNP is to square the tax-expenditure circle by cutting corporate taxes and business rates to stimulate investment, in the hope that the tax cuts will pay for themselves by stimulating growth. This looks like the wishful thinking underpinning the Reaganomics of the 1980s, which produced ballooning budget deficits. Corporation tax raised in Scotland accounts for about 7 per cent of all public expenditure incurred there, and cutting it to the Irish rate of 12.5 per cent would deprive government of 4 per cent of its revenues.[10]

Even if tax cuts did stimulate more growth, there would be a time-lag before the additional revenue could be collected. Expenditure cuts would therefore be necessary, and drastic ones if Scotland were really to match Irish spending levels of around 35 per cent of GDP, compared with its current 50 per cent. No mature welfare state has been able to cut back services to this degree, with the possible exception of New Zealand. The neo-liberal Thatcher government, notably, failed to reduce the burden of spending and taxation. The SNP, moreover, is a social democratic party and admirer of the Nordic welfare state, committed to expanding public services and extending universal provision (e.g. by abolishing university fees, bridge tolls, and prescription charges). It used to refer to the 'arc of prosperity', of thriving small states from Finland, through Ireland, to Denmark. Yet this covers a wide array of social and economic models. The Nordic countries are high tax jurisdictions, with particularly high Value Added Tax and other consumption taxes (Figure 5.3). Sweden's public expenditure amounts to about 58 per cent of GDP. These countries also have corporate tax rates of around 30 per cent (Congressional Budget Office 2005; OECD data). So combining the Irish low-tax model with the Nordic welfare state is really not possible. MacLeod and Russell (2006: 238), who take care to note that they do not speak officially for the SNP,[11] go even further, writing that 'we must look not just to Sweden and Denmark, Iceland and Ireland for models of policy innovation, but elsewhere as well – to the new countries of Europe whose flat taxes have transformed growth...' This is, to say the least, an eclectic list, combining quite incompatible social models.

An alternative to the 'low road' to competitiveness, based on tax cuts and curtailing public spending, is a 'high road' based on improvements in prod-uctivity, modernization, and promotion of high value-added production (Cooke et al. 1999). Public expenditure in this view is seen not as a burden on the productive economy but as the prerequisite to development, through

	VAT	Top income tax rate	Corporation tax	Tax burden GDP	Government spending/GDP
UK	17.5	40	28	36.6	41.9
Ireland	21	41	12.5	32.2	37.1
Sweden	25	56.5	28	48.2	57.9
Denmark	25	55	25	48.9	43.5
Norway	25	47	28	43.5	43.0
Finland	25	50	26	43.0	52.5

Figure 5.3 Selected % tax rates, 2006–7

Source: OECD, Eurostat.

investment in infrastructure and intangible assets like research, education, skills, and health (Schubert and Martens 2005). This implies that the public sector be efficient and effective rather than just be cut back. Social deprivation, poor health and lack of opportunity are seen not merely as social problems, but as a cost to the economy, necessitating social expenditure and reducing the productive workforce. Unemployment is particularly expensive and small independent nations, who have to bear the cost themselves rather than share it over a wider tax base, cannot afford a sustained and high rate of joblessness. They thus tend to invest heavily in active labour market policy, including training, re-training, and the linking of employment policies to welfare spending so that long-term welfare dependency is minimized. The data in Figure 5.4 show that the most successful small countries in Europe in recent decades have included both low-tax jurisdictions like Ireland and high-tax ones like the Nordic countries. Small, open economies do, however, tend to have larger public sectors in order to adjust to change (Rodrik 1998).

There is no single high road. Finland has emphasized high investment and standards in education, but its success has depended heavily on one sector and, indeed, on a single large enterprise, Nokia. Sweden maintains a market economy, with large corporations increasingly integrated into global markets, together with a welfare state that is generous but increasingly run on 'new public management' lines. Denmark has a network of small and

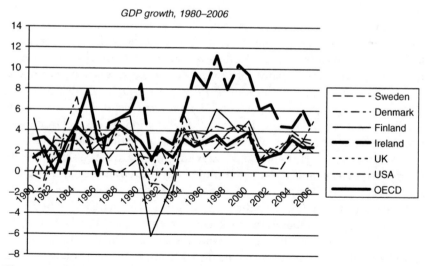

Figure 5.4 GDP growth, 1980–2006
Source: OECD.

medium-sized firms good at innovation but without a huge investment in research. Its employment strategy is based on 'flexicurity', making hiring and firing workers easy but providing generous unemployment benefits and training for those displaced (Jensen and Larsen 2005). Norway has the advantage of oil but manages this as a national resource. The Nordic group, for all their differences (Mouritzen 1996), show how national independence can be combined with social democracy, a word much-used by the SNP. Ireland, on the other hand, is far from being a social democratic state. Yet, Nordic versions of social democracy are not the traditional British social democracy, as practised by Labour governments in the 1940s, the 1960s and the 1970s, which relied heavily on public ownership and planning, together with Keynesian macroeconomic management and control of monetary policy. These instruments are largely ruled out in a modern market economy conforming to European and international competition rules and subject to global capitalism. The emphasis, rather, must be placed on 'supply side' instruments,[12] including research and development and the harnessing of economic and social actors to a common project.

SOCIAL CONCERTATION

A purely neo-liberal approach to economic management risks condemning an independent Scotland to a race to the bottom and can hardly be reconciled with a full welfare state. The state-managed alternative is largely discredited and impractical in an interdependent global economy within the European Union. A third possibility is a 'coordinated market economy', based on social partnership. This takes many forms. In the 1970s, scholars observed the return of 'corporatism' (Schmitter 1974; Streeck 2006), an idea formerly associated with right-wing and conservative movements (including both social Catholicism and Fascism) in the inter-war period. Modern corporatism was shorn of its conservative and authoritarian connotations and referred to a mode of interest representation and policy-making in which peak associations of employers and workers negotiated with government over the main issues of economic policy. There were many national varieties, including those of Germany, Austria, and the Scandinavian countries. The shared idea, however, was that within a national framework, government, capital, and labour could negotiate positive-sum bargains and avoid the collective action problems that would arise if each were to pursue its own self-interest unconstrained. Trade unions could accept lower nominal wage increases knowing that, by keeping inflation down, this would produce higher real incomes and curtail unemployment. Workers might limit private wage demands in return for an enhancement of the 'social wage' of benefits and public services. Employers could invest more if assured that wages would be controlled and government committed to long-term policies on taxation and macroeconomic stability. Government could surrender some of its autonomy in return for an enhanced capacity to deliver on policy; it could invest in education and infrastructure in the expectation that private investment would be forthcoming. Corporatist bargains might be restricted to areas of wages, investment, or taxation or go wider into social and other policies.

There was a widespread agreement by the 1980s that, in so far as the twentieth century had been the century of corporatism, it was coming to an end. It depended on representative peak associations of capital and labour, able to deliver the consent of their members, and on a government able to implement its side of the bargain. International turbulence after the oil crises of the 1970s seemed to put all this in doubt. The globalization of capitalism and the mobility of investors reduced the incentive for employers to play national corporatism, and enabled them more easily to opt out. Trade unions were in decline, more fragmented and less able to deliver the consent of their members. The crisis of Keynesian economic management meant that governments could no longer guarantee the macroeconomic stability that might encourage employers and unions to surrender immediate advantage in the interest of longer-term growth. Economic doctrine turned away from negotiated policy-making, towards a combination of unregulated markets and monetary stability. Corporatism was discredited on the left, where it was seen as undemocratic, undermining accountability, and excluding the poor and marginalized. On the free-market right, it was criticized for undermining markets, giving vetoes to entrenched interest groups and discouraging the change and innovation needed in a rapidly evolving economic order.

Yet in the mid-1980s, Peter Katzenstein (1985) observed that several smaller European states were coping with the challenge of global interdependence by developing a distinct type of social compromise and model of policy-making. Although the national variations were rather different, the common factor was an embrace of international competition to gain the advantages of large markets, together with a negotiated form of policy-making to ensure domestic adaptation while preserving their welfare states. Rather than resisting international changes and shocks or retreating into protectionism, these nations adapt to them on their own terms, while supporting international rules to protect themselves against unfair competition or abuse by larger competitors. Here was a thriving model of corporatism adapted to states whose policy autonomy seemed most at risk from global forces.

More recently, observers have noted a return to what Rhodes (2001) has called 'competitive corporatism' on the part of states faced with global challenges and the imperatives of European monetary union. Unable to manage exchange rates and constrained in their ability to run fiscal deficits, they seek to regain competitiveness by revived forms of social concertation or partnership. Since they cannot afford to maintain declining sectors or to sustain the cost of large-scale or long-term unemployment, they are dedicated to high levels of job creation, to constant transformation and upgrading of skills and to active labour market policies. Sometimes the stimulus has been provided by an external shock or crisis, such as Finland's loss of major markets with the collapse of the Soviet Union, or Ireland's economic crisis of the 1980s. In some cases, there are earlier traditions of social cooperation, in the form of corporatism, or consociational mechanisms for dealing with ethnic or religious divisions (Compston 2002*a*). Elsewhere, historic memories of civil conflict have kept alive an appreciation of the value of cooperation. Common nationality has underpinned a sense of common identity and provided a motive for collaborative action. All of these have helped the transition from a pattern of industrial relations and group politics marked by conflict, to one of partnership and the search for common interests.

These newer arrangements differ from the earlier corporatism in being looser and more flexible and not relying on peak groups of capital, labour, and government to deliver consent. Indeed they have often emerged in countries, like Ireland, where the classical preconditions for corporatism are absent. At the centre of these new forms of concertation is often a system of wage bargaining, setting the parameters for local and sectoral bargaining in order to sustain competitiveness. These are often linked to active labour market policies, to ensure a supply of qualified workers and minimize long-term unemployment. They may extend further, into the 'social wage' and non-economic policy sectors.

In Ireland, the system dates from the late 1980s when, some years after abandoning previous forms of concertation, the country was faced with an economic crisis, persistent unemployment, emigration, massive budget deficits and debt, and the European Single Market programme (O'Donnell and Thomas 2002; O'Donnell 2008). Government needed to get a grip on economic policy, while accepting the implications of European monetary union. Trade unions looked fearfully across the water at the destructive effects of Thatcherism as a mode of adaptation. Business saw the advantages of stability, a commitment to growth and a forum to discuss priorities. Seven partnership agreements followed between 1987 and 2006. While wage bargaining remains at the centre, partnership has gradually been extended to other policy fields, bringing in other actors, including the social sector whose exclusion was one of the main criticisms of old-style corporatism elsewhere. The machinery of partnership has also been extended and elaborated. A National Economic and Social Council dating from 1973 (in the earlier phase of concerted action) is a central element and was complemented in 1993 with a National Economic and Social Forum, bringing in groups that are not part of the core bargains. A Centre for Partnership and Performance looks at issues of competitiveness, while the three bodies come together in the National Economic and Social Development Office. Wage bargaining aside, this does not represent the centralized model of policy-making characteristic of old-style corporatism but a looser and more flexible arrangement, characterized as 'flexible network governance' (Hardiman 2006). Issues are taken into and out of partnership, pursued or shelved, according to circumstance. There is not one arena for partnership but several forums, with wage bargaining separated from the discussions about social priorities. Policies can be linked, and tax and employment policy have been used to ease wage bargains; but not everything is connected, so that there are fewer veto-points than in more elaborate forms of planning and concertation. The Irish model has its critics on the left, who argue that it does not promote progressive social policies, and the right, who prefer a neo-liberal form of market competition; but it has gained support across the political spectrum. Among other factors (including low corporate taxation and EU funding) it shares credit for the Irish economic miracle since the late 1980s and for the ability of Ireland to exit from the economic orbit of Britain (over sixty years after its independence) and to find its place within the new global and European order.

It is not possible to translate the Irish or comparable Nordic experiences directly into a new context, but the literature suggests some general lessons. While fully-fledged corporatism is no longer viable, weaker forms of concerted action are. New forms of concertation are less routinized and more flexible, to be used where they can produce results. Partners can exit more easily, and nobody has an absolute veto. The state remains a central presence, guiding development, providing incentives and taking the final decisions on taxation and spending. Its presence provides the 'shadow of hierarchy' to impose order on what would otherwise be a constellation of competing interests. Groups are linked in multiple ways and in various forums rather than in a single institution, so that contacts are made and renewed across a range of policy fields. Not all policies need to be agreed in partnership forums, but partnership can be extended across new fields where there are benefits in doing so, just as government can impose its will where agreement fails. There is a learning process so that successful partnership begets more partnership, networks are built and shared understandings can develop (Avdagic, Rhodes, and Visser 2005). Constant renegotiation compensates and sustains partnership despite the absence of strong organizational forms (Molina and Rhodes 2002).

Unless it were to adopt the neo-liberal and deregulated model of adaptation to global markets, Scotland would need to find its own form of social concertation and partnership. The starting point at first glance does not look propitious. Tripartite concertation in the United Kingdom gained a bad reputation after the experiences of the 1960s and 1970s. This was not entirely deserved, as negotiated incomes policy proved a relatively effective means of containing inflation without resorting to large-scale unemployment as was done in the 1980s under Margaret Thatcher. Neither side of industry, however, really developed a taste for concertation. Business was tied to the liberal model of free enterprise and, although the Confederation of British Industry was founded in 1965 as the voice of industry with government, it never built up strong collective representation. Unions have historically been wary of the state and emphasized free collective bargaining and exemption from restrictive laws rather than positive engagement (Jones and Keating 1985). Since the 1990s, the word 'partnership' has referred to the privatization of policy delivery to business interests and the use of private capital in infrastructure investment, a far cry from broad cooperation in policy-making and design. Indeed the United Kingdom has stood quite apart from the revival of social concertation in Europe since the 1990s (Compston 2002*b*). Scotland has largely followed these trends, and since devolution there has not been a revival of corporate bargaining or concerted action (Keating et al. 2009). In a devolved Scotland, policy concertation is less imperative, given that wage negotiation, taxation, and labour market policy, the centrepiece of bargains elsewhere, remain at the UK level. Policy networks tend to be sectoral, without trade-offs between fields or much scope for overarching bargains. Business does need the public goods provided by government and cannot, whatever its initial ideas after 1999, opt out of the Scottish policy network; but its main interlocutor remains the UK government, which has, under successive Conservative and Labour governments, taken a pro-business line without demanding much in return. In Scotland, there have been relatively weak efforts to harness a national discourse to a development strategy (Bond et al. 2003).

On the other hand, Ireland did not have the usual prerequisites for concerted action in the 1980s, having inherited the British model of conflictual industrial relations and a limited role for the state. Scotland, for its part, does have some of the characteristics of the partnership nations. It is of a small scale, with a high degree of personal acquaintance among elites in different fields, permitting the construction of networks and multiple points of encounter. There is a rather more consensual style of policy-making than at the UK level, the product of political culture, proportional representation and the weakness of executive government, which means that politicians have to reach out to policy networks for ideas and for implementation (Keating 2005). The minority SNP Government elected in 2007 has even more need to reach out, and partnership is part of its core philosophy.

Independence could provide further incentives to social concertation. The policy scope of the Scottish Government would now include taxation, labour market regulation and social security, encompassing the main issues to be agreed in a social pact. With monetary policy still controlled externally (whether by the Bank of England or the European Central Bank) and fiscal policy tightly constrained, adjustment to changed circumstances would have to be made in other ways, and partnership, as elsewhere in Europe, would be one obvious possibility. It is possible that independence itself would provide the external shock that was effective elsewhere in shaking up policy-making systems and provoking antagonistic groups into cooperation. This, however, is by no means an automatic result, but would require that independence be accompanied by a restructuring of the policy process, the emergence of more Scottish-oriented interest groups and a commitment to a policy style radically different from that which has prevailed in British politics.

BEYOND THE ECONOMY

A broader conception of development takes us beyond the economy as defined by increases in the Gross Domestic Product and recognizes other measures of welfare. Most modern measures of poverty are based on a relative definition, that is, one that defines the poor in relation to the rest of society rather than an unchanging absolute standard. This implies that greater social equality might be a desirable end in itself and that, where possible, growth should benefit the poor disproportionately. This is exactly the opposite of what happens in the familiar forms of competition state, in which disproportionate rewards go to those who are mobile or in higher growing sectors, and inequality may be seen as a spur to greater work effort. This is not to say that economic growth and more social equality are necessarily incompatible, but that they do not run together unless there is a conscious decision to go for an inclusive development model, underpinned by a broad coalition of support. It may also be a legitimate option for a society to forgo some economic growth in exchange for more leisure time.

Development also has an environmental dimension, which has become more salient of late. Small independent states may be under pressure to relax

environmental standards or landscape protection to attract inward investment, but this in itself amounts to a loss of overall national welfare. A broad
social welfare function, taking in the social and environmental dimensions of
development, would provide a better guide to policy than would the obses-
sion with GDP that has characterized the Scottish debate in recent years. Here
an independent Scotland could adopt its own standards and forge a social
consensus around them.

All this suggests that Scottish independence could be viable and that
Scotland could thrive in world markets, but this would require an internal
restructuring to accompany the change in the country's external relationships.
Given its mature welfare state and extensive public services, which neither the
parties nor the public seem inclined to discard, the low road to independence
is politically impractical. It would, moreover, destroy the very social investment needed for growth as well as undermining the social consensus needed
for change. Policies for concerted action, however, would require a change in
attitude by government, employers, and unions, and a transformation in their
ways of working. Government needs to be responsive and flexible and interest
groups less defensive. Otherwise concerted action ends up merely giving each
side a veto over progress and entrenching old patterns. Scotland does have the
shared national identity that has underlain the success of other small states in
world markets, but the social and economic implications of this are not clear
in a country marked by the legacy of the class politics of the industrial era.
Nationality itself has been disputed by nationalists and unionists, for whom it
is a contentious and not a unifying issue. Independence would thus require
nation-building of a new sort, around a shared project of national development. The question then arises whether, if such a project can be achieved and
institutions built to focus Scotland as a viable entity in the new European and
global order, formal independence would be needed at all.

6

Constitutional Futures: State and Nation in the Twenty-First Century

The early twenty-first century has seen competing nation-building projects within the United Kingdom, including a Scottish one and a neo-British effort. Scottish independence has remained a minority option, while very few people want to return to the old unitary state. Public opinion appears ambivalent, sympathetic to independence in some polls and hostile at others. The apparent swings in opinion might look like inconsistency but, reading deeper, they make more sense. Most Scots want more self-government within the various unions in which the nation is nested but they do not make a stark distinction between this and independence, unless it is accompanied by words like 'separate'. The case is not unique, since we see similar attitudes in other plurinational states, including Canada, Spain, and Belgium, not to mention the post-Soviet space and central and eastern Europe. Nor is it unprecedented. The relationship between state and nation in Europe has been problematic since both emerged in their modern form in the nineteenth century. After the First World War, the nation state appeared to have won out as the normal form of political order.

Nineteenth-century France is the archetype of the centralizing, unitary state, based on republican principles of civic equality and in which the *demos* underpinning democracy was identified with the state as a whole. It is not, however, necessary for the nation state to be unitary. The United States of America is a decentralized and federal state but with a strong sense of shared national identity. Pierre Trudeau's vision for Canada in the 1970s was inspired by a conception of the unitary nation as the basis for a modern democratic and liberal order, but within a federal context. In contrast to the United States, the Canadian nation was cast as multicultural, allowing immigrants to retain their own traditions, and bilingual, with an official presence of French from coast to coast. Trudeau's vision of Canada, however, was emphatically not plurinational, recognizing only one Canadian people and insisting on equal citizenship throughout the polity.

Rather than go down any of these roads, the United Kingdom operated as a union, a rather flexible concept typical of British constitutional understandings.

The Union was plurinational and asymmetrical and covered up a number of constitutional anomalies and contradictions with the useful fiction of absolute parliamentary sovereignty. Since it never established the principle of popular sovereignty, it was never necessary to define the people as in the classical republican model. For many years, this absence of popular sovereignty was an affront to modernizers and liberals, who campaigned in groups like Charter 88 for a written constitution, popular sovereignty, a bill of rights, and equal citizenship. Although devolution to the constituent nations was added to this constitutional reform menu, there was always a tension between the republican elements of Charter 88 and the multinational nature of the British state (see following text).

The conditions of the early twenty-first century are not so favourable to the concept of the mononational, sovereign state. The nation cannot be the only principle of political authority in a modern, liberal, and multi-cultural society where identity is experienced in many ways and even national identities can be multiple and overlapping. National independence no longer means what it once did in a world experiencing transnational integration and interdependence, and within a European Union that exercises supranational authority, with direct application of its laws and majority voting over a wide range of issues. There are those who argue that none of this affects the fundamentals of statehood since, whatever the new transnational institutions, they are the product of agreements among states, which have the power to withdraw if they so choose. It is similarly argued that the weakened capacity of the state is irrelevant to the essence of sovereignty, which is a normative principle referring to the ultimate locus of authority. This debate has been covered extensively in earlier works (Keating 2001*a*, *b*), where I have argued that if sovereignty is so divorced from the actual ability of states to act then it has become an empty principle of little practical use. Some of us, moreover, would argue not merely that sovereignty in practice has been heavily circumscribed but that, in plurinational states and in the European Union, the principle itself has been transformed (MacCormick 1999; Keating 2001*a*). Rather than being a unitary concept vested in the state, it is something that can be shared and divided. The concept of 'post-sovereignty' refers, not to the end of sovereignty, but to a new phase in which the meaning of sovereignty has been transformed and new forms of polity can be envisaged. The argument has been taken up widely in Europe as well as in Quebec, by sub-state nationalist movements that have abandoned classic conceptions of independence in favour of strategies to maximize self-government and autonomy within the newly emerging state and transnational order (Keating 2004).

In this context, pre-modern notions of sovereignty may be more useful than the unitary conception favoured by nineteenth-century republicans. Many nations and regions within Europe have retained such older traditions of shared sovereignty, pactism, and complex government that were elsewhere swept away during the nineteenth century, and these provide a 'usable past' to legitimate the new, multilevel dispensation in Europe. The Basques have the foral tradition, under which they enjoyed a special status under the Spanish monarchy. Catalonia has a memory of its pre-1714 status as a self-governing trading nation within a larger federation (the Kingdom of Aragon), itself part of a confederation under the Spanish monarchy. Across the former Habsburg and Ottoman lands, there are memories of more complex forms of government and accommodation that, with greater or lesser success at different periods, allowed different nationalities (as they were called from the nineteenth century) to coexist. We should, of course, avoid romanticizing these pre-modern arrangements or using anachronistic concepts like multiculturalism or multinationalism to describe them; nor were they democratic. The point is merely that they did not rely on the principle of homogeneous nationality to underpin the polity. Modernization brought democratization but at the cost of pluralism; the challenge for complex polities today is to rediscover the pluralism without losing the democracy. Scotland is particularly rich in such traditions, given the retention under the Union of much of its distinct legal system and civil society, and the scepticism in both legal and academic opinion about the Westminster principle of absolute parliamentary sovereignty (MacCormick 1999; Tierney 2004).

While an affront to reformers, Britain's untidy constitution may serve it rather well in these new conditions since by not defining nation and state very closely, it has been able to adopt a plurinational and asymmetrical constitutional settlement without worrying too much about doctrinal consistency. It is as though the United Kingdom has managed the transformation from a pre-modern state (or *ancien régime* as its detractors would have it) to a postmodern constitution without having passed through the interim of nineteenth-century modernity in which other countries are stuck. Traditional nation states like France or Spain, founded on the identity of state and nation and the principle of sovereignty vested in a unitary people, find this concept extremely difficult. This explains the difficulty of accommodation of nationalities in Spain, where there are fierce arguments over the symbolism and terminology of nation and nationality and the concept of sovereignty (Requejo 1996; Herrero de Miñon 1998; Tusell 1999; Keating and Wilson 2009). It also explains the difficulty that Canada, after Pierre Trudeau's project for a liberal and unitary Canadian identity, finds in recognizing Quebec as any more than one federal province among others (Laforest 1995; McRoberts

1997). The United Kingdom does not suffer from this kind of anguish, never having mounted a national revolution or insisted on aligning state and nation.

All this suggests that recent efforts to reinvent Britishness, complete with citizenship tests, flag-waving, and slogans, may be the wrong policies at the wrong time, a nineteenth-century formula for a twenty-first-century world. If this is true of the United Kingdom, it is equally true of its constituent parts so that arguments like those of Tom Nairn (2000), who argues that Scotland, having escaped its 'normal' destiny in the nineteenth century, should assume national independence, now may also be misplaced. We have witnessed a decline in Britishness and the old unionist doctrine is perhaps dead, but it has not been replaced by a new, hegemonic Scottish identity with clear political implications. On the contrary, the political implications of Scottishness are constantly challenged and debated.

As the idea of the nation is challenged in our times, so is that of the state. It is revealing to return to the debates on devolution in the 1970s and compare the assumptions then made about the role of government. The main report of the Royal Commission on the Constitution painted a picture of inexorable centralization and unity under the impetus of Keynesian economic management and the welfare state, putting strict limits to devolution and ruling out federalism as more suited to a nineteenth-century than a twentieth-century state (Kilbrandon Commission 1973). The dissenting report saw even less scope for diversity (Crowther-Hunt and Peacock 1973). The 1978 Scotland Act did not devolve any economic development powers, since these were regarded as essentially a matter for the centre. Nowadays, economic considerations favour decentralization, and development depends on supply-side factors that can be, and are, widely devolved. Nationalized industries, a key instrument of economic management, are almost non-existent. Conversely, while it may have been plausible in the 1970s to argue that only independence could equip Scotland with the tools needed to mount its own development project, nowadays these very powers, including policies on trade and monetary and fiscal policies, have either been taken out of the hands of states altogether or subjected to strict international constraints. It is arguable that the kinds of concerted action underpinning an autonomous political economy discussed in the previous chapter require not the trappings of statehood, but significant economic development powers and the ability to engage in social partnership, instruments open to non-sovereign polities as well as members of the United Nations.

Crowther-Hunt and Peacock (1973) argued that European integration would reduce the scope for policy divergence even further, including in educational policy, and used this to argue against legislative devolution.

Nowadays, to the contrary, European integration and sub-state devolution are widely regarded as complementary processes, transforming the state from above and below and opening up possibilities for constitutional innovation. Similarly, the idea that devolution must be contained within the nation state fails to account for the complex and multilevel system that is Europe. For some observers, the European Union is no more than an intergovernmental body composed of states that come together to pursue their mutual interests. A different conception, however, is of Europe as a union with political, economic, social, and cultural components, not to be confused with a state but more than a mere international agency. Europe in this sense includes the European Union but extends to the network of cooperation institutionalized in the Council of Europe, the Organization for Security and Cooperation in Europe, and NATO (which of course is more than a European body), as well as the patterns of transnational cooperation among states and sub-state governments. Just as the British union is an entity difficult to fit into the traditional political and juridical categories, so is the European Union that defies definition and was once famously described as an unidentified political object.

PERSPECTIVES ON THE UNION

Traditionally, Scottish opinion has been divided among nationalists, favouring a separate state; unionists, opposed to political autonomy; and home rulers, supporting a Scottish Parliament within the United Kingdom. The boundaries have always been fluid, so that Great Britain[1] has avoided the stark clashes of nationality that have marked other European countries. Nationalists have often been ambivalent about statehood, the SNP has been divided between fundamentalists and gradualists, and home rulers have come in a variety of shapes. Unionists, while opposed to political autonomy, have recognized the national diversity of the polity. After 1999, matters briefly appeared to clarify. Now that the home rule was the status quo, nationalists could unify around the slogan that 'we are all fundamentalists now', bound together on the next stage of the journey. Unionists generally abandoned their opposition to devolution and joined the ranks of the home rulers. The political offer then seemed to be twofold and simple, reinforced by the polarization of the party system, with the SNP facing Labour as the principal contenders. Yet, as we have seen, there is a broad swathe of public opinion, usually constituting a plurality if not an absolute majority and encompassing supporters of the Labour, Liberal Democrat, and Scottish National parties, favouring more self-government but falling short of independence in its classic sense. Even among SNP activists there is a willingness to work gradually towards independence, making devolution work in the meantime (Mitchell 2008). Among the leadership, there is a recognition of the limits of classic statehood and almost everybody has begun to talk the language of union, whether it is the British union, the European Union, or Alex Salmond's 'social union'.

Does this mean that the old divide between nationalists and unionists is now irrelevant? I would argue that it is still there but as a general orientation and set of preferences, which start from different premises rather than a clear difference in end points. We must understand these in order to make sense of the debate, but the difference does not in itself make a practical compromise between the positions impossible since, as so often in politics, it is possible to agree on the middle range of issues without necessarily sharing the same long-term goals.

The first perspective, which we might call the neo-nationalist, sees the United Kingdom as a framework for managing common issues in a union of self-governing nations. Scotland is presented as a historic nation, with a will to self-determination expressed recurrently since the late nineteenth century, a sociological reality, and a political community. It may have passed on the option of independent statehood in the eighteenth and nineteenth centuries but it retains the right of self-determination, either as a state or as an autonomous entity within the Union. The neo-nationalist perspective would present the Scotland–UK relationship as bilateral, based on the exchange of powers and mutual interest. It can accept radical asymmetries, while insisting that the question of how England should be governed is a matter for the English themselves. There is relatively little concern about the concept of a UK centre and no attachment to the Union in its own right. Scotland rather than the UK would be the primary framework for citizenship, although this does not preclude some redistribution across the United Kingdom and common arrangements for insuring against risk. The United Kingdom could develop along similar lines to the European Union, as an unidentified political object in continual evolution, although in this case the dynamic would be centrifugal rather than centripetal. Indeed, if and as the European Union develops and deepens, it could gradually replace the United Kingdom as the predominant union and external support system for Scottish self-government. Neo-nationalists would be relaxed about the general concept of Scottish independence, even if they accept that independence in the classic sense is no longer an option.

The second perspective I propose to call neo-unionist. This is to distinguish it from traditional unionism, which opposed elected assemblies in the peripheral nations while recognizing other forms of differentiation.

Neo-unionists accept devolution but start from a different premise from neo-nationalism, taking the United Kingdom as the primary unit and asking how power might be reordered within it. They base their analysis on the continuing existence of a British nation rooted in common values and the need to preserve these. Neo-unionists are not old-style centralists and will usually favour rebuilding the centre, while strengthening the territorial element with it and balancing the constitution more generally. This might follow the lines of German federalism, in which most taxes and much legislation are set for the whole country, with the participation of the Bundesrat, the second chamber representing the federated Länder. Neo-unionists would emphasize the need for integrative and centripetal elements to balance the centrifugal dynamics of devolution. While not necessarily calling for constitutional uniformity throughout the United Kingdom, they would tend to oppose radical asymmetries; so they might favour English regional government as a counterweight to Scottish and Welsh devolution.

Perhaps the critical difference between neo-nationalist and neo-unionist perspectives concerns the meaning and reach of citizenship and the rights that flow from this. Marshall (1992), writing at the birth of the welfare state, recognized three sets of rights. Civil rights came first and secured citizens' liberties against the state. Political rights consisted of the ability to participate in public life, including voting and standing for office. Social rights were the last to arrive and represented the right to basic welfare provision stemming from membership of the same political community. As we have seen in Chapter 2, these citizenship rights did help to underpin the British union and explain its evolution over time, even while identities remained diverse. They largely remained British-wide[2] until devolution, despite the differentiation in civil society and some instances of policy divergence.

The neo-nationalist is less concerned with British citizenship in its three dimensions, as long as the requisite rights are underpinned elsewhere. So there is no need for a British Charter of Rights as long as the European Charter applies. Social solidarity is not necessarily cast at a British level. Scotland itself, or Europe, or the world, may be seen as equally appropriate levels at which to conceive of sharing and redistribution (Keating 2009a, b). UK citizenship might then be seen rather as European citizenship is, as a bundle of specific rights and duties, but not rooted in deep identification with the state as the primary political community.

For the neo-unionist, there is a strong common citizenship, covering civil, political, and social rights, inherently equal and symmetrical and cast at the British level, implying strict limits to divergence in social entitlements. Power may be decentralized to the periphery, but within a common policy framework, with clear boundaries to the devolved sphere and a new normative underpinning for Britishness (Jeffery and Wincott 2004; Jeffery 2005). Citizen demands, it is argued, are much the same throughout the United Kingdom (Jeffery 2006). Hazell and O'Leary (1999: 43) write that 'it may be that we will also need to develop a baseline statement of social and economic rights, to give expression to our deeply felt expressions of equity; and that statement may help to define one set of boundaries beyond which devolution cannot go'.[3] The Westminster Government's evidence to the Calman Commission on Scottish Devolution clearly reflects this thinking, emphasizing common social citizenship and assumptions about public services, 'All parts of the UK regard the provision of healthcare as a fundamental part of what it means to be a citizen – devolution has responded to local needs, but it has not altered this fundamental feature of our citizenship' (Scotland Office 2008). Hazell and O'Leary (1999: 43) write of the 'need to express the common values we hold in being British and the values which make the UK a state which is worth belonging to'. Andrews and Mycock (2008: 148) write of a 'worst case scenario [of] differentiated citizenship rights underpinned by varying educational entitlements'. The Commission on Scottish Devolution (2008: 4.60) comments that 'Devolution, as it currently exists, would in principle allow for a fundamentally different welfare state in Scotland or in England, at least in relation to health or education. But there may be a case for a broadly common social citizenship across the UK. If so, does a common understanding of what that involves need to be more clearly articulated?'

These two perspectives are ideal types, and it is not always possible to fit individual proposals within them. Politicians have tried to straddle the two, as did the Labour Party in signing up to the 1988 Declaration of Right with its ringing claims of the sovereignty of the Scottish people and then putting through the Scotland Act of 1998 that bluntly reaffirmed Westminster sovereignty. The two perspectives do, nevertheless, reflect different conceptions of the logic and the boundaries of devolution since 1999. Yet, while differing in their premises, neither neo-nationalists nor neo-unionists are bound to the old conception of the nation state as unitary and centralized. This opens up new possibilities for institutional compromise and constitutional creativity. The Union can be recast in new forms and actors can agree on practical forms of change even where they start from different assumptions and have different end points. This, rather than the Diceyan certainties about parliamentary sovereignty, has been the genius of British constitutional practice.

If we move from general principles to constitutional design, there are a number of options available. All, however, are subject to some fundamental constraints, which have often frustrated their realization. First, the English need to be convinced of the merits of constitutional reform, and they have consistently shown themselves unwilling to subordinate their own power of self-government to arrangements that give the peripheral nations influence over English domestic affairs. The Union, in which the English hold 85 per cent of the parliamentary seats, just about satisfies this criterion, although since devolution there have been growing complaints about Scottish involvement in English policy. A neo-unionist reform, in which Scotland is tied back into the Union but its territorial element strengthened, is, ironically, less likely to appeal in England since it would put in question the assumption that England is somehow a unitary state. It follows that any extension of self-government to Scotland is likely to mean less influence for Scotland at the centre. This has been the historic dilemma for the Union, recognized in the settlement of 1998, which set up the Scottish Parliament but reduced the number of Scottish MPs. That compromise retained full rights for Scottish MPs in Westminster, including voting on English matters and running English-based departments, but these issues will become more contentious as devolution deepens.

Second, under any settlement, the national composition of the United Kingdom gives England the overwhelming share of population and wealth, and Scotland will always be the weaker party. This does not mean it has no influence, but that Scots must realistically appraise their negotiating position. Common institutions, ostensibly based on equal or proportional influence, are likely to work to the advantage of the larger and stronger party. Third, any constitutional settlement for an asymmetrical union will contain anomalies. The question is whether we can live with these anomalies and whether those in a reformed system will be more intolerable than those that already exist. Some of the anomalies raised by devolution are posed, not by the project of limited Scottish self-government, which is a familiar idea in many federal and composite states, but from the peculiar nature of the British parliamentary constitution. Accommodating Scotland within the conventions of Westminster supremacy has always been difficult. Unionism worked in the past by combining recognition of plurinationality with the centralization of ultimate power. Devolution has stretched this arrangement further, by seeking to combine home rule at the periphery with parliamentary sovereignty at the centre in an essentially unchanged form in a way that satisfies neither neo-nationalists, who emphasize Scottish sovereign rights, nor neo-unionists, who argue that the centre should itself change in order to recognize the new territorial dispensation.

Finally, the relationships between the two levels of government will be affected both by constitutional arrangements and by the political climate. If the two sides are pursuing radically different constitutional agendas, with a Scottish Government seeking independence and the UK Government to rebuild a British nation, then almost any issue could become the basis for a constitutional dispute. With an acceptance of the realities of shared sovereignty and the limits of independence, constitutional politics could be restrained and attention focused on more concrete and immediate issues.

Despite the reluctance of the parties to adapt Westminster to devolution, the central regime has seen a number of important changes in recent years, tending towards a new understanding of governing modes and of constitutionalism (King 2007). European integration and the limited entrenchment of the European Convention for the Protection of Human Rights and Fundamental Freedoms have constrained parliamentary sovereignty while not attacking it head on. Courts have shown greater willingness to restrain government in accordance with statute and broader principles of justice. Backbenchers are more ready to buck the whips. The conventions of 'club government' and the informal ways of the old political and administrative elites are giving way to more formal modes of regulation and transparency (Moran 2003). The wider programme of constitutional reform demanded by reformers has not materialized, and the limited imagination of governing parties is typified by the Labour Government's 2007 White Paper (Secretary of State for Justice and Lord Chancellor 2007), which ignored the big issues of devolution, Europe, and the House of Lords. Yet there is consistent pressure to make the electoral system more proportional and to reform the House of Lords. A British Charter of Rights has been floated by both main parties. This is not to say that further devolution can take place only in the context of comprehensive constitutional reform. The chances of agreement on a constitutional package of items at the same time are extremely remote, and different elements enjoy priority at different times and places. Constitutional reform has been possible in the United Kingdom only in a piecemeal and incremental fashion. It is important, however, to think of how the various elements being dealt with at one time related to each other, and how one reform can open up opportunities for others.

FEDERALISM

Federalism covers a wide variety of systems, but its essential feature is the division of the state into self-governing units, a directly-elected federal legislature, a federal executive, and a constitutionally entrenched division of power such that neither tier can intrude upon the competences of the other. So there is both a central state, with reach across all the constituent territories and direct links with the citizens, and a territorialized tier of government. There is a longstanding theory that federalism only works in relatively homogeneous states, where the units represent just territory and not national identities, and that it should be symmetrical (Tarleton 1965). Otherwise, the federated units will assume sovereign powers to themselves and the system will be unstable. This view is strongly influenced by the experience of the United States but also finds support in the arguments of Dicey and others against Irish and Scottish home rule. More recent analyses, however, have emphasized the value of federalism, often in asymmetrical and complex forms, in managing national pluralism (Requejo 1996; Karmis and Norman 2005; Burgess and Pinder 2007; Kymlicka 2007).

There have been advocates of a federal United Kingdom since the nineteenth century. Ideas of Imperial Federation briefly flourished around 1900 (Burgess 1995; Kendle 1997; McConnel and Kelly 2006), and for many years a federal United Kingdom has been the official policy of the Liberal Party/Liberal Democrats. Federalism looks clear in principle, it would allow equal treatment for the parts of the United Kingdom, and it would provide the basis for a clean constitutional division of powers. In practice, there are several possible versions, all of which have drawbacks. A federation of the four nations would be extremely unbalanced, and the English Parliament would rival that of the United Kingdom. Another possibility is to divide England into regions. Yet it is difficult to see these being given the wide range of exclusive powers possessed by the Scottish Parliament or Northern Ireland Assembly, or even the National Assembly for Wales. Such a federation might work if the UK Parliament were to extend its powers of oversight and pass framework laws within which local parliaments and assemblies could work, as happens in some federations, notably Germany. This would be consistent with the neo-unionist logic of maintaining common social provisions throughout the United Kingdom but would represent a significant reduction from the present powers and status of the Scottish Parliament. One of the few efforts to establish a system of symmetrical devolution for Great Britain, Crowther-Hunt and Peacock's minority report (1973) for the Kilbrandon Commission gained no political backing because of this objection. The Institute for Public Policy Research's proposed constitution (1991) for the United Kingdom was similarly unionist in inspiration, seeking to downgrade Scotland to the same status as an English region, with the same amount of policy discretion in both, circumscribed by overarching UK laws and policy.

If a full federal arrangement is not appropriate, some federal principles might nevertheless be relevant. One is that the constitutional arrangement be entrenched so that Westminster could no longer change it unilaterally and by ordinary law. The present convention is that London will 'normally' not overrule the Scottish Parliament on devolved matters, but it insists on a residual claim to do so (Scotland Office 2008). It is commonly objected that this entrenchment is impossible since Westminster cannot bind a future Parliament and that the principle of parliamentary sovereignty itself is the one thing that Parliament cannot change. This is a weak and ahistorical argument. Westminster has surrendered sovereignty many times, in the case of decolonization and the independence of Ireland, not to mention European matters.[4] It might be argued that the independence of Ireland and the colonies was a one-off matter in which the United Kingdom renounced its jurisdiction, and that an internal reorganization of the state is another matter. Yet it was by no means obvious before the Statute of Westminster, or even the Second World War, that Dominion status meant full independence; rather, it was a way of reorganizing the Empire while keeping its external framework intact. As late as 1982, the constitution of Canada had to be amended by the British Parliament, a legacy of the settlement of 1867; but nobody suggested that Westminster had any real choice in the matter once it had received the bill from Canada. Westminster has also bound itself by conventions; indeed, without these we would have no constitution at all. So Parliament does not prolong its own life except in times of war; the monarch signs acts of Parliament and acts only on the advice of ministers; and a host of other understandings govern everyday political life. It would be equally possible to establish a convention to the effect that the powers of the Scottish Parliament could be changed only with the consent of the Parliament itself. Putting this into a Westminster law might not give it extra legal force but as a declaratory act could give force to the convention, whose violation would thus give rise to a constitutional crisis. So the violation of the convention that the Lords would not obstruct the budget gave rise to the constitutional crisis of 1910 and a clarification in law.

A looser arrangement is confederation, in which self-governing units come together to manage affairs in common. There is no directly elected federal legislature or executive, but common institutions answer to the respective constituent governments. A confederal United Kingdom would reflect the neo-nationalist perspective, with the Union as a framework for selected common policies rather than the focus of citizen loyalty. Scotland would lend powers to the centre rather than receiving them from it. It is sometimes suggested that the (British) Isles could form such a union, bringing Ireland back into the fold while letting Scotland move out of the existing Union and into a looser one.[5] Yet it is unlikely that either Ireland or England would subordinate their present autonomy merely to accommodate Scotland. Not even the prospect of bringing the two parts of Ireland together seems a strong enough motive, and there is almost no political will to link the Scottish and Irish constitutional questions. The English political class, effectively in control of the Westminster Parliament, would not welcome an additional supranational element between them and the European Union. Some such pan-Isles community might be a possible outcome of Scottish independence and there presently exists the British–Irish Council (or Council of the Isles), but neither of these is likely to develop on confederal lines.

SOVEREIGNTY-ASSOCIATION

An option falling between independence and internal constitutional reform would be Scottish independence combined with a special association with the rest of the United Kingdom. This would follow neo-nationalist logic by making Scotland the focus for sovereignty and identity, with no state centre in the usual sense. Relations between Scotland and the United Kingdom would be essentially bilateral. Puerto Rico has the status of freely associated state with the United States, giving it full internal self-government but no standing in foreign and defence policy. Puerto Ricans have US citizenship but cannot vote in presidential or congressional elections. This is a special case of a colonial territory seized from Spain in 1898, and the historical circumstances are quite different from those of Scotland. The freely associated state is challenged both by supporters of full independence and by those favouring becoming a state of the US federation; but the former option would lose the advantages of the association, notably the right of Puerto Ricans to move to the mainland, while the latter is unacceptable in the US Congress, since it would bring in a predominantly non-English-speaking territory.

More relevant to Scotland would be the proposals of the Basque First Minister Ibarretxe of the Basque Nationalist Party (PNV) for a 'freely-associated state' (Keating and Bray 2006) and the various proposals for sovereignty-association or partnership in Quebec. Under the Ibarretxe Plan, powers reserved to the central Spanish state would include Spanish nationality; defence and the armed forces; arms and explosives; currency; customs and tariffs; merchant marine and air navigation; and international relations, without prejudice to the Basque Country's ability to project itself abroad in areas of its own competence. The Spanish state could pass framework laws in the areas of criminal law; commercial law; civil law, except for foral[6] law and family law; intellectual and industrial property; and weights and measures. The Spanish police forces would enforce Spanish state laws. All matters not reserved to the centre would belong to the Basque Country, and the Plan lists a series of exclusive Basque competences covering domestic policy fields. Shared areas of responsibility include social security, this at the insistence of Ibarretxe's left-wing coalition partners, who wanted a continued link with statewide insurance, state enterprises, and property rights. The *concierto económico*, by which the Basque Country raises nearly all its own taxes and negotiates a payment to Madrid for common services, would continue. There would be provision for 'direct' Basque representation in the institutions of the European Union, although it is not clear how this would work. Early drafts of the Plan proposed that the Basque Country could become an associate or partner of the EU, inspired by the proposal of French Basque (but not nationalist) politician Alain Lamassoure in the lead-up to the Convention on the Future of Europe. Lamassoure's proposal, however, never amounted to more than a form of administrative decentralization and was further watered down in its application. Later drafts of the Ibarretxe Plan dropped the reference and suggested that Basques would participate in the Spanish delegation, with the policy line presumably decided in bilateral negotiation. The principle of bilateralism would also be extended to other matters of common interest.

Sovereignty-association was a scheme designed by the Parti Québécois (PQ) for the referendum of 1980 to bring together the separatist and confederalist wings of the movement and appeal to the centre ground (Balthazar 1992). There would be a customs union, free movement of capital and persons, a common currency, and possibly joint management of transport systems, including Air Canada and the railways (McRoberts 1988). Common matters would be handled by joint institutions, in most of which Quebec and Canada would have parity, although in others the side with the predominant interest could have a larger say. After the failure of the referendum, the PQ moved to an accommodation with the rest of Canada but then, under the leadership of Jacques Parizeau, back to separatism. The idea of association was discredited and the very word was regarded as tainted, but the concept was not formally abandoned and in various ways it kept creeping back in, to moderate the party's image and to deal with the practical problems of independence (Bergeron 1991; Langlois 1991). In the second referendum, in 1995, it was proposed that Quebec become sovereign after making an offer of partnership with the rest of Canada, a compromise between Parizeau and the more moderate Lucien Bouchard, leader of the Bloc Québécois, and the Action Démocratique du Québec. The partnership could cover internal and international trade; international representation, with the possibility of Canada and Quebec speaking with a single voice in international bodies; transport; defence; financial institutions; fiscal and budgetary policy; environment; arms and drug trafficking; postal services; and any other matters that might raise common interests.[7] There would be a joint Council of Ministers, representing both sides equally; a parliamentary assembly representing the two sides according to population; and a Court. Quebec would retain the Canadian dollar, but there were no specific provisions for managing it. This, arguably, would amount to a confederation, although the term was avoided.

None of these plans was put to the test. Spanish central politicians refused to countenance the Ibarretxe Plan on the grounds that it violated the constitution and Spanish sovereignty and so was a non-starter. Canadian federalist politicians rejected association in 1980 and insisted after the referendum of 1995 that future referendums not refer to such a prospect, on the grounds that they merely confused the issue of independence.

Some form of sovereignty-association is not inconceivable in the Scottish case but would be less urgent than in Canada-Quebec because the European Union would take care of many of the common interests and externalities. Indeed the EU could make sovereignty-association particularly difficult, since it would presumably not give Scotland a seat in the Council of Ministers. The two sides would then have to agree constantly on the position to take at the Council, an arrangement unlikely to satisfy either, but particularly the United Kingdom. It might be that Scotland and the United Kingdom would agree to share a currency, some regulatory institutions, and even a defence force, but it is difficult to see why Westminster, unless it put a very high premium on keeping Scotland on side, would agree to Scottish influence in these matters, when it can presently set policy on its own. At the limit, Scotland could just accept this reality and allow Westminster the predominant or final say in matters of common interest as the price of gaining effective independence in other matters.

The more attenuated forms of independence fade, through partnership, sovereignty-association, and confederalism, into the stronger forms of devolution, giving Scotland more powers but leaving the link with the United Kingdom in place. The Allaire Report, which was briefly the official policy of the Quebec Liberal Party[8] and then became the inspiration for the *Parti Action Démocratique du Québec* (ADQ), was a response to the PQ's promise of sovereignty with partnership (Laforest 2004). It proposed that Quebec assume all powers not specifically reserved to the Canadian federation, which would be limited to foreign affairs, customs and tariffs, defence and security, and the currency and fiscal equalization. The ADQ did support the Yes side in the referendum of 1995 but declared that there should thereafter be a ten-year moratorium on independence referendums, since extended indefinitely. The party now adheres to the principle of 'autonomy' defined as a special relationship with Canada based on Allaire (Charron 2007; Action Démocratique du Québec 2008). In practice, this form of radical decentralization is rather difficult to distinguish from its sovereignty-association competitor, which proposed a similar list of powers for the new association, with the exception that Allaire wanted to keep fiscal equalization. This caused particular outrage in the rest of Canada, and it is difficult to imagine why other Canadians would consent to transfer resources to a Quebec that had moved to a loose confederal arrangement. Leaving this aside, the end points of both strategies looked remarkably similar, the difference being over how to get there, with Allaire wanting to negotiate half-way out of Canada and the PQ to leave and then negotiate half-way back in. This is not a trivial point. A constitutional rupture followed by agreement would be a very different matter politically from an internal constitutional reform. It would create antagonisms and polarize opinion, forcing politicians to stress the dividing line between independence and less radical options rather than the continuum between them. This could hamper cooperation in building new forms of partnership. In 2008, the PQ attenuated its aims still further, deferring a prompt referendum in favour of a 'national conversation', an idea presumably borrowed from Scotland, further blurring the distinctions.

Another approach is functional, starting with the changes under way in the relationship between social and economic change, public policies and territory, captured under the heading of the 'new regionalism' (Keating 1998). Much of the relevant literature is rooted in economic and social functionalism and ignores politics, and little of it addresses nationality questions. Ohmae (1995) proclaims the 'end of the nation-state', to be replaced by the regional economy; but his vision of the region is a curious combination of neo-liberal and mercantilist elements, dedicated to a narrow vision of economic growth and the suppression of social expenditure. Scott (1998) recognizes the political implications of the rise of economic regions and the need for some kind of management of these new spaces, in his concept of 'regional directorates'. Gagnon (2001) more explicitly links these ideas to the rise of neo-nationalisms, positing the 'regional state' as an alternative to classic statehood in the case of Quebec. The regional state in this sense would be a polity equipped with the competences to pursue the kind of economic, social, and cultural policies for which small units are, in the new global order, often best equipped. It would leave matters of defence and currency, together with other matters of common interest, to the wider level. Of course, the term 'region' would never run in Scotland (and is not much easier in Quebec), but the idea points away from classic preoccupations with constitutional matters towards a consideration of the practical powers and resources that might be needed to undertake a specific social and economic project.

EVOLVING UNIONS

There is no ready-made concept for a reforged British Union that could satisfy both centre and periphery and stabilize the constitutions. Yet, federation, confederation, sovereignty-association, and functional autonomy provide elements for building an evolving order based on a series of unions within which Scotland would be nested. This is not a matter of recasting the United Kingdom as a federation with a clear division between centre and periphery, but of shifting powers gradually to recognize the constitution of Scotland as an emerging political space, the growing demands for self-determination, and the needs of social and economic development. If the neo-unionist perspective points towards cooperative federalism and a stronger but territorialized centre, the neo-nationalist points to confederal principles or something on the lines of sovereignty-association. A strengthening of competences would serve to make the Scottish Parliament the main focus of political life in Scotland and the main object of political competition. Interest groups would adopt a stronger Scottish focus and strengthen their Scottish presence so that Scotland became the main arena for social exchange and compromise. A Scottish model of development could then emerge of the sort discussed in the previous chapter. This does not necessarily imply a separate state, as the experience of Quebec and Flanders shows, but nor can that be ruled out in the longer term. As the UK level gradually becomes residual, there might be a slow move towards Scottish independence, *de facto* and eventually *de jure*; but alternatively a new territorial balance might emerge and an asymmetrical settlement eventually stabilize.

7

Beyond Devolution: Evolutionary Change

There is no blueprint for a new constitutional settlement for Scotland, and none of the existing models seem to fit the bill. The nearest we can come to a philosophy is the concept of union, a protean idea that points us in the direction of asymmetry, negotiation, pactism, and shared sovereignty. Yet while defying the Cartesian logic of much continental constitution-making, such a fuzzy concept is consistent with British constitutional tradition. So is the idea of evolutionary change, the gradual adaptation of constitutional arrangements to changed demands and conditions. This does not mean that proposals for further change should be a mere shopping list, to be mixed and matched at will. The previous chapter suggested two visions and directions of travel. The neo-nationalist vision focuses on Scotland and its need to negotiate a deal within the various unions in which it is nested; the end point may or may not be independence but could be based on confederal principles. The neo-unionist vision starts from the premise that Great Britain (if not the United Kingdom) remains a nation state with common citizenship and largely similar demands across its territory; the end point is a strengthened Union. In practice, of course, particular ideas may be supported by different people for different reasons, just as devolution itself was supported by nationalists as a stepping-stone to independence and by unionists as a way to safeguard the future of the United Kingdom. This is the price of constitutional agreement.

Scottish devolution has represented more than the 'regional decentralization' found in unitary states like France or Italy. It rests upon a modernized and politicized national identity, the re-emergence of a political community and the creation of a new polity. This is not the nation state of the past, with its rigid boundaries and the internalization of nearly all political exchange and policy-making within them. Scotland is, rather, an open polity nested in wider social, economic, and political systems. Yet self-government does imply a form of boundary-building in the strengthening of a Scottish level of action, to which political, social, and economic actors are at least loosely bound and from which they find it difficult to exit. With weak devolution, actors find it easier to circumvent devolved institutions and take matters directly to the centre, or to ignore the devolved level altogether, on the grounds that it does not control the competences of interest to them. Stronger forms of self-government bind actors in more strongly since they depend on the policies and public goods produced by devolved governments and available only from them. This provides an incentive for the range of social and economic interests to engage in politics there, so encouraging political exchange and laying the basis for the kind of social concertation outlined in Chapter 6. So stronger self-government is not merely a matter of allocating competences on grounds of technical efficiency but of polity-building and making Scotland the level at which key social compromises are struck and at which trade-offs can be made among policy objectives.

Self-government in an interdependent world is not merely a matter of Scotland being autonomous from Westminster but of it having the ability to tackle social and economic problems; the distinction has sometimes been framed as between 'autonomy from' and 'power to'. There is little evidence that most Scots seek more autonomy in order to become a force in world affairs, or to change foreign and defence policy. Rather, the challenge is to find the instruments for an economic and social project that can combine economic competitiveness with social cohesion and environmental responsibility. There is a growing preference that the reference point for such a project be Scotland and not just a territorially undifferentiated United Kingdom. The policy tools are not those of the classic nation state, such as control of external trade and tariffs or even monetary and macroeconomic policy. Nor are grand development plans in vogue, or extensive state control over the economy. The emphasis is rather on steering, selective intervention, social partnership, and building physical, human, and social capital. Since the policy tools cannot all be found within Scotland (even in the case of independence), a self-governing nation will need the capacity to act within wider arenas, be they British, European, or global.

FISCAL MATTERS

Devolution in 1999 perpetuated the Barnett Formula, a non-statutory device whereby Scottish devolved expenditure is determined by two different principles: historic levels for the base and population for the increment in each spending round. It was never intended as a permanent arrangement and has been widely criticized, not least by Lord Barnett himself. Although electors voted for tax-varying powers in 1999, Labour governments at Westminster were afraid of the consequences of fiscal devolution and limited the discretion of the Scottish Parliament to the three pence on or off standard rate of income tax. In practice, this power is almost unusable, given the costs of collection and its high political visibility. Centralization of taxation confuses the electorate about who is really responsible for public services; surveys under the Labour–Liberal Democrat coalition regularly showed most people thinking that Westminster had the greatest say over matters like health and education. It also allows the parties to play political games, with the nationalists blaming Westminster for not providing money and Labour, after 2007, accusing the SNP Government of not increasing spending on public services by the same percentage as in England, although this is the automatic effect of the Barnett Formula.

The 1999 settlement is rooted in neo-unionist assumptions about the scope for, and likelihood of, Scottish policy differentiation. The block funding system in principle gives Scotland full discretion in the spending of its funds, and there is little evidence of Whitehall interfering here. Yet it is assumed that Whitehall and Holyrood are committed to the same broad pattern of welfare spending and the balance between taxation and charges to fund it.[1] The advisers to the unionist Calman Commission (Independent Expert Group 2008) seemed to accept the same logic, treating the matter of taxation as a largely technical matter. Other observers have been concerned that the devolved administrations might not keep up to UK-wide standards in public services (Hazell and O'Leary 1999). In fact, given the social democratic consensus in Scotland, the real danger is the reverse. A UK Government might seek to privatize the welfare state or bring in charges for public services or private insurance in health, so cutting the Barnett consequentials and forcing Scotland, without its own tax powers, to follow.

Nor can the Scottish Government strike its own balance between public spending and taxation, the central choice in a modern democracy. Fiscal discretion would give the Scottish Government greater flexibility in its policy instruments, matching tax incentives and spending and shaping its own welfare settlement through allowances. It would also provide an incentive for policies encouraging growth (Thomson et al. 2008). At present, any additional revenues accruing from Scottish growth and employment benefit the UK Government, while rising unemployment does not cost the Scottish exchequer anything directly. Scotland could shape its own welfare settlement, choosing the high-cost or the low-cost road to development (Chapter 5) and taking responsibility or credit for the outcome. Taxation powers would also be a crucial element in polity-building, helping to make the Scottish Parliament the centre of attention and sharpening political choice at elections. It would draw in interest groups to the Scottish policy arena and make this a real forum for social compromise and exchange, encouraging the emergence of new forms of social partnership such as those sketched out in Chapter 5. In recent years, the case for giving tax-raising powers to the Scottish Parliament has been increasingly accepted, but the underlying rationale and the choice of instruments remains in contention.

The most thoroughgoing form of devolution is full fiscal autonomy, as exists in the Basque Country and Navarre,[2] under the historic *concierto económico*. This allows the Basque provinces to raise all the main taxes, including personal income tax, corporation tax, value added tax (VAT), and excise duties.[3] This revenue is mostly passed on to the Basque Government, which then negotiates with the Spanish Government an agreed share (the *cupo*) for common services, including defence, foreign affairs, and the royal household. Unemployment insurance and pensions come under a different regime, financed by contributions. There is some tax harmonization, with agreed limits on variation of taxes to preserve the Spanish internal market, while EU law further limits variations in VAT. The Basque Country does not fully participate in the equalization system among the Spanish autonomous communities which, given its higher income levels, is a big advantage.[4] It lost out in the 1980s and early 1990s when it went through a serious crisis of industrial decline but was able to use its fiscal discretion to good effect in designing policies for recovery and modernization. The Basques were also able to use their balance of power in the Spanish Parliament, to force a favourable revision of the *concierto* at a point at which the balance to be transferred to Madrid was in danger of becoming a negative amount.[5]

Another option is assigned taxation, under which Scotland would receive a specific share of a range of taxes in Scotland, but without the power to change the rates or coverage. Such a system existed in Northern Ireland under the Stormont regime, where the main taxes were assigned but subject to an 'imperial contribution' for common services. In the face of economic crisis, however, the arrangement was regularly changed so that the imperial contribution ceased to be the first charge on revenue and eventually disappeared altogether, with Stormont receiving substantial transfers from Westminster. The first drafts of the current Northern Ireland Act provided for assigned revenues but balanced this with a provision for the UK Government to make transfers, which emptied the provision of significance. It was deleted after complaints from Northern Ireland parties who feared that a future UK Government might abandon them to their own resources. If assigned taxes in Scotland were to be balanced by a system for fiscal equalization and redistribution, the provision would similarly be meaningless. If there were no equalization then Scotland would be dependent on its own resources but without the ability to use taxation rates innovatively to pursue its own priorities, arguably the worst of both worlds.

In a system of tax-sharing, as in Germany, most taxes are harmonized across the federation, but the two levels of government set the levels and coverage jointly. Such an arrangement would be consistent with the neo-unionist argument for a strong role for the centre, combined with strong territorial influence within it. This is an unlikely possibility for Scotland, since Westminster will not subordinate its discretion over taxes to a joint decision with the Scots. That would leave neither level really autonomous or responsible, something that is increasingly recognized as problematic even in the German system of cooperative federalism.

A more likely prospect is fiscal devolution under which Scotland could vary the rate and possibly the coverage of certain taxes. Some taxes, such as fuel and excise duties or road tax, could be handed over completely. The major taxes on sales, incomes, and business would be divided into a UK and a Scottish share, with some discretion over the Scottish rate. Sales taxes are a problem since in the United Kingdom they were replaced in the 1970s by Value Added Tax (VAT), which is mandatory in the European Union, with variations in the rate limited by European regulations. Differential sales taxes within the United Kingdom could cause economic distortions, with cross-border shopping if, for example, a Scottish Government were to tax alcohol more heavily; this already happens between England and France.

Differential rates of business taxation seemed at one stage to be ruled out under EU competition and regional policy provisions since they counted as state aids. After a series of cases in the Azores and the Basque Country, however, the European Court of Justice ruled that tax variations were legal if brought in by an authority with 'institutional, procedural and economic autonomy' (Official Journal of the European Union 2008/C/285/98). The condition, however, is that there be no compensation from central government for lost revenue, which is much easier to assure under conditions of full fiscal autonomy. A proposal to cut Northern Ireland's corporation tax to compete with the lower rate prevailing in the Republic of Ireland came into difficulties, as it would be almost impossible to ensure that an equivalent amount had been deducted from the block grant. Even if the technical problems were to be overcome, there remains a danger of a race to the bottom if devolved governments are free to set their own rates to try to attract industry, and a fiscally-autonomous Scottish Parliament might wish to agree on provisions with Westminster to avoid this.

This leaves personal income tax as the prime candidate for real variation. Federal systems typically divide income taxes into a federal and sub-federal element, with each level having discretion over the rates and allowances. Variations in income tax could provoke migration or cross-border commuting, but these would be limited. More generally, governments know that raising taxes too much will drive away taxpayers, while cutting them will deprive them of revenues, so they tend to stay in line with their neighbours. So fiscal devolution in Europe has not generally led to large disparities in tax levels.

Fiscal decentralization is difficult, to the point that many Scottish commentators have suggested that the problems are insuperable; but it is widely practised around the world. Other systems of devolved government (including Spain, Belgium, and Italy) have often started off keeping finance centralized but have moved on to fiscal decentralization both for technical reasons and in order to diffuse the political pressure away from the centre. The Spanish autonomous communities other than the Basque Country and Navarre receive 30 per cent of income taxes, 35 per cent of VAT, and 40 per cent of excise taxes collected in their regions, together with inheritance tax, gaming tax, and some special taxes on transport and energy (Girón 2007). Their main discretion is over the rates and allowances on income tax. Italian regions have a small margin of discretion over income and business taxes, but discussions are under way about introducing more 'fiscal federalism'. Regions also have considerable discretion in health service and other charges. Belgian regions have control over a range of consumption and licensing taxes and a limited discretion at the margin over income taxes. Federal countries including Switzerland, Canada, and the United States give the lower levels much broader discretion over the scope and scale of taxation.

In any arrangement short of independence, there would be some redistribution of resources across the United Kingdom, through the automatic effect of central government expenditure and explicit fiscal equalization among territories. Such redistribution can be justified on both economic and social grounds. By pooling resources across a wide area, states can insure against asymmetrical shocks, provide automatic stabilizers, and secure the unity of the labour market. It may also be in the interest of prosperous areas to encourage growth in poorer regions because it develops statewide markets and many of the benefits of growth return to them in the form of demand for their goods and services. This was the rationale for redistributive regional policy spending in European countries and more recently for the European Union's Structural Funds, small though these are in comparison with overall levels of public spending. More crucially, however, territorial redistribution and fiscal equalization represent an effort of national solidarity, providing funding to different territories, taking into account their resources and their needs. This implies a strong sense of social citizenship associated with a neo-unionist conception of the nation. The economic rationale for some territorial redistribution might survive in a looser form of union or confederation without a strong shared citizenship. The social rationale, however, would be undermined and Scotland might be obliged to fund its own welfare settlement with its own resources. If fiscal autonomy were to be introduced without changes in the responsibilities of the devolved government, then the United Kingdom would retain large spending competences in Scotland and there would be a lot of implicit territorialization based on the location of beneficiaries. Such expenditures do feature in the calculations of fiscal gains and losses in the GERS reports, although they are not part of the transfers under the Barnett Formula. Were devolution to extend a long way into social security these transfers would either disappear or have to be incorporated into an equalization formula.

Fiscal equalization implies that each territory should be able to provide the same level of services, taking into account both its resources and its needs. Resources include wealth and taxable income, and full equalization would provide that one penny on income tax should produce the same revenue everywhere, with the central government topping up where necessary. This, however, would encourage poorer regions to raise higher taxes, knowing that other regions would pay. Richer regions therefore tend to demand that their poorer compatriots make an equivalent 'fiscal effort', a concept that cannot easily be quantified but which refers to the pain that taxpayers should feel from increased taxes. It is also argued that a system of full fiscal equalization does not give poorer regions an incentive to develop their own economies, since the result would be the loss of support from the centre. Resource equalization may therefore be less than full. Equalizing for need is even more difficult, since it requires a measure of standard needs across the state, even though governments may be providing different services. The factors used to calculate need are often proxies, such as demographic balances, or sparsity of population, which can be assumed to impose additional costs; but they may also be items that could equally be considered matters of policy choice, such as minority language education or universal social services. In the revised Spanish statutes of autonomy, regions have tried to incorporate principles of fiscal distribution favourable to themselves, variously stressing population numbers, population density, ageing or young populations, sparsity of population, immigration, or GDP. Catalonia stipulates that fiscal transfers must not change the overall GDP rankings of regions. Andalucia refers to the 'historic debt' due to alleged under-funding in the past. Most try to stipulate that they are entitled to a specified share of state investment. At the time of writing, this was all waiting to be resolved in a new finance law that would lay down some consistent principles.

Unionists on the centre-left have argued against fiscal decentralization on the grounds that it would promote inequality (Walker 2002), and some have claimed that the present system for allocating spending among the nations and regions of the United Kingdom is based on need.[6] Yet the only attempt ever to calculate relative need was the Needs Assessment Study carried out in the late 1970s in anticipation of devolution but never used. The present arrangements are the outcome of a historical process and *ad hoc* political decisions. So equalization mechanisms would have to be invented from scratch, as would the basic principles for dealing with needs and resources. These would need to be grafted on to the present mechanisms, allowing time for adjustment. The basis could be provided by an independent body charged with calculating the figures and providing scenarios. The settlement, however, would have to be negotiated by the UK and Scottish governments, and probably the other devolved governments as well. This would inevitably be conflictual, and it would be desirable for a multi-year formula to be agreed, to avoid annual recriminations. It would be important to have a source of data independent of both levels of government, especially in view of the controversies that have arisen with GERS. The Commonwealth Grants Commission, which advises government on grant distribution among the Australian states, has often been cited as a model.

So fiscal equalization is an eminently political rather than a technical matter. It has become a salient political issue in many European countries as the old economic justification breaks down in the face of international and European integration. Citizens in recipient regions can spend their increased incomes anywhere, while the wealthy regions complain that transfers are an unacceptable burden, hampering their ability to compete in international markets. In plurinational states, the shared identity that underpinned inter-territorial solidarity may also be weakening. Typically, the response of wealthy regions has not been to propose the abolition of all transfers but to make them more transparent and to limit their incidence, so that poorer regions are forced to face up to their own responsibilities. The issue is always complicated by disputes about the magnitude and direction of transfers and over who is subsidizing whom. A new fiscal system for Scotland will therefore depend on what kind of union it is intended to serve.

The Scottish Parliament is unusual among devolved legislatures in its lack of an ability to borrow. This has constrained its ability to finance capital projects other than through the Treasury's preferred Private Finance Initiative/Public Private Partnership model, which has been criticized by the SNP. Were Scotland to rely more on its own taxes then borrowing powers would be appropriate to cope with fluctuations in revenue caused by economic conditions. A radical solution would be to allow the Scottish Parliament to borrow freely, as happens in Canada, where the provinces are disciplined only by the bond markets. This would violate UK Treasury assumptions about counting public debt as a whole, and probably European rules as well. Less radically, the Scottish

Parliament could be given borrowing powers and the ability to balance borrowing and spending over time, while putting into place procedures for limiting overall public debt, as Spain and its regions did in order to meet the Maastricht criteria. Another possibility is to allow revenue bonds, under which capital projects could be financed by borrowing, with the capital changes the first call on revenues. This would be suitable for roads and bridges (although the SNP has decided that these will be free) and some other public facilities.

The treatment of North Sea oil revenues is a particular case, for strong political reasons. Scottish nationalists have persistently played on the injustice of Scotland's not gaining the benefits of oil taxes even while Westminster politicians, leaving oil out of the account, claim that Scotland is subsidized by England. UK governments have argued that oil is a resource that belongs to the whole of the United Kingdom and not a part of it. This reasoning looks rather selective. Scotland suffers from various economic disadvantages due to its remote location, climate, and difficult topography. Its advantages include the possession of natural resources, and it would only seem reasonable to include them in the balance. On the other hand, taxation of oil is not an ideal revenue source for sub-state governments, as the experience of the province of Alberta, with its highly unstable revenues, shows. It would certainly be a poor basis for the maintenance of a developed welfare state such as exists in Scotland. As in the independence scenario, the best use for oil revenues might be for a stabilization or investment fund and to help with economic diversification and life after oil. There would be a case, therefore, for Scotland to have access to a share of oil revenues, especially so as to benefit from periods of high oil prices, with the bonanza shared with the UK Treasury. If an elaborate system of fiscal equalization were in place, these benefits might disappear, with Scotland becoming a net contributor to UK revenues. There could, however, be provisions for a share of oil revenues to be taken out of these calculations in recognition of the special status of natural resources, with the surpluses going into the long-term stabilization fund. The idea of a Scottish endowment, giving the country a permanent legacy from its oil era, has also been canvassed.

The 1999 settlement contains another anomaly that reflects the assumption that welfare policies would not diverge. This concerns what happens to UK-funded programmes when Scotland changes the relevant policy. When the Scottish Parliament introduced free personal care for the elderly, Whitehall refused to pass on the savings made on attendance allowances on the grounds that this was not Scotland's money and had never been part of the block. Later, it refused to pass on savings made on council tax benefits should the Scottish Parliament adopt local income tax, arguing that these are tied to council tax and not to Scottish needs. This is a serious restriction on the ability of the Scottish Parliament to legislate within its sphere of competence. It also means that Scottish taxpayers are helping to meet the bill for benefits in England which are not available in Scotland. Energy in general is a reserved UK competence, but renewable energy policy is devolved. This means that if Scotland refuses to build new nuclear power stations (as it has done), any subsidies to nuclear power generation will not attract Barnett consequentials, nor will Scotland get compensation.[7] Subsidies to encourage renewable energy, however, will have to be paid out of Scottish revenues. A similar issue has arisen in Canada where provinces, notably Quebec, have complained that, if they decline to participate in federal spending programmes in areas of their own jurisdiction, they risk losing money. To compensate for this, there have been provisions for provinces to continue to receive the money that would have been spent by the federal government as long as they are pursuing their own programmes with similar or compatible objectives (Richer 2007). The failure of constitutional reform over the years has meant that this has never been entrenched, but successive federal governments have repeated their commitment to the principle. A similar provision would certainly allow Scotland to reclaim attendance allowances or council tax benefits.

THE WELFARE STATE

The welfare state is one of the pillars of the British nation, representing the principle of statewide solidarity and redistribution, and most cash transfers, including pensions, unemployment benefits, and social security, are excluded from devolution. The argument is twofold. First, the British nation is the appropriate unit of social solidarity. Second, it makes practical sense to pool risks over the wider area, given the vagaries of demographic change and asymmetrical economic shocks. This is consistent with practice elsewhere in Europe. Devolving social security has been seen on the left particularly as an attack on social solidarity, narrowing the basis for redistribution, appealing to more egotistical local sentiments, and allowing wealthy regions to desolidarize from their poorer neighbours. It is also associated with the 'race to the bottom', as regions and localities cut social overheads in order to attract investment. Even the Basque Ibarretxe Plan left social security and unemployment insurance at the Spanish level, at the insistence of the left-wing coalition partner. In the United States, decentralization of welfare is historically associated with the political right.[8]

Yet decentralization is not necessarily anti-solidarity if the local level is more solidaristic than the state itself, as has been argued of Quebec

(Noël 1999). In this case, the locus of solidarity might be changed, but not the principle. The smaller west European democracies are in practice more solidaristic than larger states, as well as more generous with overseas aid. One of the forces pushing for Scottish devolution is the rise of other forms of solidarity and, in particular, a strengthening of the territorial dimension in the face of declining class identities. Already there are signs of the gradual development of a distinct Scottish model of public service provision, tending towards universalism as against the selectivism that prevails in England, and less reliant on markets and private delivery (Keating 2005). In the absence of control over income-support programmes, however, this has often taken the form of extending free provision to all regardless of means.

As noted earlier, the 1998 Scotland Act differed from its 1978 predecessor in devolving most of the instruments of economic development, in line with changing conceptions about the spatial economy and the drivers of growth. Its conception of the welfare state, however, remained rather traditional, distinguishing between cash payments, which remained with Westminster, and social services, which are devolved. Modern thinking about social and economic policy, however, stresses the linkages between the welfare system and labour market policy and the need to use both constraint and incentives to get unemployed people back into work. For neo-liberal economists, this takes the form of 'workfare' in which there is no alternative to work for the able-bodied; but social democratic governments practise similar policies under the labels of active labour market policy and social inclusion. The old distinction between unemployment insurance based on contributions and income support derived from taxation – a staple of the old 'male breadwinner' model of the welfare state – makes less sense in modern social and economic conditions and is also breaking down. There has, in consequence, been a series of experiments in new forms of social policy, including the New Deal in the early days of the Labour Government, and the Community Allowance schemes piloted from 2008.

There has been a growing argument from progressive social groups and agencies that Scotland needs now to forge its own packages of social intervention and support, allowing it to combine instruments in new ways adapted to local circumstances. This represents a significant change from the traditional social democratic preference for centralization. More neo-liberal commentators have noted that devolving social security would provide a strong incentive for Scottish governments to get people into work, since they would save on welfare payments and, assuming fiscal devolution, gain the tax benefits. Devolving social security and unemployment benefits could allow Scotland to design its own package of measures to ensure social equity and efficient labour markets, as happens in some of the smaller European democracies. More broadly, devolving the range of tax, welfare, and labour market policies could draw more actors into the policy process and encourage the sort of social partnership outlined earlier (Chapter 5). All this suggests that a devolved social welfare system would look rather different from the present one and would need to be more responsive to external shocks and linked to other policy instruments. Under these conditions, a new compromise could be struck between accommodating global markets and self-government.

Under enhanced devolution, this is not an all-or-nothing issue as it would be under independence, since it would be possible to divide the social protection system in various ways. Pensions, which might be presented as matters of mutual insurance rather than social solidarity, might be left at the UK level and financed jointly. The rest of social security might be devolved, allowing Scotland a significant margin to design its own package of social services and cash payments. There might also be a shared stabilization fund to be drawn down in case of unemployment crises and asymmetrical shocks. An alternative model would be to retain the basic framework for social support at the UK level but to give the Scottish Government administrative autonomy in managing measures, with the discretion to raise standards at its own expense.

REGULATORY POLICY

Under advanced devolution, the United Kingdom would remain an economic and monetary union, within the wider European Union. Until the 1980s this implied an active role in fiscal and monetary policy for the central government, together with extensive public ownership and an industrial policy. Developments since then have transformed the role of government, with some powers going to the market, some to the European Union, and some to independent regulatory agencies. This has already facilitated a much more permissive devolution of economic policy in 1998 than that envisaged in the Scotland Act of 1978. Nationalized industries have almost disappeared. Instruments of regional development policy, such as innovation, knowledge transfer, inward investment, training, as well as infrastructure, are more easily devolved, as are institutions such as Scottish Enterprise. Other policy fields have been kept at the centre but entrusted to semi-independent agencies in one of the most striking transformations of British government over recent years. These have served to promote transparency, surveillance, and central control, patrolling the newly liberalized economy and promoting competition and price control in formerly nationalized utilities in place of informal direction and influence (Moran 2003). Yet while this arguably amounts to a constitutional change, it has not been linked to reforms of territorial government. One way of looking at the regulatory state, whether at the European or UK level, is as a form of depoliticization, taking out of partisan politics issues that are best left to technical experts, and setting the neutral rules by which other actors play. From this perspective, it does not really matter, except for technical and efficiency reasons, at which level regulatory agencies are located. As we have seen, even some supporters of Scottish independence would leave these UK regulatory institutions in place.

Another view, reinforced by the exposure of regulatory failure in the banking crisis of 2008, is that regulation raises pre-eminently political issues of policy choice and that these have a territorial dimension. This feeds demands for a Scottish level of regulation, or a Scottish input to UK regulation. There have been suggestions that Scotland could have its own competition authority, working within British and European legislation, but paying particular attention to conditions within Scotland. The revised Statute of Autonomy for Catalonia, adopted in 2006, gives the devolved government responsibility for competition in matters entirely within Catalonia, and establishes a competition authority.[9] If this is considered one level of regulation too much, then Scotland could take over the entire responsibility, within the limits of EU law. The Financial Services Authority could be given a territorial remit, particularly crucial given the role of Edinburgh as a financial centre. Railway regulation could be devolved, as in effect the railways have been in a series of steps after 1999. Responsibility for regulation of utilities could be devolved or shared. Assuming that the United Kingdom does not enter the Euro any time soon, monetary policy will remain the responsibility of the Bank of England, which since 1997 has had independence from the government. It lacks, however, any territorial element in the composition of its board or its operational criteria. Under advanced devolution, it might be converted into a Bank of Britain, with representatives of the devolved territories on its board and a remit to consider the territorial impact of its decisions.

The regulation of broadcasting has proved a particularly sensitive issue, given the importance of radio and television to nation-building, representations of the nation in fact and fiction, and coverage of political events. This is consistent with experience in other stateless nations, although in those cases there is often a language issue. Since devolution there have been complaints that not enough programming is made in Scotland and that Scottish viewers and listeners are subject to news items affecting only England, distorting the political debate. The Scottish Broadcasting Commission (2008) recognized these criticisms and recommended a new Scottish network and that more production should be located in Scotland. It was more circumspect about the devolution aspects, warning that its review should not become a surrogate for the constitutional debate. It did, however, call for a stronger Scottish input into BBC decision-making and broadcasting regulation, more accounting on the part of the BBC to the Scottish Parliament, and the appointment of Scottish representatives on the regulatory agency, Ofcom. If this did not work, then devolution of broadcasting might be considered.

Energy regulation and policy is of particular salience, given the importance of oil and of wind and wave power to Scotland. The Scottish Parliament, which has opposed new nuclear power stations, can stop them only by using planning powers, criticized by many as a misuse of powers. The financial anomaly has been discussed above. This is another example of the distortion of policy choices and incentive by the division of functions and points towards the complete devolution of energy regulation to the Scottish level, with cooperation where necessary.

THE WEST LOTHIAN QUESTION

Among the supposed anomalies arising from devolution, none has received more attention than the West Lothian Question (WLQ). Originally posed by Tam Dalyell in the 1970s, the conundrum is that after devolution Scottish MPs at Westminster can continue to vote on English and Welsh matters, while neither they nor English and Welsh MPs can vote on the equivalent Scottish issues. It has never been clear what sort of 'question' the WLQ is. The Spanish and Italian languages have separate words for question in the sense of issue (as in the Middle Eastern question) and question as interrogative (one that demands an answer). Dalyell clearly thought that it had no answer and that the only alternatives were no devolution or Scottish independence. Gladstone lost sleep on the issue over his Irish Home Rule bills in the nineteenth century, without coming to a satisfactory conclusion. Under the Stormont regime the number of Northern Irish MPs was cut to below their population share, but only once did they determine the composition of a government.[10] The 1978 Scotland Act ignored the WLQ altogether, while the 1998 Act compromised by reducing the number of Scottish MPs to their population-based share. Public indignation at the WLQ anomaly has been limited, perhaps because it is just one more democratic oddity in a system that allows parties to gain absolute majorities on a minority of the vote and even (in 1951 and February 1974) while gaining fewer votes than their rivals; and where the second chamber still has a hereditary element. It has, however, exercised English politicians and media and, were the powers of the Scottish Parliament to be extended, the grievance would rankle more. Gladstone's various bills excluded Irish MPs from Westminster, then included them, and then reduced their number. None of these resolves the issue, since excluding Scottish MPs altogether would end the Union, while reducing their number leaves the principle unchanged.

The most widely canvassed answer is an in-and-out system whereby Scottish MPs do not vote on purely English or English-and-Welsh matters. Various arguments have been raised against this from a neo-unionist perspective (Bogdanor 2007; Hazell 2008). First, it is said to be impossible to define English bills, since most laws have a mixture of UK and English or Welsh items. This is really a matter of drafting, since bills and their clauses already have territorial application clauses and it would not be impossible to group them better or to separate bills so as to make matters clearer. That would have the added advantage of making the statute book more coherent and legible. Second, it is argued that English bills have implications for Scotland, as in the legislation for top-up university fees, which faced Scotland with the challenge of following suit or finding the money elsewhere. (In fact, Scottish MPs happily voted this bill through, their votes being decisive, precisely because it did *not* affect them.) This argument is strongly unionist, since it implies that representatives from one jurisdiction should have a vote in another one every time a bill with spillover effects is introduced. Indeed the logical corollary would be to allow Westminster MPs to vote on Scottish matters such as free personal care or abolition of university fees, since these decisions put them under pressure to follow suit. A related argument is that Scottish MPs have a legitimate interest in English legislation, since the English financial allocations are the basis on which the Barnett consequentials, determining the Scottish budget, are based. Bogdanor (2007) argues that Scottish MPs could legitimately vote on any move towards insurance-based health provision in England on these grounds. This is to make a constitutional principle out of a funding formula that has no statutory basis, was originally introduced as a short-term expedient, and is widely agreed to be in need of reform. If a new formula for tax-sharing and equalization were to be introduced, this is indeed a matter in which Scottish MPs would have a legitimate interest, but this does not require them to vote on the organization of public services in England.[11]

A fourth argument is that, were Scottish MPs debarred from voting on English matters, the government could lose its majority over much of its legislative programme. As Bogdanor (2007) claimed, such an idea 'undermines the principle of collective responsibility according to which a government must command a majority on all of the issues that come before

Parliament, not just a selection of them'. This implies that a single UK-wide majority should give authority to legislate in all the parts of the United Kingdom, precisely the principle to which Scots objected during the 1980s and 1990s and which gave the decisive impulse to devolution. More widely, it accepts the idea that governments should always have the power to whip legislation through the House of Commons. Constitutional reformers have long argued that strong executive government based on minorities of the popular vote is itself an anomaly, which should be addressed by introducing proportional representation (PR) at Westminster – Bogdanor (1984) is himself a longstanding advocate of this. With PR, governments would be obliged to seek wider Commons support for their legislation, through coalition or negotiating on individual items of legislation, a situation that already exists in the Scottish and Welsh legislatures and the London Assembly. Without the Scottish MPs, such coalitions would have to include a majority in England. Finally, it is argued that an in-and-out system would create two classes of MP, although it is not clear why this is a problem and it is arguable that there are already two classes: those who can vote on domestic matters affecting their constituents and those who cannot. More seriously, it is argued that there would be progressive separation of English business within Westminster and a delinking of the arenas of English and Scottish politics, leading perhaps to Scottish independence. This is indeed possible, but that is an issue to be examined on its own merits. If the current version of unionism requires that Scottish MPs vote on English issues, then it is in serious trouble, just as it was when English MPs could legislate for Scotland.

If Labour has ignored the WLQ, the Conservative Party has tried to square the circle by allowing the constituent nations their own forum but giving Westminster the final say. The Alec Douglas Home report, which briefly became party policy in the late 1960s, proposed an elected Scottish Assembly to take the committee stage and second reading debate of Scottish bills, whose final stages would be taken at Westminster, where the governing majority would prevail. In 2008, Kenneth Clarke proposed a special procedure for English bills. Second reading would be taken in the whole House, where the government would command its normal majority. Committee and Report stages, where amendments can be made, would be taken in an English Grand Committee. At third reading, bills would come back to the whole House, which could not reverse the amendments but could still vote out the entire bill (Conservative Party Democracy Task Force 2008). Clarke's rationale was that the principles of legislation would be set by government, while the details could be shaped by English opinion. It is difficult to see how this would address the WLQ, as long as Scottish MPs could vote on the general principles, or how one could distinguish between the essence and the detail.

It is unlikely that the Labour Government would have regarded university top-up fees as a matter of detail, to be settled by the English MPs. Presumably, 'wrecking amendments', intended to destroy a bill, would have to be disallowed at the committee stage.

A more confederal perspective on the Union would have fewer problems with asymmetry or the in-and-out principle, seeking to separate out clearly English from Scottish business as far as possible, even if a perfect distinction cannot always be made. More problematic, perhaps, is the question of Scottish ministers in the central government. For decades, there was always a Scottish MP in the Ministry of Agriculture, although agriculture came under the remit of the Scottish Office, and between 1974 and the late 1990s the minister responsible for oil was a Scottish member.[12] On the other hand, Scottish MPs are never appointed to the English department of education, and the presence of Scottish MPs in government as a whole from the 1950s to the 1990s was so small that the issue hardly arose. During the 1990s, while the number of Conservative MPs in Scotland diminished, a high proportion of them served in the government, including the Cabinet, while the incoming Labour Government in 1997 contained a disproportionate number of Scots. Robin Cook was disowned by his party leader in the 1990s when he suggested that, as a Scottish MP, he could not serve as Secretary of State for Health after devolution, and another Scottish MP, John Reid, did go on to hold this post, later becoming Home Secretary with mainly English responsibilities. As devolution deepens, this would become more difficult and a convention is likely to develop barring Scottish MPs from these posts. This still leaves the Prime Minister, the Chancellor of the Exchequer and the economic ministers, who have responsibilities both for UK affairs and for domestic English policy. It would not be possible, while asymmetrical devolution exists, to bar Scottish MPs from these positions, although it could become increasingly difficult for them to serve. Again, more self-rule for Scotland entails less influence at the centre.

REBUILDING THE CENTRE

In any scheme short of full independence, there will still be a centre; but its character would be very different under neo-unionist assumptions or more confederal assumptions. The former would point towards mechanisms for resolving conflicts and for cooperation on selected matters of common interest. The latter would look to joint policy-making over wide areas and strong common institutions.

One widely canvassed option is a reformed parliamentary second chamber to replace the House of Lords and based upon the nations and regions. In a strongly unionist scheme, the chamber could be directly elected and given broad powers to ensure that territorial interests were not neglected across the legislative field. A less unitary alternative would see it nominated by devolved and local governments and given powers over matters affecting the constitutional settlement, helping to entrench the devolution of power. The difficulty here would be to balance the devolved nations and England. In the absence of an English national government or regional governments, its nominees would have to come from local government, which does not have the constitutional standing of the Scottish Parliament or Welsh and Northern Ireland assemblies. In any case, the debates on reforming the House of Lords in recent years have focused on the balance between elected and appointed members, with the political tide flowing strongly towards election. The devolved territories have not featured largely in this debate – more evidence of the separation between devolution and other items of the constitutional agenda – but it is not likely that public opinion would be enthusiastic about appointment or indirect election.

Mechanisms for cooperation and conflict-resolution at the executive level follow the same logic, depending on whether the aim is more separation or binding together. In the early years of Scottish devolution, relations between the Scottish Executive and Whitehall departments were largely informal, based upon existing civil service linkages and the common party affiliation of Labour ministers. With the arrival of the SNP in the renamed Scottish Government, party connections ceased and the moribund mechanisms for formal cooperation were revived. These consist of a memorandum of understanding, a series of concordats in policy fields, and Joint Ministerial Committees (JMCs), which had atrophied with the exception of that on Europe. JMCs potentially have a number of roles. A neo-unionist perspective would have them coordinate policy across levels in order to avoid excessive divergence while providing a stronger territorial voice in an essentially unified policy system. It has also been suggested that more coherence might be secured through passing framework laws at Westminster to set the limits for policy divergence. This is a feature of some federal systems, such as Germany and Spain, but not of the Scottish devolution settlement where, by and large, whole areas of policy were devolved along with the administrative machinery. Framework laws would thus represent a constraint on existing levels of Scottish autonomy in favour of a rebuilt union at the centre. The model of stronger devolution, and even more the confederal idea, implies that Scotland will become the principal political arena in which social compromises are forged and inter-sectoral policies developed.

Even a more confederal perspective (extending to sovereignty-association) would have a role for intergovernmental mechanisms to deal with spillovers and externalities, so that governments can recognize mutual interests in coordination where appropriate. This could apply, for example, to environmental policies or cross-border transport infrastructure, or to policies that might provide incentives for people to move across the border merely to take advantage of different regulations. All constitutional options would also need mechanisms to resolve disputes between the two levels, whether about finance, competences, or the costs imposed on one government by the actions of the other. Whatever roles intergovernmental machinery is to fulfil, it would require more formal procedures and mechanisms for exploring differences. It could be possible to commission outside research and advice on financial or legal points in dispute, so as to inform debate. The ultimate decision in such bodies, however, would be political and reflect the balance of power and influence. In a more open system, each side could be restrained by the need to carry opinion with it and, once again, the salience of the independence issue would affect the climate.

Another mechanism for resolving disputes is the judiciary, which has played an important role in the evolution of Canadian federalism and Spain's 'state of the autonomies' (Aja 2003). There has long been a suspicion of judicial intervention in politics in Britain, but over recent decades the courts have become more important in restraining executive government and interpreting European law (both from the European Union and the European Convention for the Protection of Human Rights and Fundamental Freedoms – ECHR). The Scotland Act provides that competence disputes be resolved by the courts and, ultimately, the Judicial Committee of the Privy Council, although between 1999 and 2008 not a single case reached that far. Nor were there any challenges by the centre to the powers of the Scottish Parliament. A stronger devolution settlement, by entrenching the powers of the Scottish Parliament, could provide for appeal against both Holyrood and Westminster legislation on the grounds that it strayed into fields belonging to the other. Such a reciprocal guarantee could force Westminster to craft its legislation more clearly and, through jurisprudence, secure the boundaries between the reserved and the devolved spheres. It would, of course, challenge the principle of Westminster sovereignty; but this is inherent in any federal-type arrangement. Parliament has already come very close to limiting the application of the doctrine through EU law and the ECHR, although it has sought to deny the implications. The courts can declare a UK or English law to be non-compliant with the ECHR, and Parliament is then invited to bring the law into line through an emergency procedure. Laws of the devolved assemblies, on the other hand, can be struck down directly by the courts for non-compliance with the Convention. While the courts can strike down Westminster statutes as non-compliant with EU law, successive governments have consoled themselves with the doctrine that they have only 'lent' powers to the EU or that they could withdraw altogether. All this suggests that the doctrine of parliamentary sovereignty is not an obstacle to stronger constitutional entrenchment, a view supported by the Steel Commission (2006).

A WRITTEN CONSTITUTION?

Many critics of the devolution settlement have called for clarity and stability in a written constitution. This dovetails with a campaign running since the 1980s through Charter 88 (later renamed Unlock Democracy), the Institute for Public Policy Research (1991), and others. Such a constitution would be based on the sovereignty of the people, not Parliament, and would limit the scope of government, democratize the system, protect civil liberties, and democratize the state. Gordon Brown dropped approving hints, as did the Green Paper, *The Governance of Britain* (Secretary of State for Justice and Lord Chancellor 2007), but shied away from a commitment. Reformers, nonetheless, still look to a comprehensive package of changes that would incorporate the devolution settlement in a formalized order.

The idea is in many ways appealing and could help to entrench the settlement on generally federal principles. The traditional objections that Westminster cannot bind itself by higher law are rather beside the point. A constitution could be adopted and affirmed by referendum and special procedures provided for its amendment. The deeper problem is how a single constitution would sit on a plurinational and asymmetrical state. The principle of popular sovereignty requires that the people, or *demos*, be defined for the first time. If it were the people of the United Kingdom, that would undermine Scottish understandings about sovereignty and represent a unionist move. If sovereignty were vested in the constituent nations, we would have in effect a confederal order. It would also imply recognizing England as a sovereign nation, something that reformers have been very reluctant to do. The Institute for Public Policy Research (1991) draft constitution seeks to resolve the problem through English regional government but only at the cost of reducing the Scottish Parliament's powers to those of an English region. English regional government, however desirable, is not the answer to the United Kingdom question; it is the answer to a question about the internal organization of England (Keating 2006b). The problem is magnified when we move from Great Britain to Northern Ireland since the constitution would need to incorporate the Good Friday Agreement, with its provisions for people to express multiple loyalties and for the province to secede and join the Republic of Ireland. If there were a secession clause for Northern Ireland, then it would seem inconsistent not to include one for Scotland, given that successive British governments have not denied the Scottish right to independence. There would also be demands, as there have been in Quebec, that constitutional amendments require not just a special statewide majority but consent from each of the constituent nations.

One demand that has attracted some support across the political spectrum is for a British Bill of Rights. It is favoured on the liberal left as part of the Charter 88 agenda on civil liberties, and by the Conservative Party as a way of undermining the European Charter for the Protection of Human Rights and Fundamental Freedoms (ECHR). Labour ministers see it as a way of restraining rights by balancing them with duties and as a contribution to their Britishness agenda, with a preamble stating British values. Herein lies the problem. Both the Conservatives and Labour appear to see a British charter as a nation-building device, much as Pierre Trudeau used the Charter entrenched in the 1982 Constitution to build a pan-Canadian identity and citizenship against the claims of Quebec. Nationalists and many federalists in Quebec rejected the Charter precisely on these grounds and not because of its substantive provisions, which indeed closely resembled those in Quebec's own charter. A UK Charter (i.e. not just British) that linked rights to Britishness could not work in Northern Ireland, where the whole basis of the settlement is about separating human rights from national identities. Nor would it get an easy reception in Scotland. The problem is recognized but not resolved by the House of Lords and House of Commons Joint Committee (2008). They prefer the title 'UK Bill' rather than 'British Bill' on the grounds that some people do not consider themselves British, but English, Scottish, Irish, or Welsh. This merely begs the question of what 'UK' used as an adjective covers, if it is to be more than a geographical expression. Indeed, they go on to say that 'there is an inevitable and entirely appropriate link with national identity. A national bill of rights is an expression of national identity and the process of drawing one up deliberately invites reflection on what it is that "binds us together as a nation", what we regard as of fundamental importance, and which values we consider to guide us. It is potentially a moment of national definition' (Joint Committee on Human Rights 2008: 96). JUSTICE (2007) explicitly excludes Northern Ireland from its proposed bill, which is defined as British, but it says nothing whatever about the implications in Scotland and addresses only the English legal system. The ECHR, on the other hand, is delinked from nationality and nationalism, represents a more universal conception of rights and is more easily adaptable to slightly different traditions and requirements in various parts of Europe. Since the ECHR is already binding on the Scottish Parliament, it is difficult to see what a UK Charter could add, except to restrict Scottish policy-making in favour of statewide uniformity.

At present the ECHR is entrenched in UK law in a way that purportedly preserves parliamentary sovereignty. The courts cannot strike down laws, but merely refer them back to Parliament, which is invited to amend the offending clauses by fast procedure. It is, however, directly applicable in the devolved institutions. In Canada the 'notwithstanding' clause allows both federal and provincial governments to opt out of some provisions of the Charter; the Parti Québécois when in power used it as a blanket exception, while taking care to abide by Quebec's own Charter. If a UK or British Charter were to follow the ECHR procedure by allowing Westminster but not Holyrood to opt out, its unitary purpose might be undermined as the same rights could be more strongly entrenched in Scotland than in England and Wales.

The written constitution and charter of rights might thus be part of a neo-unionist strategy to reform the union, restrain the executive, and enhance the territorial dimension of the polity. It is more difficult to reconcile with the neo-nationalist strategy or a confederal conception, not because of any difference over the substance of democracy or rights, but because of the differing assumptions about nationality, sovereignty, and the locus of authority. It might therefore be better for human rights advocates to press for an extension and deepening of the European instrument rather than get involved in the project to recreate a British nation.

More generally, this all shows the difficulty in making explicit matters that can be managed in practice without raising questions of high principle and consistency all the time. There are also practical problems in the 'big bang' approach of taking the whole constitutional agenda together. This creates so many interlinked problems and veto points that agreement can become impossible except at founding moments such as independence, defeat in war, or emergence from authoritarian rule. Canada has been trying to agree its constitution on and off since the middle of the nineteenth century. The 1982 repatriation of the constitution was pushed through without the consent of Quebec and has remained a grievance since. Efforts to address it in the Meech Lake Accord during the 1980s were rebuffed in English Canada and among the aboriginal people for offering unilateral concessions to Quebec and omitting their grievances. When the agenda was widened in the subsequent Charlottetown Accord, it created even more conflict points, with the result that the deal was voted down both in Quebec and in the rest of Canada (Lusztig 1995). The British approach to constitutional reform, by contrast, has been piecemeal, often impelled by political opportunism and low politics, as with successive extensions of the franchise, reform of the House of Lords, or devolution. Constitutional conventions emerge, they are challenged, and they change, often without worrying too much about the doctrinal implications. Efforts to pull it all together quickly run into their own contradictions, as with Dicey's (1912, 1961) to reconcile his concept of the rule of law with that of parliamentary sovereignty, or to insist that Parliament was sovereign but that it could not legislate Irish Home Rule.

THE EXTERNAL DIMENSION

Defence and foreign policy, core competences of the sovereign state, cannot be transferred to Scotland short of full independence. Nor is there much public demand for a Scottish defence force or diplomatic presence even among supporters of the softer independence options. During the Cold War, security was not a partisan issue as Britain's main defence posture was subsumed within NATO, although a section of Scottish opinion was opposed to nuclear weapons and inclined to neutralism, and an independent Scotland's security would continue to be assured by collective means through Euro–Atlantic institutions. This explains why the classic issues of defence and diplomacy have had a relatively low profile in the Scottish debate. Yet there have been controversies, as UK governments face accusations of excessive subservience to US interests and are reluctant to pursue a stronger European defence pillar unless it is firmly under NATO. Foreign wars, notably in Iraq, have been contentious domestically, as has the renewal of the Trident missile system. Under stronger devolution, these would continue to be Westminster responsibilities, but it would be impossible to prevent the Scottish Parliament or Government from expressing dissenting views. Foreign and security policy could then be a source of contention, if not of jurisdictional competition.

Great issues of peace and war do not, however, exhaust the scope of external relations. While classical diplomacy represents the prerogative of the sovereign state, devolved and federated governments have been active abroad as the implications of their domestic competences cannot be contained at home. 'Paradiplomacy' refers to the growing net of international activities of sub-state governments; the term 'proto-diplomacy' refers to those of independence-seeking governments that are searching for external support for their projects (Duchacek, Latouche, and Stevenson 1988; Michelmann and Soldatos 1990). Paradiplomacy may be focused on cultural issues, especially in stateless nations with their own language as in Catalonia or Quebec; on economic matters such as inward investment, technology, and markets, and to positioning in the international trading system; and on political issues including alliances with other regions and nations, policy learning, and influence within international regimes and networks. Catalonia has a wide array of overseas representation but with a flexible structure and in partnership with private actors and civil society. The aim is not merely the projection of Catalan interests but the internationalization of Catalonia. Quebec for many years has practised an active paradiplomacy, as has Flanders.

Scotland is already involved in a large number of external activities, geared to attracting inward investment, forming alliances with other devolved territories in Europe, sharing experiences and policy ideas, and promoting Scottish culture. More recently, there have been efforts to mobilize the Scottish diaspora in North America. Many of these have been pursued in cooperation with the Foreign Office, other government departments, and the British Council. Scotland has its own office in Brussels (discussed in the following) and staff in British embassies in key countries. These initiatives, which extend domestic competences abroad, do not necessarily conflict with British diplomatic priorities, although there have been regular arguments with English interests over the promotion of inward investment. There is further scope for Scottish paradiplomacy, as Scotland has name recognition and arouses an active interest elsewhere. It could be particularly effective by stressing the international linkages of all sectors of Scottish society without regard to political affiliation. There are also possibilities for a formal Scottish presence in international bodies such as UNESCO, since education and culture are already fully devolved. Catalonia has a memorandum for cooperation with UNESCO since 2002 and has sought a greater presence, without seeking to displace Spain, while Quebec participates as a member of La Francophonie and is recognized within the Canadian delegation to UNESCO.[13] A very advanced model is provided by Belgium, where the regions and language communities have responsibility for the external projection of their domestic responsibilities, subject to protection of Belgian diplomatic and foreign policy priorities and obligations (Brassinne 1994). Such functionally based plurinational paradiplomacy (Aldecoa 1999) could be more extensive the more Scotland moves to the confederal pole, although a neo-unionist perspective might see it as a barrier to British nation-building and seek to confine it to specific economic and cultural matters.

Proto-diplomacy is another matter, since it is more politicized and will bring Scotland into more direct confrontation with the UK Government. This is partly because of clashes on specific issues, including economic policies and competences, but perhaps even more so on the symbolic claims to sovereignty and precedence made by a Scottish government that aspires to independence. The experience of Quebec, Catalonia, and the Basque Country shows that paradiplomacy can work even when a nationalist government is in office, as long as the independence question is parked; but as soon as it is raised, then almost any issue can become the occasion for the rehearsing of competing sovereignty claims and the right to speak definitively for the nation.

THE EUROPEAN DIMENSION

Minority nationalists across the continent have invested heavily in the ideal of a united Europe (Keating 2004). For some, Europe lowers the cost of independence and allows full national sovereignty – the policy of the SNP. For others, Europe permits a loosening of the state framework and opens pathways to new forms of polity based on shared and diffused sovereignty. Some of these possibilities are ideological, as Europe provides a new discursive space into which to project aspirations and to frame the national project. Nationalists can point to the transformation of sovereignty within the European Union, or to the coexistence of nations within a broader union, as lessons for domestic politics. A commitment to Europe serves to ward off accusations of separatism and even allows minority leaders to portray state elites as narrow-minded nationalists. They retrieve historical memories of pactism and divided power to show how their own pluralist traditions mesh with the European project.

Other possibilities are more concrete and reached their apogee in the Europe of the Regions concept during the 1990s. The idea was that, as regions consolidated and the Commission encouraged them as a level for policy, a 'third level' of government might emerge, and eventually even a three-level federalism of Europe, state, and regions. In the (Maastricht) Treaty on European Union of 1992, the regions gained two key concessions: a consultative Committee of the Regions; and a provision allowing regions to represent their states in the Council of Ministers, where this is permitted under domestic law. Neither, however, met the demands for devolved regions or stateless nations for a distinctive place as more than decentralized administration. A few years later, a group of Regions with Legislative Powers was formed to demand a special status as bodies that shared the responsibilities of member states in the transposition of EU directives and laws. They made little progress in the Convention on the Future of Europe or the ill-fated draft constitutional treaty, and other members of the Committee of the Regions refused to accept their claims. There have been occasional suggestions that regions could gain a status as 'regions of Europe' (Drèze 1993), but this has not advanced. French politician Alain Lamassoure proposed that regions could become 'partners of the Union', an idea taken up in early versions of the Ibarretxe Plan; but the idea was reduced to a limited form of tripartite partnerships. More generally, the move to constitute regions as a third level failed (Elias 2008) because of the heterogeneity of regions themselves, which have a very different status in different countries; the reluctance of member states to surrender power; and the lack of interest within the Commission which, contrary to a once-popular view, does not have an interest in undermining states and making common cause with regions. Given this, the options for non-state territorial governments have been reduced to two: working through the mechanisms of consultation and lobbying around the EU policy process; and gaining a stronger influence over the bargaining stance of their state within the Council of Ministers.

The EU policy process is a complex one in which a multiplicity of actors intervene at all stages – initiation, negotiation, and implementation (see Chapter 3) – and devolved governments that are present in the right places may be able to exert influence. The Committee of the Regions (CoR) is one forum, although its performance has been less than inspiring. Its membership is heterogeneous, including stateless nations, federated governments, and municipalities, so that it is difficult to agree on matters of substance. Municipalities refuse to accept any differentiation of status and in most member states the notion of a stateless nation is regarded as an oxymoron. Much of CoR's time is spent on negotiating compromise resolutions, which are then passed on to the Commission, Parliament, and Council of Ministers rather than focusing on a key policy issue. The European Parliament is another forum, although as a devolved rather than independent nation, Scotland's representation there is limited to seven members, about to be reduced to six – proportionately less than half the number for small independent states.

There is a great deal of scope for territorial lobbying in Brussels, with a dense network of groups and states and non-state governments. These can be effective where the latter are well-organized, with good policy ideas, and able to intervene during the policy elaboration phase, while ideas are being considered in the Commission or going back and forward to national delegations. Scotland is represented by a Scottish Government EU Office, while the pre-devolution body, Scotland Europa, provides a platform for Scottish interests more broadly (Bulmer et al. 2002). The Scottish Government Office is linked closely to the UK Permanent Representation as part of the 'UKREP family' predicated on a close identity of interest between Scotland and the United Kingdom. This may be an effective vehicle for paradiplomacy, although questions have been raised as to the effectiveness of Scottish lobbying, notably in a leaked report by the head of the Brussels Office. As Scotland moves into proto-diplomacy, seeking its own place in Europe distinct from the United Kingdom, this becomes much more difficult. Another avenue of influence is through inter-territorial networks and alliances. Scotland has been quite active in partnerships across Europe, although these are of varying effectiveness, depending on how well focused they are (as explained above). There is also a dense network of inter-regional associations, which wax and wane over time according to the political agenda and the work that regions are prepared to put into them.

Further possibilities exist 'downstream', in the implementation of EU laws and directives. Generally speaking, the EU has insisted that any variation permitted in the application of directives be exercised only at the member state level, but Scotland has already gained some concessions in the application of Common Agricultural Policy reform (Keating and Stevenson 2006). The Lamassoure proposal for partners of the Union gave rise to a very limited programme for tripartite agreements among the Commission, the member state and a region; but this could in principle be expanded, as part of the EU's new commitment to a regional strategy under the Leipzig agreement of 2007. Scotland, since devolution, has often let the UK Parliament transpose directives in devolved matters, but it could systematically assume this responsibility for itself and take the opportunity to dovetail EU and domestic policies more closely.

The centre of power, however, remains in the Council of Ministers; developments in recent years, including the draft constitutional treaty and the Lisbon Treaty, have tended to reinforce the intergovernmental rather than the supranational nature of the Union. This puts a premium on the ability of devolved and federated governments to work through their host states. The strongest sub-state influence is Belgium where there is a list of competences, from exclusive federal matters to exclusive regional or community ones. The composition of the Belgian delegation in the Council of Ministers follows this, so that on some matters the regions and communities appear alone; during the Belgian presidency, regional ministers have even chaired the Council. Where regional or community matters are at stake, all the relevant governments must agree, otherwise Belgium has to abstain. This gives priority to horizontal agreement among the federated units, with only a weak power of vertical coordination by the centre. In Germany there is a similar division of matters, with the Länder attending the Council as appropriate, although the central government is never excluded. The negotiating line is agreed among the governments concerned, with the Länder, if necessary, voting by majority in the Bundesrat. This produces a horizontal form of coordination, which is then modified by vertical negotiation with the federal level. Spain has a weaker system, in which the autonomous communities are present in certain formations of the Council of Ministers[14] alongside the central government. The final decision on the negotiating line belongs to the centre.

Weaker still is the UK system, according to which the devolved governments may attend the Council of Ministers where their competences are at stake, but only at the invitation of the centre. The negotiating line is discussed within the Joint Ministerial Committee (Europe), but London has the final say. When governments at both levels were dominated by the same party there was a strong incentive to agree in public, and Scottish ministers believed that cleaving to the UK line was the best way to retain influence. This was bound to cause tensions when the two levels of government are controlled by different parties, and there have been calls to formalize the relationship (Wright 2005). Such a formal procedure for European matters would complement a more general move to constitutionalized mechanisms for managing the relationship between Scotland and the United Kingdom, but would need to take into account the peculiar nature of UK devolution. The German model, in which the Länder agree policy within their sphere, is not appropriate due to the asymmetrical nature of the settlement and the fact that the UK Government also speaks for England. A version of the Belgian system would be possible in which, in matters of their exclusive competence, the agreement of the devolved territories would be needed to establish the UK line, although it would be difficult to persuade any UK Government to accept such a territorial veto. Moreover, even if agreement is reached in one policy sector, this might be traded off in a package deal across sectors at another stage, for example, in the European Council, representing heads of government. It would, nonetheless, be possible to give the devolved governments a more formal role and even a veto in key policy areas, if this were accompanied by an understanding that European policy is about bargaining and compromise. The veto would then be more of a bargaining chip within the JMC (Europe). It would work only if the possibility of vetoes represented a threat more than a practice providing an incentive for the parties to agree. Short of a veto, procedures in the JMC could provide for formal votes or statements of position and for dissent on the part of devolved governments from the UK line. This would be a political rather than a legal mechanism, bringing the issue to public attention and letting governments gain the political benefits or bear the political costs of disagreement.

The Europe of the Regions movement may have run out of momentum, but it did establish a complementarity between changing patterns of government at the supranational and the sub-state level. The radical devolution strategy would be helped by further moves to European integration and the strengthening of supranational elements of the EU, including the European

Parliament, the Commission, and the rise of transnational lobbies. This would provide a level of policy-making with a degree of autonomy from the member states and thus open to other influences. By the same token, potential for conflict will expand the more EU and Scottish devolved competences are both extended, thus increasing their overlap. A British policy of opting out of extensions of EU competences might reduce the scope for conflict over Europe, bringing matters back within the domestic system; but if Scotland were committed to closer European integration, this itself could become a matter of contention. For example, were Scotland to gain more responsibilities in labour market and welfare matters, it might be inclined to opt into the Charter of Rights and other expressions of the social Europe. Europe, rather than purely domestic matters, could thus prove the breaking point for the Union, as Scotland seeks its own place within the EU, or England seeks to rid itself of a Scottish veto and secure its own semi-detached form of membership. Moving from one union, the United Kingdom, into a direct relationship with another, the European Union, could thus become the form that Scottish independence assumes.

THE FUTURE OF UNION

Scotland has long faced a strategic dilemma within the Union. It could go for more self-government at the risk of reducing its influence at the centre; or it could renounce self-government in favour of building influence in London, through intermediaries like Scottish Office ministers, civil servants, MPs, and political parties. For three hundred years, autonomy was subordinated to access, a choice made more or less explicitly after Scottish Home Rule was placed on the agenda in the late nineteenth century. English opinion could accept this as long as Scottish affairs were marginal within the United Kingdom and Scottish autonomy confined to elements of 'low politics'. Devolution was a compromise, giving Scotland limited self-government but leaving arrangements at the centre largely unchanged, apart from a reduction in the number of Scottish MPs. Yet the old dilemma has not gone away, and it remains true that more Scottish autonomy means less influence at the centre. The reaction to Scottish devolution within England has not, interestingly, been to oppose it and demand a return to unity. It has, rather, been to accept the consequences that Scots should have less influence at the centre. The Unionist parties have so far been largely unable to face this conclusion, since it implies that devolution affects the central state itself; hence the proliferation of anomalies like the West Lothian Question. Two directions of travel are possible: a neo-unionist effort to re-integrate the UK state and nation on more territorially sensitive terms, or a confederalist move towards a looser union. Ironically, neo-unionism is likely to be less acceptable to English opinion than more radical Scottish devolution, as it would imply a continued and even strengthened Scottish role at the centre and a concomitant limitation on the ability of the English majority to govern their own affairs untrammelled. It also requires the re-building of a British nation. The more likely level of travel is therefore towards a looser and more asymmetrical union.

8

Scotland and the Future of Union

The study of nationalism has been bedevilled by two tendencies. One is to generalize from a few cases into a theory of the whole. The other is to claim that one's own case is an exception to a general rule, itself expressed as an ideal-type of unitary national state. This kind of exceptionalism has long been endemic to national histories, where the case in question is explained by the absence of a 'bourgeois revolution', or of an industrial revolution, or of a thoroughgoing process of national integration. One is tempted to think that the only thing that national histories have in common is their claim to exceptionalism. In complex, compound states, where the link between state and nation is problematic, this tendency is particularly pronounced. Spanish (including Catalan and Basque) scholars have long insisted on the particular nature of their own state, while blithely contrasting it with a supposedly unitary and conflict-free state called England (Vicens Vives 1970; Sorauren 1998; Tusell 1999; Riquer 2000). Complex states compounded of historically, culturally, and institutionally distinct segments are rather more common than one might suppose from reading the standard political science literature about national integration and politics. Territorial politics, in a broader sense, is ubiquitous, albeit expressed and managed in different ways (Keating 2008a). The British 'union state' is one such form. It bears same resemblance to forms found in other states, but its particular configuration is distinct. We must therefore understand it in a comparative frame.

Comparative studies in social science generally look for parsimonious explanations that work, *mutatis mutandis*, everywhere. Such approaches have fared poorly in the study of nationalism, since the phenomenon is so varied and so tied to specific contexts. Case studies, on the other hand, look for complexity and the interaction of factors in specific places and across time. This book has taken the form of a case study but within a wider conceptual framework derived from comparative analysis. Scotland is not a grand historical exception but a nation that, like others, has followed its own particular route to the global prospect of modernity. Earlier chapters have examined the Union as an intellectual project and analysed its evolution according to functional logic, mass opinion, elite strategy, and institutional evolution. The picture is of a changing political reality, with periods of integration alternating with assertions of particularity.

The Union has been described as 'intellectually incoherent' (McLean and McMillan 2005) but, while there may be justification for the claim in purely logical terms, this surely sets the bar too high for constitutional settlements in general. These have the purpose of laying down general principles of political authority and citizenship, but also of accommodation and coexistence, and intellectual inconsistency is often the price to pay. Even the supposedly rational and coherent American and French constitutions are prey to constant interpretation and, in the latter case, amendment and supersession. The genius of British unionism was precisely that it was understood rather differently in different places. The remarkable thing, perhaps, is that it survived the transition to mass politics, democracy, and social citizenship, all factors that would seem to point to unity and uniformity. It is, perhaps, as some (Bulpitt 1983; Nairn 2006) would have it, an *ancien régime*, bearing strong traits of pre-modern politics; but it has managed the transition to a 'postmodern' order of diffused authority, mixed sovereignty, and diversity better than states that have become stuck in a nineteenth-century form of modernity marked by Jacobin uniformity or constitutional rigidity. It is now in a process of profound restructuring. This is not a matter of the short-term ups and downs of the SNP, the outcomes of individual elections, or even a putative referendum, but a longer-term adjustment. The death of nationalism has been pronounced many times, as it has in Quebec; but it is an ever-present force in Scottish politics, as are the various currents of unionism, structuring social and political institutions. The old form of unionism is, indeed, in crisis, as the tortuous efforts of unionism to articulate what in the past could be taken for granted show. Yet, unionism has not given way to an alternative intellectual hegemony based on a putative Scottish nation state. On the contrary, the language of union is ever-present, whether in discussions of the European Union, the 'social union' or formulations about 'these islands', or the North Atlantic community.

This is partly because of the functional dependence of Scotland, with England, the other nations of the United Kingdom, Europe, and the global trading world. The economic logic of the Union has shifted, from providing access to imperial and global markets, to managed dependency, protection, and transfers, then to the new policies of 'competitive regionalism', and decentralized development strategies. The welfare state has not, as some feared and others hoped, been cut down, but it has been reshaped and social solidarity can no longer rely on the class and British-national ties that under-pinned it in the past. New conceptions of social welfare are linked to labour markets and competitiveness, and the question is raised as to how solidarity can be maintained in a climate of international competition. It is no longer clear, to pitch the claim at the minimal level, that large states are the best way to achieve all this. On the other hand, the degree of functional interdependency makes the independent nation state alternative ever less meaningful.

Mass opinion has shifted towards a self-identification that is primarily Scottish but strong elements of Britishness remain, as shared historical memory, political identification, and voting behaviour. Elite strategies have diverged between the nationalist and the unionist, but neither is unambiguous or entirely successful. Nationalists have sought to accentuate the Scottish but have been curiously uninterested in nation-building, tending to take the nation for granted. They have also appropriated the language of union for reassurance and as a new external support system for an independence that would, compared with the ideal-type nation state, be highly attenuated. Unionists, having over a period of thirty years abandoned the idea that unionism is incompatible with any elected assembly for Scotland, have sought a new union but struggled to give it shape or meaning. Both sides have sought to build a political division around the issue of independence, but public opinion remains resistant to this Manichean framing of the question, preferring the fuzzy middle ground and seeking to mix and match the various components of statehood to order.

Scotland has emerged over recent decades as a new polity. It has governing institutions and elements of statehood enough to justify McCrone (2001*b*) in dropping the qualifier 'stateless' from the second edition of his book on the sociology of the nation. Institutional dynamics are self-reinforcing. Scotland has its own civil society and is gradually developing its own policy communities around the main issues (Keating, Cairney, and Hepburn 2008; Keating 2009*d*). A distinct model of political and social citizenship may be emerging. The argument for independence has, in one sense, been won, since almost nobody, not even the most ardent unionist, argues that Scottish independence would be either illegitimate or unfeasible. The controversies, rather, turn on its desirability, given the alternatives. Neither is the population of the majority nation, England, unduly exercised about the possibility of Scottish secession. This marks Scotland off from otherwise comparable cases in Belgium, Spain, or Canada. Yet the teleology of statehood, that this is the ultimate aim or inevitable end of nation-building, is misleading, a generalization from one phase of history. It also abstracts from important questions about the actual capacity of national units to realize collective goals, which might or might not be helped by becoming formally independent states. The case of Kosovo is an extreme example but it is difficult to argue that, by becoming formally independent, it endowed itself with a capacity for action greater than that enjoyed currently by Scotland.

The international environment can also be interpreted in two ways. On the one hand, in an integrated Europe and world trading order, independence for small units becomes more viable; on the other hand, it may become less necessary to the extent that autonomist strategies can be pursued within wider frameworks. There is another consideration: that Scottish independence would be profoundly destabilizing in Europe as a whole, given the other regions or stateless nations that would see it as a precedent. While Scottish independence could be a relatively clear-cut affair, with few disputes about borders or who belongs, this would not be the case in Flanders or the Basque Country. Catalonia, which has managed to combine nation-building with a non-separatist strategy for autonomy, would also be under pressure to rupture with Spain. A Scotland that aspired to play a full part in Europe could not ignore these wider ramifications.

Independent or not, Scotland finds itself in much the same geo-political, geo-strategic, and geo-economic position as an Atlantic and European periphery caught between competing poles. There is the UK pole which, as Ireland has found, will continue to be important. This to a large extent means England, although the potential for alliances and exchange of experience with Northern Ireland, Wales and, eventually perhaps, English regions can provide an alternative perspective. There is the European pole, focused on the European Union. An earlier chapter has explored the relationship of Scotland to Europe and the choices of whether to follow England in a semi-detached relationship, or to seek entry into the core. If the latter is chosen, then Scottish independence is the only way to achieve it; but it is an independence that would immediately be heavily qualified by the European framework. There is the North Atlantic pole, dominated by the United States, although British governments have insisted, with ever less plausibility, on a special relationship that allows them a real influence in this sphere. This is not merely a geo-strategic choice or a matter of security policy, but also a choice of social and economic models. Ireland has also been torn between the European and the North Atlantic poles and, after an apparent period of Europhilia, has now become more Atlanticist in its politics and social models. There is a weaker northern European pole, expressed in the Nordic grouping, which the SNP tried to extend into the concept of the 'arc of prosperity' to encompass Ireland during its boom times.

If we merely consider Scotland's position and options, then a wide choice appears to open on the more confederalist side. Europe's Atlantic periphery is home to an extraordinary variety of constitutional forms. Norway and Iceland opted for full independence in 1905 and 1944, respectively, while maintaining cultural ties to other Nordic states and remaining outside the European Union. Greenland gained home rule from Denmark in 1979 and, while remaining part of the Danish state, withdrew from the EU. Denmark joined the (then) European Communities in the wake of the United Kingdom in 1973, given its strong trading dependence, but has then practised a form of semi-detached membership that is often more symbolic than real, opting out of the Euro and common policies but then shadowing them anyway. The Republic of Ireland became a self-governing dominion in 1922 and left the Commonwealth in 1949, but over recent years has entered into common arrangements with the United Kingdom for the government of Northern Ireland, which itself has a unique and complex constitutional arrangement. The Faroe Islands have a strong degree of self-government within Denmark but are not part of the EU and regularly contemplate the prospect of full independence. The Canaries and Azores have special status, including a distinct fiscal regime, within Spain and Portugal, respectively. The Channel Islands and the Isle of Man are part of the possessions of the British Crown but not part of the United Kingdom or of the EU, a status that European law manages to pass over with only the occasional tension. There is, therefore, a wealth of examples of how to mix and match self-government and sovereignty claims – the product of incomplete state-building and management of this part of the European periphery.

There are other examples of stateless nations and regions[1] building autonomous and distinct political and social institutions without separating from the host state. There is a longstanding Catalan tradition, dating from the late nineteenth century, of seeking stronger national autonomy but without breaking with Spain. This spirit, shared by moderate nationalists and many socialists, is represented in the autonomy statute of 1980 and its 2006 revision, with their strong nation-building elements. Quebec politics is divided between 'federalists' and 'sovereigntists', but both are committed to nation-building and their precise constitutional visions have often seemed to converge. The 1995 referendum was fought between a sovereigntist platform that proposed separating from Canada in order to negotiate half-way back in, and a Quebec federalist platform that promised a special status with more autonomy without first breaking with the state. Flemish politicians, not just those from explicitly nationalist parties, have sought to strengthen institutions and common identities but have been very cautious, for both principled and practical reasons, about seeking their own state. In these cases, it is difficult to see a definitive moment in which the constitutional problem will be resolved. It has become, rather, a matter of ordinary politics, although more prominent at some times than at others. Scotland could, and probably will, follow this line, whether under officially nationalist or unionist leadership. Nationalists will be forced to curtail their ambitions while unionists are already showing a willingness to move (Brown and McLeish 2007).

The problem becomes much more difficult when the reference point is not just Scotland but the United Kingdom and its constitution. The key question here is not so much the extent of Scottish autonomy but rather the weight of Scottish influence at the centre. Devolution represented an incremental adjustment of the old union by transferring most matters previously handled by the Scottish Office under administrative devolution to the new Parliament and government, but leaving the rest of the UK constitution essentially untouched. It also left intact the old union dilemma, that Scottish interests could seek more autonomy at home or more access to the centre but not both. Some would seek to resolve this problem by rebuilding the centre around common understandings of state and political and social citizenship, with the territorial dimension of the UK state more strongly articulated but policy divergence curtailed (Jeffery 2006). This, however, is likely to satisfy neither Scotland nor England. Scottish opinion seems to be pushing for more autonomy and recognition of national distinctiveness. The point here is not that Scots want substantive policies to diverge from those in England but rather that the frame of reference for debating them and making the trade-offs inherent in public policy is Scotland. The institutional effect of devolution, like administrative devolution before it, is to strengthen the Scottish arena and frame.

For their part, the English elite and, increasingly, public opinion are coming to resent Scottish influence at the centre. This does not take the form of a coherent English counter-project, whether as a demand for an English Parliament or for regional devolution. While Scotland is consolidating as a functional unit and set of institutions, English trends appear to be pulling apart. The south-east of England consistently comes across as the deviant region in UK statistics, with Scotland coming somewhere in the middle. It has been portrayed as one of the global city regions (Sassen 2001) with connections across the world and in many ways detached from its national hinterland. Demands for a territorial rebalancing in England, by reviving regional policy or restraining development in the south, have fallen on deaf ears under successive governments. Proposals for regional government, which would not have resolved the essential asymmetry of the UK constitution but could at least have represented a response to differentiated territorial needs within England, failed at the first referendum in the North East in 2004. The regional allies that Scotland and Wales might have found to rebalance the polity have not appeared. Scotland thus faces a centralized England, dominated by its richest part, with the English periphery now the neglected partner of the Union. This England does not, however, have its own government but lies athwart the Westminster constitution, resisting federalist ideas in the interest of retaining its notional supremacy.

Relations with the European Union could be another breaking point. The Europe of the Regions movement, which seemed for a time to offer a 'third way' between independence and devolution, has rather stalled. Sub-state territories continue to be active in EU affairs, but there is no constitutional recognition of stateless nations or 'legislative regions'. If this road continues to be barred while Europe expands its powers, then independence in Europe might be more attractive. In this case, Scotland would be better to move into the inner core of Europe rather than playing at the margins of both British and European politics, but this would require a considerable restructuring within Scotland, both economic and political.

I have argued above that more differentiation at the centre is possible, for example, by addressing the West Lothian Question. The institutional anomalies created by devolution can thus find some institutional answers, but only if the Westminster parties accept the implications. If English elites and English opinion insist that the central constitution remain essentially untouched by devolution then their only real option is to constitute themselves as a new nation state. The end of the United Kingdom is unlikely to come about from the secession of Scotland as long as the Scots have other options. It is more likely, strange to say, to come from the secession of an England that is no longer prepared to pay the political or economic price of union.

Notes

CHAPTER 1

1. The Peace of Westphalia entrenched the principle of *cuius regio, eius religio,* first elaborated at Augsburg in the previous century. This, rather than the idea of national sovereignty, was the central meaning of the Peace.
2. The (Anglican) Church of Ireland was disestablished in 1869. The Church of England was disestablished in Wales in 1922.
3. The loss of the remaining Spanish colonies in 1898 provoked a state crisis and the rapid rise of Catalan and Basque nationalisms. The French Fourth Republic fell over decolonization problems, including the question of whether Algeria was a colony or part of the state itself.
4. This referred to the Irish and not the Scottish Union.
5. The 1970s, for all their subsequent image, were a time when Scotland was doing relatively well within the United Kingdom.
6. I have used this rather convoluted formulation to acknowledge that nationhood is a subjective feeling and often contested.
7. McCrone (2001*b*) captures a similar idea when, in the second edition of his book on the sociology of Scotland, he drops 'stateless' from the title.

CHAPTER 2

1. The continuing problems of English intellectuals in discussing Britain are illustrated by Tony Judt's book (2005) on Europe in which he regularly loses his normal sure touch when referring to his own country, frequently mentioning Britain and then qualifying it with 'at least in England'.
2. Haseler (1999) firmly believes that it was for the benefit of the English.
3. Haseler (1999: 33) claims that the United Kingdom 'became a perfect instrument for the English ruling classes. It was a useful front for England and Englishness.'
4. This, however, was also true of the French possession of Algeria.
5. The French Empire came unstuck on this very problem.
6. Even the noted nationalist R.B. Cunninghame Graham styles his address NB in correspondence in the National Library of Scotland.
7. More recently, Lunn (1996: 87) notes that 'The use of the term "English" as a synonym for "British" is more than just a slovenly application of the word. It represents a series of assumptions about the natural right of England to speak for Britain' – yet in the rest of his own chapter, Britain and England are used interchangeably.
8. Independent Crofters' MPs were elected in 1885 but soon moved in the Liberal orbit.
9. Referring still to the British–Irish Union.

10. Pittock (2008) asserts that before the First World War Scotland's *per capita* income was 120 per cent that of the United Kingdom; but no source is cited.

11. Imperial expenditure was for the armed forces and the national debt, it being assumed that in a self-governing Scotland under Home Rule all other items would fall on the Scottish budget.

12. Although the idea that Jacobites were Scottish nationalists is an invention of Victorian romanticism.

13. There is a revealing exchange between Sir Douglas Haddow, Permanent Secretary of the Scottish Office, and John Mackintosh, MP, in the minutes of the Select Committee on Scottish Affairs, 19 May 1969, in which Haddow admits that the system benefits Scotland but hopes that his answer will not 'come to the notice of English colleagues of members of this committee'.

14. As late as 2007 appeared Robert Lacey's *Great Tales from English History*, subtitled *A Treasury of True Stories of the People Who Made Great Britain Great*. Since Lacey promises future histories of the Scots, Irish, and Welsh, it may be that the subtitle was the work of a careless editor.

15. The case was *MacCormick* v. *Lord Advocate*. MacCormick had challenged the right of the Queen to use the title Elizabeth II in Scotland. The Court dismissed the case on the grounds that the matter came under the royal prerogative. Lord President Cooper commented: 'The principle of the unlimited sovereignty of Parliament is a distinctively English principle which has no counterpart in Scottish constitutional law. It derives its origin from Coke and Blackstone, and was widely popularized during the nineteenth century by Bagehot and Dicey, the latter having stated the doctrine in its classic form in his *Law of the Constitution*. Considering that the Union legislation extinguished the Parliaments of Scotland and England and replaced them by a new Parliament, I have difficulty in seeing why it should have been supposed that the new Parliament of Great Britain must inherit all the peculiar characteristics of the English Parliament but none of the Scottish Parliament, as if all that happened in 1707 was that Scottish representatives were admitted to the Parliament of England. That is not what was done. Further, the Treaty and the associated legislation, by which the Parliament of Great Britain was brought into being as the successor of the separate Parliaments of Scotland and England, contain some clauses which expressly reserve to the Parliament of Great Britain powers of subsequent modification, and other clauses which either contain no such power or emphatically exclude subsequent alteration by declarations that the provision shall be fundamental and unalterable in all time coming, or declarations of a like effect. I have never been able to understand how it is possible to reconcile with elementary canons of construction the adoption by the English constitutional theorists of the same attitude to these markedly different types of provisions.'

    He added, however, that neither the English nor the Scottish courts were competent to enforce this provision.

16. There is a similar debate in Canada over the historic status of Quebec and whether there was ever a bi-national understanding of confederation (McRoberts 1999; Romney 1999; Laforest 2004).

17. English commentators tend to the singular, emphasizing the English act, which brought Scotland into the existing constitution. Scots tend to use the plural, to make the point that it required the consent of both parliaments, or write instead of the Treaty of Union.

18. I have dealt at length elsewhere with the prejudicial tendency to describe stateless nations as 'ethnic' in order to distinguish them from nations with their own states (Keating 2001*a*, 2001*b*).

19. There is often a further twist in the argument to the effect that, if stateless nations are not different, they have no right to self-government; if they are different, they must be ethnic and deviant from normal universal values, and so again have no right to self-government.

20. In this, I concur with Morton (1999: 53), although he erroneously cites me (Keating and Bleiman 1979) as sustaining the old line that Scottish nationalism did not emerge until the 1960s.

CHAPTER 3

1. The percentages supporting Scottish independence were 51 per cent in Scotland and 48 per cent in England.

2. Thirteen per cent thought that England would be better off, 22 per cent that it would be worse off, and 60 per cent that it would make no difference (ICM, January 2007).

3. Sixty-nine per cent in England and 71 per cent in Scotland wanted the union between England and Scotland to continue, while 24 per cent and 23 per cent, respectively, wanted it to come to an end (ICM, Britishness Survey, December 2007).

4. YouGov Survey, April 2007. Fourteen per cent of people believed that an independent Scotland would establish border controls with England, and 70 per cent thought that it would not.

5. Hussein and Miller (2006) also run the two issues together; but this is in the context of studying the English in Scotland, an issue related to, but by no means identical with, the institutional relationship of Scotland to the United Kingdom.

6. For example, how the process of buying a house 'differs' in Scotland, which itself implies an English norm.

7. There is a great deal of evidence of this in Quebec (Keating 2001*a*, 2001*b*).

8. The ICPS surveys in Catalonia ask voters about their constitutional preferences along similar lines to those in Scotland, finding that only about 17 per cent support independence. When, in the same survey, respondents are asked their opinion about the hypothetical 'independence of Catalonia', double the number regularly declare themselves favourable (ICPS, various years).

9. Voters are familiar with the term 'country' as applied to Scotland, but 'state' implies a big change.

10. This disposes of an old idea that the Scottish periphery would prefer rule from London on the grounds that it is further away and more even-handed than Edinburgh.

11. In earlier surveys, the question was asked of the Scottish Parliament, but the change to Executive does not seem to have affected responses. Since 2007, the Executive is known as the Scottish Government.
12. The survey even showed that a fifth of those who think that Scotland does better out of the Union favour independence, although the numbers here are too small to be reliable.

CHAPTER 4

1. The historic nationalities were exempted from the requirement on the grounds that they had voted for autonomy in the 1930s.
2. At present, students from other European countries pay only the same as the Scottish students, which means, since 2008, that they pay no fee.
3. This is not to be confused with the Council of Europe's Charter for the Protection of Human Rights and Fundamental Freedoms. The EU Charter mainly concerns social rights.
4. Indeed it is a sector of very limited economic importance for Scotland as a whole.

CHAPTER 5

1. This is the secondary spending that arises when people on the public payroll spend their salaries on goods and services.
2. It was christened the Barnett Formula by David Heald, after Joel Barnett, Financial Secretary to the Treasury in the late 1970s. Lord Barnett himself has frequently disowned it, insisting that it was a temporary expedient to which he had given little thought, rather than a spending formula (interview in *Holyrood*, April 2008).
3. The Scottish Executive (2003a) claimed that 'Within the United Kingdom the levels of expenditure vary from one constituent part to another, reflecting the needs rather than the tax capacity of an area.'
4. The figures quoted above are the original calculations, not adjusted backwards to take account of the rectifications made in recent GERS reports.
5. The term is used even when the currency in question is the Euro or the Pound.
6. Ohmae is more useful for stating the model in its starkest form than for his illustrations, which merely serve to show the limitations of his knowledge; his cases of dynamic regional states stretch from Singapore (a modern city-state) to the totally implausible case of Wales.
7. Thomson, Mawdsley, and Payne (2008) included Iceland among their positive examples, just a few months before its financial collapse.
8. This is the figure usually cited, but if we include oil revenues in the GDP calculation, it is several percentage points lower.
9. This is a rather polemical paper, with little hard evidence to back the claims, but it made a splash politically.

10. It does not appear that SNP calculations for oil revenues have taken account of this cut, which would presumably apply to oil.
11. Since Russell was an SNP candidate and later became a minister in the Scottish Government.
12. The term 'supply side' was misused in the name of 'Reaganomics' in the 1980s to justify tax cuts. These were in fact neo-Keynesian demand-side measures, which worked in the short run by stimulating consumer demand.

CHAPTER 6

1. In using the term Great Britain I am, of course, excluding the Irish case.
2. Equal British rights did not, of course, apply in Northern Ireland.
3. There is an interesting asymmetry in their argument since it appears that these restrictions would bind the devolved assemblies and not Westminster. So, in the unlikely event of Scotland wishing to privatize the health service, it would be prohibited, but no such restriction would apply for England.
4. This is more contentious since Westminster would claim the right to withdraw from the EU but, short of this revolutionary measure, it is bound by EU law and jurisprudence.
5. The idea recalls the proclamation of Catalan nationalist Macià, who, after the fall of the Spanish monarch in 1931, proclaimed the independence of Catalonia as part of an Iberian confederation, in which the inclusion of Portugal would ensure that the constituent units really were independent; unfortunately, he did not consult the Portuguese.
6. This refers to the traditional civil law enshrined in old compacts between the Basque provinces and the Spanish state and recognized, in a rather unclear manner, in an annex of the 1978 Constitution.
7. The texts are reproduced in Lachapelle, Tremblay, and Trent (1995).
8. It is clear that the then Liberal Premier of Quebec, Robert Bourassa, had never intended it as more than a bargaining chip with the rest of Canada.

CHAPTER 7

1. In an earlier contribution (Keating 1999), I argued that policy divergence was in practice limited by the existence of a common UK market, security area, and welfare state. This has since been taken up to make a neo-unionist case against enhanced devolution, which is not quite what I intended.
2. Since the provisions in Navarre are so similar, we will refer here only to the Basque Country.
3. The reason why it is the historic territories and not the Basque Parliament that raise the taxes is historical, since it is they who are the holders of this historic right.
4. Figures published by the Spanish Government in 2008 showed that the Basque Country made a net fiscal contribution of 0.59 and 1.35 per cent of revenues (dependent on two methods of calculation) to the centre, while the figures for

Catalonia were 6.5 and 8.7 per cent, respectively (Instituto de Estudios Fiscales 2008). This is despite the fact that the Basque Country had a higher *per capita* GDP.

5. They were able to get the excise taxes counted as own revenue, thus providing them with something to hand over.

6. Before devolution, the Scottish Council Foundation asserted that: 'A process of "equalisation on the basis of need" underpins the UK public expenditure system. That results in net transfers, broadly, from the prosperous South East to other parts of the country' (Scottish Council Foundation 1997:27).

7. Government may claim that the nuclear industry must pay its own way, but it has not done so in the past if the cost of decommissioning and waste disposal is taken into account, and it is unlikely that it will do so in the future.

8. The massive decentralization of welfare under the Clinton administration represented the abandonment of the traditional Democratic faith in big federal government.

9. *Estatuto de autonomía de Cataluña*, article 154, Barcelona: Generalitat de Catalunya.

10. In 1973, they renounced the Conservative whip, allowing Labour to take power as a minority government in February 1974. During the next parliament (October 1974–9), all the territorial parties engaged in bargaining for advantage after Labour lost its small majority.

11. The matter was well put by a young Gordon Brown and Henry Drucker (1980: 127), 'It is scandalous for the British Treasury to deny that it is capable of devolving any powers to levy tax when so many other countries do it. Most of all, a revised Scotland Act could embody some form of "in-and-out" principle. Under such a principle the remaining Scottish MPs at Westminster would not be allowed to take part in the proceedings of the House when it was debating English or Welsh domestic matters.'

12. This followed a pledge given by Harold Wilson before the election of February 1974.

13. Partly to downplay the proto-diplomatic implications of Quebec's membership, the bilingual province of New Brunswick was also admitted.

14. A formation is defined by the matter at stake, for example, agriculture or environment.

CHAPTER 8

1. At the margin, the difference between a stateless nation and a region is hard to draw. Brittany, for example, is usually described, even by autonomists, as a region, while in Catalonia public opinion is divided on how to characterize the territory.

Bibliography

Action Démocratique du Québec (2008), 'Pour un Québec autonome', www.adq.qc.ca.

Aja, Eliseo (2003), *El Estado Autonómico. Federalismo y hechos diferenciales*, 2nd edition, Madrid: Alianza.

Albareda i Salvadò, Joaquim and Pere Gifre i Ribes (1999), *Historia de la Catalunya moderna*, Barcelona: Edicions de la Universitat Oberta de Catalunya.

Aldecoa, Francisco (1999), 'Towards Plurinational Diplomacy in the Deeper and Wider European Union (1985–2005)', in Francisco Aldecoa and Michael Keating (eds.), *Paradiplomacy in Action. The External Activities of Subnational Governments*, London: Frank Cass.

Alesina, Alberto and Enrico Spolaore (2003), *The Size of Nations*, Cambridge, Mass.: MIT Press.

Alexander, Wendy (2003), *Chasing the Tartan Tiger: Lessons from a Celtic Cousin?*, London: The Smith Institute.

Allan, Grant, Brian Ashcroft, and Maria Plotnikova (2007), 'Public Spending and Scottish Devolution: Crowding out, or Crowding in?', *Working Paper No. 5*, Glasgow: Centre for Public Policy for Regions.

Anderson, Benedict (1983), *Imagined Communities: Reflections on the Origins and Spread of Nationalism*, London: Verso.

Andrews, Rhys and Andrew Mycock (2008), 'Dilemmas of Devolution: The "Politics of Britishness" and Citizenship Education', *British Politics*, 3.2: 139–55.

Artola, Miguel (1999), *La Monarquía de España*, Madrid: Alianza.

Ascherson, Neal (2006), 'The Last Druid of Ancient Britain', in Tom Nairn (ed.), *Gordon Brown. Bard of Britishness*, Cardiff: Institute of Welsh Affairs.

Ashcroft, Brian and James H. Love (1993), *Takeovers, Mergers and the Regional Economy*, Edinburgh: Edinburgh University Press.

Aughey, Arthur (2001), *Nationalism, Devolution and the Challenge to the United Kingdom State*, London: Pluto.

Avdagic, Sabina, Martin Rhodes, and Jelle Visser (2005), 'The Emergence and Evolution of Social Pacts: A Provisional Framework for Comparative Analysis', *European Governance Papers* (EUROGOV), No. 05-01, www.connex-network.org.

Badie, Bertrand (1995), *La fin des territoires. Essai sur le désordre international et sur l'utilité sociale du respect*, Paris: Fayard.

Baird, Sandy, John Foster, and Richard Leonard (2007), 'Scottish Capital: Still in Control in the 21st Century', *Scottish Affairs*, 58: 1–35.

Balthazar, Louis (1992), 'L'évolution du nationalisme québécois', in Gérard Daigle and Guy Rocher (eds.), *Le Québec en jeu. Comprendre les grands défis*, Montreal: Presses de l'Université de Montréal.

Bartolini, Stefano (2005), *Restructuring Europe*, Oxford: Oxford University Press.

Bechhofer, Frank and David McCrone (2007), 'Being British: A Crisis of Identity?', *The Political Quarterly*, 78.2: 251–60.

Béland, Daniel and André Lecours (2008), *Nationalism and Social Policy. The Politics of Territorial Solidarity*, Oxford: Oxford University Press.

Beran, Harry (1998), 'A Democratic Theory of Political Self-Determination for a New World Order', in Percy B. Lehning (ed.), *Theories of Secession*, London: Routledge.

Bergeron, Gérard (1991), 'Le devenir de l'état du Québec', in Louis Balthazar, Guy Laforest, and Vincent Lemieux (eds.), *Le Québec et la restructuration du Canada, 1980–1992*, Sillery (Quebec): Septentrion.

Beveridge, Craig and Ronald Turnbull (1989), *The Eclipse of Scottish Culture*, Edinburgh: Polygon.

Billig, Michael (1995), *Banal Nationalism*, London: Sage.

Birch, A.H. (1977), *Political Integration and Disintegration in the British Isles*, London: Allen and Unwin.

Birch, Kean and Andrew Cumbers (2007), 'Public Spending and the Scottish Economy: Crowding Out or Adding Value?', *Scottish Affairs*, 58: 36–56.

Blondel, Jean (1974), *Voters, Parties, and Leaders. The Social Fabric of British Politics*, revised edition, Harmondsworth: Penguin.

Bogdanor, Vernon (1984), *What is Proportional Representation?*, Oxford: Martin Robertson.

—— (2007), 'Tory Plans for an "English Parliament" Will Wreck the Union', *The Observer*, 4 November.

Bond, Ross (2006), 'Feeling Scottish: Its Personal and Political Significance', *Briefing No. 3*, Leverhulme Trust research programme on Nations and Regions, Edinburgh: Institute of Governance.

—— and Michael Rosie (2006), 'National Identities in the UK: Do They Matter?', *Briefing No. 16*, Leverhulme Trust research programme on Nations and Regions, Edinburgh: Institute of Governance.

—— David McCrone, and Alice Brown (2003), 'National Identity and Economic Development: Reiteration, Reinterpretation and Repudiation', *Nations and Nationalism*, 9.3: 371–91.

Brassinne, Jacques (1994), *La Belgique fédérale, Dossiers du CRISP, 40*, Brussels: Centre de recherche et d'information socio-politiques.

Braudel, Fernand (1986), *L'Identité de la France*, Paris: Arthaud-Flammarion.

Brockliss, Laurence and David Eastwood (eds.) (1997), *A Union of Multiple Identities: The British Isles, c. 1750–1850*, Manchester: Manchester University Press.

Brook, Keith (2002), 'Trade Union Membership: An Analysis of Data from the Autumn 2001 LFS', *Labour Market Trends*, July: 343–54.

Brown, Alice, David McCrone, Lindsay Paterson, and Paula Surridge (1999), *The Scottish Electorate: The 1997 General Election and Beyond*, London: Macmillan.

Brown, Gordon (2006), 'The Future of Britishness', lecture to the Fabian Society, 14 January (www.fabians.org.uk).

Brown, Tom and Henry McLeish (2007), *Scotland. The Road Divides. New Politics, New Union*, Edinburgh: Luath.

Bryant, Christopher (2006), *The Nations of Britain*, Oxford: Oxford University Press.

Bryce, James (1887), letter to *The Times*, quoted in Ian McBride, 'Ulster and the British Problem', in Richard English and Graham Walker (eds.), *Unionism in Modern Ireland*, London: Macmillan.

Buchanan, Allen (2004), *Justice, Legitimacy, and Self-Determination. Moral Foundations for International Law*, Oxford: Oxford University Press.

Bulmer, Simon, Martin Burch, Catríona Carter, Patricia Hogwood, and Andrew Scott (2002), *British Devolution and European Policy-Making*, London: Palgrave.

Bulpitt, James (1983), *Territory and Power in the United Kingdom. An Interpretation*, Manchester: Manchester University Press.

Burgess, Michael (1995), *The British Tradition of Federalism*, London: Leicester University Press.

——and John Pinder (eds.) (2007), *Multinational Federations*, London: Routledge.

Butterfield, Herbert (1968), *The Whig Interpretation of History*, Harmondsworth: Penguin (first published Bell, 1931).

Campaign for a Scottish Assembly (1988), 'A Claim of Right for Scotland', in Owen Dudley Edwards (ed.), *A Claim of Right for Scotland*, Edinburgh: Polygon.

Campbell, R.H. (1954), 'Income', in A.K. Cairncross (ed.), *The Scottish Economy*, Cambridge: Cambridge University Press.

——(1955), 'Changes in Scottish Incomes, 1924–49', *The Economic Journal*, 65.258: 225–40.

——(1980), *The Rise and Fall of Scottish Industry, 1707–1939*, Edinburgh: John Donald.

Charron, Christian (2007), 'La vision autonomiste de Mario Dumont, ou le rapport Allaire revisité', *Québec-Politique.com*, 5 May, http://www.quebec-politique.com/article455.html.

Civardi, Christian (2002), *L'Écosse contemporaine*, Paris: Ellipses.

Clark, Samuel (1995), *State and Status. The Rise of the State and Aristocratic Power in Western Europe*, Montreal: McGill-Queen's University Press.

Colley, Linda (1992, 2003), *Britons. Forging the Nation 1707–1837*, London: Pimlico, 1st edition, 2nd edition.

——(1999), 'Britishness in the 21st Century', Downing Street Millennium Lecture, www.number-ten.gov.uk.

Colls, Robert (2002), *Identity of England*, Oxford: Oxford University Press.

Colomer, Josep M. (2006), *Grandes imperios, pequeñas naciones*, Barcelona: Anagrama.

Commission on Scottish Devolution (Calman Commission) (2008), *The Future of Scottish Devolution within the Union: A First Report*, presented to the Presiding Officer of the Scottish Parliament and to the Secretary of State for Scotland, on behalf of Her Majesty's Government.

Compston, Hugh (2002a), 'The Strange Persistence of Policy Concertation', in Stefan Berger and Hugh Compston (eds.), *Policy Concertation and Social Partnership in Western Europe*, Oxford: Berghahn.

Compston, Hugh (2002*b*), 'Policy Concertation in Western Europe: A Configurational Approach', in Stefan Berger and Hugh Compston (eds.), *Policy Concertation and Social Partnership in Western Europe*, Oxford: Berghahn.

Congressional Budget Office (2005), *Corporate Tax Rates: International Comparisons*, Washington: US Congress.

Conservative Party Democracy Task Force (2008), *Answering the Question. Devolution, the West Lothian Question and the Future of the Union*, London: Conservative Party.

Cooke, Philip, Patries Boekholt, and Franz Tödtling (1999), *The Governance of Innovation in Europe: Regional Perspectives on Global Competitiveness*, London: Pinter.

Coppieters, Bruno and Richard Sakwa (eds.) (2003), *Contextualizing Secession. Normative Studies in Comparative Perspective*, Oxford: Oxford University Press.

Crammond, Edgar (1912), 'The Economic Position of Scotland and Her Financial Relations with England and Ireland', *Journal of the Royal Statistical Society*, LCCV.II: 157–82.

Crowther-Hunt, Lord and Alan Peacock (1973), *Royal Commission on the Constitution, 1969–73, Volume 11, Memorandum of Dissent, Cmnd. 5460–1*, London: HMSO.

Curtice, John (2005), 'Devolution and Britishness', ESRC Devolution and Constitutional Change Programme, *Devolution Briefings*, 35.

—— (2008), 'How Firm are the Foundations? Public Attitudes towards the Union in 2007', in Thomas Devine (ed.), *Scotland and the Union 1707–2007*, Edinburgh: Edinburgh University Press.

Cuthbert, Jim and Margaret Cuthbert (2007), Open Letter to Wendy Alexander on GERS, www.cuthbert1.pwp.blueyonder.co.uk.

Cuthbert, Margaret and Jim Cuthbert (2008), 'Opening Up the Books on the True State of Scottish Finances', *Sunday Herald*, 22 June.

Dahrendorf, Ralf (1982), *On Britain*, London: British Broadcasting Corporation.

Dalyell, Tam (1977), *Devolution: The End of Britain?*, London: Jonathan Cape.

Danson, Mike (1990), 'The Scottish Economy: Revisiting the Development of Underdevelopment', Economics and management working papers, no. 17, Paisley: Paisley College.

Dardanelli, Paolo (2005), *Between Two Unions. Europeanisation and Scottish Devolution*, Manchester: Manchester University Press.

Davidson, Neil (2000), *The Origins of Scottish Nationhood*, London: Polity.

Davies, Norman (1999), *The Isles. A History*, London: Macmillan.

de Pablo, Santiago and Ludger Mees (2005), *El Péndulo Patriótico. Historia del Partido Nacionalista Vasco (1895–2005)*, Barcelona: Crítica.

Deutsch, Karl (1966), *Nationalism and Social Communication. An Inquiry into the Foundations of Nationality*, 2nd edition, Cambridge, Mass.: MIT Press.

Devine, Thomas (2003), *Scotland's Empire, 1600–1815*, London: Allen Lane.

—— (2005), 'The Modern Economy. Scotland and the Act of Union', in T.M. Devine, C.H. Less, and G.C. Peden (eds.), *The Transformation of Scotland. The Economy since 1700*, Edinburgh: Edinburgh University Press.

—— (2008a), 'Three Hundred Years of the Anglo-Scottish Union', in Thomas Devine (ed.), *Scotland and the Union 1707–2007*, Edinburgh: Edinburgh University Press.

—— (2008b), 'The Spoils of the Empire', in Thomas Devine (ed.), *Scotland and the Union 1707–2007*, Edinburgh: Edinburgh University Press.

Dicey, Albert Venn (1912), *A Leap in the Dark. A Criticism of the Principles of Home Rule as Illustrated by the Bill of 1893*, 3rd edition, London: John Murray.

—— (1961), *Introduction to the Study of the Law of the Constitution*, 10th edition, with introduction by E.C.S. Wade, London: Macmillan.

—— and Robert Rait (1920), *Thoughts on the Union between England and Scotland*, London: Macmillan.

Dickson, Tony, Jim Brown, Keith Burgess, Tony Clarke, John Foster, Peter Smith, and Wille Thompson (eds.) (1980), *Scottish Capitalism. Class, State and Nation from before the Union to the Present*, London: Lawrence and Wishart.

Dion, Stéphane (1991), 'Le nationalisme dans la convergence culturelle. Le Québec contemporain et le paradoxe de Tocqueville', in R. Hudon and R. Pelletier (eds.), *L'engagement intellectuel. Mélanges en l'honneur de Léon Dion*, Sainte-Foy: Presses de l'Université de Laval.

Drèze, Jacques (1993), 'Regions of Europe', *Economic Policy*, 17: 265–307.

Drucker, H.M. and Gordon Brown (1980), *The Politics of Nationalism and Devolution*, London: Longman.

Duchacek, Ivo, Daniel Latouche, and Garth Stevenson (eds.) (1988), *Perforated Sovereignties and International Relations*, New York: Greenwood.

Durkheim, Emile (1964), *The Division of Labour in Society*, New York: Free Press.

Dyson, Kenneth (1980), *The State Tradition in Western Europe: A Study of an Idea and Institution*, Oxford: Martin Robertson.

Elias, Anwen (2008), 'Whatever Happened to the Europe of the Regions? Revisiting the Territorial Dimension of European Politics', *Regional and Federal Studies*, 18.5: 483–92.

Erskine May, Thomas (1906), *The Constitutional History of England since the Accession of George the Third, 1760–1860*, 3 volumes, London: Longmans, Green.

Ferguson, William (1977), *Scotland's Relations with England: A Survey to 1707*, Edinburgh: John Donald.

—— (1998), *The Identity of the Scottish Nation. An Historic Quest*, Edinburgh: Edinburgh University Press.

Ferguson, Yale H. and Richard W. Mansbach (1996), *Polities: Authority, Identities, and Change*, Columbia: University of South Carolina Press.

Ferrera, Maurizio (2006), *The New Boundaries of Welfare*, Oxford: Oxford University Press.

Finer, Samuel (1974), *Comparative Government*, Harmondsworth: Penguin.

Finlay, Richard (1992), ' "For or Against?": Scottish Nationalists and British Empire, 1919–30', *The Scottish Historical Review*, LXXI, 1.2: 184–206.

—— (1998), 'Caledonia or North Britain? Scottish Identity in the Eighteenth Century', in Dauvit Broun, R.J. Finlay, and Michael Lynch (eds.), *Image and Identity. The Making and Remaking of Scotland through the Ages*, Edinburgh: John Donald.

Finlay, Richard J. (1997), *A Partnership for Good? Scottish Politics and the Union since 1880*, Edinburgh: John Donald.

Firn, John (1975), 'External Control and Regional Policy', in Gordon Brown (ed.), *The Red Paper on Scotland*, Edinburgh: Edinburgh University Student Publications Board.

Fortin, Pierre (1992), 'Les conséquences économiques de la souveraineté du Québec: analyse exploratoire', *Commission d'étude des questions afférents à l'accession du Québec à la souveraineté, Exposés et Études, volume 4*, Quebec: Assemblée Nationale du Québec.

Fraser, Douglas (2008), 'Independent Scotland Should Keep Troops in British Army', *The Herald*, 16 January.

Frey, Bruno S. and Reiner Eichenberger (1999), *The New Democratic Federalism for Europe: Functional, Overlapping, and Competing Jurisdictions*, Cheltenham: Edward Elgar.

Fry, Michael (1987), *Patronage and Principle. A Political History of Modern Scotland*, Aberdeen: Aberdeen University Press.

—— (2001), *The Scottish Empire*, East Lothian: Tuckwell Press.

—— (2006), *The Union. England, Scotland and the Treaty of 1707*, Edinburgh: Birlinn.

Gagnon, Alain-G. (2001), 'Le Québec, une nation inscrite au sein d'une démocratie étriquée', in Jocelyn McClure and Alain-G. Gagnon (eds.), *Repères en mutation. Identité et citoyenneté dans le Québec contemporain*, Montreal: Québec-Amérique.

Gall, Gregor (2005), *The Political Economy of Scotland. Red Scotland? Radical Scotland?*, Cardiff: University of Wales Press.

Gamble, Andrew (1988), *The Free Economy and the Strong State. The Politics of Thatcherism*, Basingstoke: Macmillan.

Gardiner, Michael (2004), *The Cultural Roots of British Devolution*, Edinburgh: Edinburgh University Press.

Garvin, Tom (2004), *Preventing the Future. Why was Ireland So Poor So Long?*, Dublin: Gill and Macmillan.

Gendron, Claude and Daniel Desjardins (1992), 'Le dollar canadien et un Québec souverain: certains aspects juridiques', *Commission d'étude des questions afférents à l'accession du Québec à la souveraineté, Exposés et Études, volume 4*, Quebec: Assemblée Nationale du Québec.

Girón Reguera, Emilia (2007), 'La incidencia de la reforma de los estatutos de autonomía en la financiación autonómica', *Revista Española de Derecho Constitucional*, 80: 75–111.

Goldsmith, Lord (2008), *Our Common Bond. Report of Citizenship Review*, London: Ministry of Justice.

Greenfeld, Liah (1992), *Nationalism. Five Roads to Modernity*, Cambridge, Mass.: Harvard University Press.

Gurtubay, Alfredo (2001), *La dimensión exterior del autogobierno vasco. Representatividad, capacidad contractual y responsabilidad pública internacional a través de los derechos históricos*, Oñati: Instituto Vasco de Administración Pública.

Habermas, Jürgen (1998), 'Die postnationale Konstellation und die Zukunft der Demokratie', in *Die postnationale Konstellation. Politische Essays*, Frankfurt: Suhrkamp, pp. 91–167.

Haddow, Douglas (1969), Oral Evidence, Select Committee on Scottish Affairs, 19 May.

Haggith, Toby (1998), 'Citizenship, Nationhood and Empire in British Official Film Propaganda, 1939–45', in Richard Weight and Abigail Beach (eds.), *The Right to Belong. Citizenship and National Identity in Britain, 1940–1960*, London: I.B. Tauris.

Hansen, Lene (2002), 'Sustaining Sovereignty: The Danish Approach to Europe', in Lene Hansen and Ole Wæver (eds.), *European Integration and National Identity: The Challenge of the Nordic States*, London: Routledge.

Hardiman, Niahm (2006), 'Politics and Social Partnership: Flexible Network Governance', *The Economic and Social Review*, 37.3: 343–74.

Harvie, Christopher (1995), *Scotland and Nationalism. Scottish Society and Politics, 1707–1994*, 2nd edition, London: Routledge.

Haseler, Stephen (1996), *The English Tribe. Identity, Nation and Europe*, London: Macmillan.

Hazell, Robert (2008), 'Hokey Cokey Votes on English Laws', *Guardian*, 3 July.

—— and Brendan O'Leary (1999), 'A Rolling Programme of Devolution: Slippery Slope or Safeguard of the Union', in Robert Hazell (ed.), *Constitutional Futures. A History of the Next Ten Years*, Oxford: Oxford University Press.

Heald, David (1983), *Public Expenditure: Its Defence and Reform*, Oxford: Martin Robertson.

—— (1992), 'Formula-Based Territorial Public Expenditure in the United Kingdom', *Aberdeen Papers in Accountancy*, W7, Aberdeen: University of Aberdeen.

—— and Alastair McLeod (2002*a*), 'Beyond Barnett? Financing Devolution', in John Adams and Peter Robinson (eds.), *Devolution in Practice. Public Policy Differences within the UK*, London: IPPR.

—— —— (2002*b*), 'Public Expenditure', in Law Society of Scotland, *The Laws of Scotland. Stair Memorial Encyclopaedia*, Edinburgh: Butterworths.

Hearn, Jonathan (2000), *Claiming Scotland. National Identity and Liberal Culture*, Edinburgh: Polygon.

Heater, Derek (2006), *Citizenship in Britain. A History*, Edinburgh: Edinburgh University Press.

Heath, Anthony (2005), 'Is a Sense of British Identity in Decline?', ESRC Devolution and Constitutional Change Programme, *Devolution Briefings*, 36.

—— and Jane Roberts (2008), 'British Identity: Its Sources and Possible Implications for Civic Attitudes and Behaviour', *Citizenship Review Research*, London: Ministry of Justice.

Herbert, Stephen (2006), 'Attitudes to the Scottish Parliament and Devolution', *SPICe Briefing 06/23*, Edinburgh: Scottish Parliament.

Hechter, Michael (1975), *Internal Colonialism. The Celtic Fringe in British National Development, 1536–1966*, London: Routledge and Kegan Paul.

Hechter, Michael (1985), 'Internal Colonialism Revisited', in Edward Tiriakian and Ronald Rogowski (eds.), *New Nationalisms of the Developed West*, Boston: Allen and Unwin.

Heffer, Simon (1999), *Nor Shall My Sword. The Reinvention of England*, London: Weidenfeld and Nicholson.

Herrero de Miñon, Miguel (1998), *Derechos históricos y constitución*, Madrid: Taurus.

House of Lords and House of Commons Joint Committee on Human Rights (2008), *A Bill of Rights for the UK? Twenty-ninth Report of Session 2007–08*, HL Paper 165-I, HC 150-I.

Howe, Stephen (2000), *Ireland and Empire. Colonial Legacies in Irish History and Culture*, Oxford: Oxford University Press.

Hroch, Miroslav (1985), *Social Preconditions of National Revival in Europe: A Comparative Analysis of the Social Composition of Patriotic Groups among the Smaller European Nations*, Cambridge: Cambridge University Press.

Hussein, Asifa and William Miller (2006), *Multicultural Nationalism. Islamophobia, Anglophobia, and Devolution*, Oxford: Oxford University Press.

Hutchison, I.C.G. (2001), *Scottish Politics in the Twentieth Century*, London: Palgrave.

Independent Expert Group (2008), *First Evidence to the Commission on Scottish Devolution*, Edinburgh: Commission on Scottish Devolution.

Institute for Public Policy Research (1991), *The Constitution of the UK*, London: IPPR.

Instituto de Estudios Fiscales (2008), *Balanzas Fiscales de las Comunidades Autónomas Españolas con el Sector Público Estatal*, Madrid: Ministerio de Economía y Hacienda.

Jeffery, Charlie (2005), 'Devolution, Social Citizenship and Territorial Culture: Equity and Diversity in the Anglo-Scottish Relationship', in William L. Miller (ed.), *Anglo-Scottish Relations from 1900 to Devolution*, Oxford: Oxford University Press.

—— (2006), 'Devolution and Divergence: Public Attitudes and Institutional Logics', in John Adams and Katie Schmueker (eds.), *Devolution in Practice 2006*, Newcastle: IPPR North.

—— and Daniel Wincott (2004), 'Devolution in the United Kingdom: Statehood and Citizenship in Transition', *Publius: The Journal of Federalism*, 36.1: 3–18.

Jellinek, Georg (1981), *Fragmentos de Estado*, translation of *Uber Staatsfragmente*, Madrid: Civitas.

Jensen, Hans and Jørn Neergaard Larsen (2005), 'The Nordic Labour Markets and the Concept of Flexibility', in Carlos Buhigas Schubert and Hans Martens (eds.), *The Nordic Model: A Recipe for European Success?*, EPC Working Paper 20, Brussels: European Policy Centre.

Johnston, Thomas (1952), *Memories*, London: Collins.

Joint Committee on Human Rights (2008), Joint Committee of House of Lords and House of Commons on Human Rights, *A Bill of Rights for the UK? Twenty-ninth Report of Session*, HL 165-1, HC 150-1, London: The Stationery Office.

Jones, Barry and Michael Keating (1985), *Labour and the British State*, Oxford: Oxford University Press.

Jones, Peter (2002), 'Scotland at the Starting Line', in Jo Eric Murkens with Peter Jones and Michael Keating, *Scottish Independence. A Practical Guide*, Edinburgh: Edinburgh University Press.

Judt, Tony (2005), *Postwar: A History of Europe since 1945*, London: William Heinemann.

JUSTICE (2007), *A British Bill of Rights. Informing the Debate*, London: JUSTICE.

Karmis, Dimitrios and Wayne Norman (2005), 'The Revival of Federalism in Normative Political Theory', in Dimitrios Karmis and Wayne Norman (eds.), *Theories of Federalism. A Reader*, London: Palgrave.

Katwala, Sunder (2005), *Fabian Review*, 117.4.

Katzenstein, Peter J. (1985), *Small States in World Markets: Industrial Policy in Europe*, Ithaca, NY: Cornell University Press.

Kearney, Hugh (1995), *The British Isles. A History of Four Nations*, Cambridge: Cambridge University Press.

Keating, Michael (1975), *The Role of the Scottish MP*, PhD thesis, Glasgow College and CNAA.

—— (1988), *State and Regional Nationalism. Territorial Politics and the European State*, London: Harvester-Wheatsheaf.

—— (1998), *The New Regionalism in Western Europe. Territorial Restructuring and Political Change*, Aldershot: Edward Elgar.

—— (2001*a*), *Plurinational Democracy. Stateless Nations in a Post-Sovereignty Era*, Oxford: Oxford University Press.

—— (2001*b*), *Nations against the State. The New Politics of Nationalism in Quebec, Catalonia and Scotland*, 2nd edition, London: Palgrave.

—— (2004), 'European Integration and the Nationalities Question', *Politics and Society*, 31.1: 367–88.

—— (2005), *The Government of Scotland. Public Policy-making after Devolution*, Edinburgh: Edinburgh University Press.

—— (2006*a*), 'Irish Explanations', *European Political Science*, 5.4: 434–40.

—— (2006*b*), 'From Functional to Political Regionalism. England in Comparative Perspective', in Robert Hazell (ed.), *The English Question*, Manchester: Manchester University Press.

—— (2008*a*), 'Thirty Years of Territorial Politics', *West European Politics*, 31.1–2: 60–81.

—— (2008*b*), 'Culture and Social Sciences', in Michael Keating and Donatella della Porta (eds.), *Approaches and Methodologies in the Social Sciences. A Pluralist Perspective*, Cambridge: Cambridge University Press.

—— (2008*c*), 'Territorial Autonomy in Nationally Divided Societies. The Experience of the United Kingdom, Spain, and Bosnia and Herzegovina', Conference on Assessing Territorial Pluralism, Queen's University, Kingston, Ontario.

—— (2009*a*), 'Social Citizenship, Devolution and Policy Divergence', in Scott Greer (ed.), *Citizenship Rights in the United Kingdom*, London: Policy Press.

—— (2009*b*), 'Spatial Rescaling and the Future of Welfare', *Social Policy Review*, 2.1.

—— (2009*c*), 'Putting European Political Science Back Together', *European Political Science Review*, 1.2.

—— (2009*d*), 'The Territorialisation of Interest Representation: The Response of Groups to Devolution', in Ben Seyd and John Curtice (eds.), *Devolution and Identity in the United Kingdom*, Manchester: Manchester University Press.

Keating, Michael and Alex Wilson (2009), 'Renegotiating the State of Autonomies: Statute Reform and Multi-level Politics in Spain', *West European Politics*, 32.3: 534–56.

—— and David Bleiman (1979), *Labour and Scottish Nationalism*, London: Macmillan.

—— and Linda Stevenson (2006), 'Rural Policy in Scotland after Devolution', *Regional Studies*, 40.3: 397–408.

—— and Zoe Bray (2006), 'Renegotiating Sovereignty; Basque Nationalism and the Rise and Fall of the Ibarretxe Plan', *Ethnopolitics*, 5.4: 347–64.

—— Paul Cairney, and Eve Hepburn (2008), 'Territorial Policy Communities and Devolution in the United Kingdom', *Cambridge Journal of Regions, Economy and Society*, 1.2: 1–16.

Kellas, James (1973), *The Scottish Political System*, Cambridge: Cambridge University Press.

Kelly, Ruth and Liam Byrne (2007), *A Common Place*, London: Fabian Society.

Kemp, Alexander and Linda Stephen (2008), *The Hypothetical Scottish Shares of Revenues and Expenditures from UK Continental Shelf, 2000–2013*, Aberdeen: University of Aberdeen.

Kendle, John (1997), *Federal Britain. A History*, London: Routledge.

Kendrick, Steve (1989), 'Scotland, Social Change and Politics', in David McCrone, Stephen Kendrick, and Pat Straw (eds.), *The Making of Scotland. Nation, Culture and Social Change*, Edinburgh: Edinburgh University Press.

—— Frank Bechhofer, and David McCrone (1985), 'Is Scotland Different? Industrial and Occupational Change in Scotland and Britain', in Howard Newby, Janet Bujra, Paul Littlewood, Gareth Rees, and Teresa L. Rees (eds.), *Restructuring Capital: Recession and Reorganization in Industrial Society*, London: Macmillan.

Kerevan, George (2006), 'Reinventing Scotland', *Prospect*, 129.

—— (2007), 'Banking on Victory for the Scottish Nationalists', *The Spectator*, 12 April.

Kidd, Colin (1993), *Subverting Scotland's Past. Scottish Whig Historians and the Creation of an Anglo-British Identity, 1689–c. 1830*, Cambridge: Cambridge University Press.

—— (1999), *British Identities before Nationalism. Ethnicity and Nationhood within the Atlantic World, 1600–1800*, Cambridge: Cambridge University Press.

—— (2008), *Union and Unionisms*, Cambridge: Cambridge University Press.

Kilbrandon Commission (1973), *Royal Commission on the Constitution, 1969–73, Volume 1, Report, Cmnd. 5460*, London: HMSO.

King, Anthony (2007), *The British Constitution*, Oxford: Oxford University Press.

Krugman, Paul (2003), 'Second Winds for Industrial Regions?', *The Allander Series*: Glasgow, Fraser of Allander Institute, University of Strathclyde.

Kymlicka, Will (2007), *Multicultural Odysseys*, Oxford: Oxford University Press.

Lacey, Robert (2007), *Great Tales from English History. A Treasury of True Stories of the People Who Made Great Britain Great*, New York: Back Bay Books.

Lachapelle, Guy, Pierre P. Tremblay, and John E. Trent (eds.) (1995), *L'impact référendaire*, Sainte-Foy: Presses de l'Université du Québec.

Lafont, Robert (1967), *La révolution régionaliste*, Paris: Gallimard.

Laforest, Guy (1995), *Trudeau and the End of a Canadian Dream*, Montreal: McGill-Queen's University Press.

—— (2004), *Pour la liberté d'une société distincte. Parcours d'un intellectuel engagé*, Sainte-Foy: Presses de l'Université Laval.

Lagasabaster Herrarte, Iñaki and Iñigo Lazcano Brotóns (1999), 'Derecho, política e historia en la autodeterminación de Euskal Herria', in Mikel Gómez Uranga, Iñaki Lagasabaster, Francisco Letamendía, and Ramón Zallo (eds.), *Propuestas para un nuevo escenario: Democracia, cultura y cohesión social en Euskal Herria*, Bilbao: Fundación Manu Robles-Arangiz.

Langlois, Simon (1991), 'Une société distincte à reconnaître et une identité collective à consolider', Commission sur l'avenir politique et constitutionnel du Québec (Bélanger-Campeau), *Document de travail, numéro 4*, Quebec: Commission.

Lee, C.H. (1995), *Scotland and the United Kingdom. The Economy and the Union in the Twentieth Century*, Manchester: Manchester University Press.

—— (2005), 'Economic Progress: Wealth and Poverty', in T.M. Devine, C.H. Lee, and G.C. Peden (eds.), *The Transformation of Scotland*, Edinburgh: Edinburgh University Press.

Lee, Simon (2006), 'Gordon Brown and the "British Way"', *The Political Quarterly*, 77.3: 369–78.

Lobo, Ricard (1997), 'La devolución de la soberanía', in Xavier Bru de Sala, Gemma Garcia, Anna Grau, Ricard Lobo, Magda Oranich, Martí Parellada, Augustí Pons, and Josep-Maria Puigjaner, *El modelo catalán. Un talante político*, Barcelona: Flor del Viento.

Lovering, John (1999), 'Theory Led by Policy: The Inadequacies of the "New Regionalism"', *International Journal of Urban and Regional Research*, 23.2: 379–90.

Lunn, Kenneth (1996), 'Reconsidering Britishness', in Brian Jenkins and Spyros Sofos (eds.), *Nation and Identity in Contemporary Europe*, London: Routledge.

Lusztig, Michael (1995), 'Constitutional Paralysis: Why Canadian Constitutional Initiatives Are Doomed to Fail', *Canadian Journal of Political Science*, XXVI.4: 747–72.

Lynch, Peter (1996), *Minority Nationalism and European Integration*, Cardiff: University of Wales Press.

Lythe, Charlotte and Madhavi Majmudar (1982), *The Renaissance of the Scottish Economy?*, London: Allen and Unwin.

MacCormick, Neil (1999), *Questioning Sovereignty. Law, State and Nation in the European Commonwealth*, Oxford: Oxford University Press.

—— (2000), 'Is There a Scottish Path to Constitutional Independence?', *Parliamentary Affairs*, 53: 721–36.

—— (2005), 'New Unions for Old', in William L. Miller (ed.), *Anglo-Scottish Relations from 1900 to Devolution*, Oxford: Oxford University Press.

Macinnes, Allan L. (2007), *Union and Empire: The Making of the United Kingdom in 1707*, Cambridge: Cambridge University Press.

—— (2008), 'The Treaty of Union: Made in England', in Thomas Devine (ed.), *Scotland and the Union 1707–2007*, Edinburgh: Edinburgh University Press.

Mackay, Donald and David Bell (2006), 'The Political Economy of Devolution', *Series Economy no. 12*, Edinburgh: The Policy Institute.

Mackinnon, James (1907), *The Union of England and Scotland*, London: Longmans, Green, and Co.

Mackintosh, John (1973), 'Review of James Kellas, The Scottish Political System', *Political Quarterly*, 44: 368.

MacLeod, Dennis and Michael Russell (2006), *Grasping the Thistle: How Scotland Must React to the Three Key Challenges of the Twenty-First Century*, Glendaruel: Argyll Publishing.

Magnette, Paul and Kalypso Nicolaïdes (2005), 'Coping with the Lilliput Syndrome: Large vs. Small States in the European Convention', *European Law*, 11.1: 83–102.

Mahoney, James and Dietrich Rueschemeyer (2003), 'Comparative Historical Analysis: Achievements and Agendas', in James Mahoney and Dietrich Rueschemeyer (eds.), *Comparative Historical Research*, Cambridge: Cambridge University Press.

Maitland, Frederick William (1908), *The Constitutional History of England*, Cambridge: Cambridge University Press.

Major, John (1993), 'Forword by the Prime Minister', in Secretary of State for Scotland, *Scotland and the Union*, Edinburgh: HMSO.

Marquand, David (1981), 'Club Government – The Crisis of the Labour Party in the National Perspective', *Government and Opposition*, 16.1: 19–36.

——(1995), 'How United is the United Kingdom?', in Alexander Grant and Keith Stringer (eds.), *Uniting the Kingdom?: The Making of British History*, London: Routledge.

Marsden, Gordon (2005), 'Only Connect', *Fabian Review*, 117.4.

Marshall, T.H. and T. Bottomore (eds.) (1992), *Citizenship and Social Class*, London: Pluto.

Mattila, Mikko (2004), 'Contested Decisions: Empirical Analysis of Voting in the European Council of Ministers', *European Journal of Political Research*, 43.1: 29–50.

—— and Jan-Erik Lane (2001), 'Why Unanimity in the Council? A Roll Call, Analysis of Council Voting', *European Union Politics*, 2.1: 31–52.

McConnel, James and Matthew Kelly (2006), 'Devolution, Federalism and Imperial Circuitry: Ireland, South Africa and India', in Duncan Tanner, Chris Williams, W.P. Griffith, and Andrew Edwards (eds.), *Debating Nationhood and Governance in Britain, 1885–1939*, Manchester: Manchester University Press.

McCrone, David (1992 and 2001*b*), *Understanding Scotland. The Sociology of a Nation*, 1st edn, 2nd edn, London: Routledge.

——(2001*a*), 'Who are We? Understanding Scottish Identity', in Catherine Di Domenico, Alex Law, Jonathan Skinner, and Mick Smith (eds.), *Boundaries and Identities: Nation, Politics and Culture in Scotland*, Dundee: University of Abertay Press.

——(2006), 'Scotland and Europe: Examining the Myths', talk given to the 6th annual conference of the Hansard Society Scotland, Edinburgh: Institute of Governance.

McCrone, Gavin (1965), *Scotland's Economic Progress, 1951–60*, London: Allen and Unwin.

——(1969), *Scotland's Future. The Economics of Nationalism*, Oxford: Blackwell.

——(1975), 'The Economics of Nationalism Re-Examined', confidential paper, Edinburgh: Scottish Economic Planning Department.

—— (2007), Oral evidence to Scottish Parliament Finance Committee, 16 January.

McEwen, Nicola (2006), *Nationalism and the State. Welfare and Identity in Scotland and Quebec*, Brussels: PIE/Peter Lang.

McGarry, John and Michael Keating (2006) (eds.), *European Integration and the Nationalities Question*, London: Routledge.

McLean, Iain (1995), 'Are Scotland and Wales Over-represented in the House of Commons?', *Political Quarterly*, 66.3: 250–68.

—— and Alistair McMillan (2005), *State of the Union. Unionism and the Alternatives in the United Kingdom since 1707*, Oxford: Oxford University Press.

McLaren, John and Richard Harris (2007), 'Measuring the Growth of the Scottish Economy', *Working Paper no. 10*, Glasgow: Centre for Public Policy for the Regions.

McRoberts, Kenneth (1988), *Quebec. Social Change and Political Crisis*, 3rd edition, Toronto: McClelland and Stewart.

—— (1997), *Misconceiving Canada. The Struggle for National Unity*, Toronto: Oxford University Press.

Michelmann, Hans J. and Panayotis Soldatos (eds.) (1990), *Federalism and International Relations: The Role of Subnational Units*, Oxford: Clarendon.

Midwinter, Arthur (2007), *Background Paper on Expenditure and Revenue in Scotland*, Scottish Parliament Finance Committee, Edinburgh: Scottish Parliament.

—— Michael Keating, and James Mitchell (1991), *Politics and Public Policy in Scotland*, London: Macmillan.

Mill, John Stuart (1972), *On Liberty, Utilitarianism, and Considerations on Representative Government*, London: Dent.

Miller, David (1995), *On Nationality*, Oxford: Clarendon.

—— (2001), 'Nationality in Divided Societies', in Alain-G. Gagnon and James Tully (eds.), *Multinational Democracies*, Cambridge: Cambridge University Press.

Mitchell, James (1990), *Conservatives and the Union. A Study of Conservative Party Attitudes to Scotland*, Edinburgh: Edinburgh University Press.

—— (1996), *Strategies for Self-government. The Campaigns for a Scottish Parliament*, Edinburgh: Edinburgh University Press.

—— (2003), *Governing Scotland. The Invention of Administrative Devolution*, London: Palgrave.

—— (2008), 'Who are the SNP?', 2008 Annual Donaldson Lecture, SNP Conference.

Molina, Oscar and Martin Rhodes (2002), 'Corporatism: The Past, Present, and Future of a Concept', *Annual Review of Political Science*, 5: 305–31.

Moore, Margaret (2001), *The Ethics of Nationalism*, Oxford: Oxford University Press.

Moran, Michael (2003), *The British Regulatory State. High Modernism and Hyper-Innovation*, Oxford: Oxford University Press.

Moreno, Eduardo and Francisco Martí (1977), *Catalunya para españoles*, Barcelona: DORESA.

Morgan, Kenneth (1980), *Rebirth of a Nation. Wales, 1880–1980*, Oxford: Oxford University Press.

Morton, Graeme (1999), *Unionist Nationalism: Governing Urban Scotland, 1830–1860*, East Lothian: Tuckwell.

Mouritzen, Hans (1996), 'Polarity and Constellations', in Hans Mouritzen, Ole Waever, and Hakan Wiberg (eds.), *Integration and National Adaptations: A Theoretical Inquiry*, Commack, NY: Nova Science.

Murkens, Jo (2002), *Scottish Independence. A Practical Guide*, Edinburgh: Edinburgh University Press.

Nairn, Tom (1977), *The Break-up of Britain: Crisis and Neo-nationalism*, London: New Left Books.

—— (2000), *After Britain. New Labour and the Return of Scotland*, London: Granta.

—— (2006), *Gordon Brown. Bard of Britishness*, Cardiff: Institute of Welsh Affairs.

—— (2007), 'Union on the Rocks', *New Left Review*, 43: 117–32.

Nicholas, Siân (1998), 'From John Bull to John Citizen: Images of National Identity and Citizenship on the Wartime BBC', in Richard Weight and Abigail Beach (eds.), *The Right to Belong. Citizenship and National Identity in Britain, 1930–1960*, London: I.B. Tauris.

Noël, Alain (1999), 'Is Decentralization Conservative?', in Robert Young (ed.), *Stretching the Federation. The Art of the State in Canada*, Kingston: Institute of Intergovernmental Relations, Queen's University.

NU Health Care (2003), *Doctor's Orders. The Health of the Nation Index*, Eastleigh: Norwich Union Health Care.

O'Donnell, Rory (2008), 'The Partnership State: Building the Ship at Sea', in Maura Adshead, Peader Kirby, and Michelle Millar (eds.), *Contesting the State. Lessons from the Irish Case*, Manchester: Manchester University Press.

—— and Damian Thomas (2002), 'Ireland in the 1990s: Policy Concertation Triumphant', in Stefan Berger and Hugh Compston (eds.), *Policy Concertation and Social Partnership in Western Europe*, Oxford: Berghahn.

Office for National Statistics (2008), *Regional Trends*, 30, Basingstoke: Palgrave-Macmillan.

Ohmae, Kenichi (1995), *The End of the Nation State. The Rise of Regional Economies*, New York: Free Press.

Oneto, G. (1997), *L'invenzione della Padania. La rinascita della communità più antica d'Europa*, Bergamo: Foedus.

Paasi, Anssi (2002), 'Place and Region: Regional Worlds and Words', *Progress in Human Geography*, 26.6: 802–11.

Page, Edward (1978), 'Michael Hechter's Internal Colonial Thesis: Some Theoretical and Methodological Problems', *European Journal of Political Research*, 6.3: 295–317.

Paterson, Lindsay (1994), *The Autonomy of Modern Scotland*, Edinburgh: Edinburgh University Press.

—— (2002a), 'Is Britain Disintegrating? Changing Views of "Britain" after Devolution', *Regional and Federal Studies*, 12.1: 21–42.

—— (2002b), 'Governing from the Centre: Ideology and Public Policy', in John Curtice, David McCrone, Alison Park, and Lindsay Paterson (eds.), *New Scotland, New Society?*, Edinburgh: Edinburgh University Press.

—— (2003), 'The Survival of the Democratic Intellect: Academic Values in Scotland and England', *Higher Education Quarterly*, 57: 67–93.

—— (2006), 'Sources of Support for the SNP', in Catherine Bromley, John Curtice, David McCrone, and Alison Park (eds.), *Has Devolution Delivered?*, Edinburgh: Edinburgh University Press.

—— Alice Brown, John Curtice, Kerstin Hinds, David McCrone, Alison Park, Kerry Sproston, and Paula Surridge (2001), *New Scotland, New Politics?*, Edinburgh: Polygon.

—— Frank Bechhofer, and David McCrone (2004), *Living in Scotland. Social and Economic Change since 1980*, Edinburgh: Edinburgh University Press.

Pierson, Paul (2004), *Politics in Time: History, Institutions and Social Analysis*, Princeton, NJ: Princeton University Press.

Pittock, Murray (1999), *Celtic Identity and the British Image*, Manchester: Manchester University Press.

—— (2008), *The Road to Independence? Scotland since the Sixties*, London: Reaktion.

Pocock, J.G.A. (1975), 'British History: A Plea for a New Subject', *Journal of Modern History*, 47.4: 601–28.

Powell, David (2002), *Nationhood and Identity: The British State since 1800*, London: Taurus.

Pulzer, Peter (1972), *Political Representation and Elections in Britain*, 2nd edition, London: Allen and Unwin.

Qvortrup, Mads (2001), 'Functionalism in Practice: Nordic Lessons for the British-Irish Council', *Regional and Federal Studies*, 11.1: 27–38.

Redwood, John (1999), *The Death of Britain?*, London: Macmillan.

Reicher, Stephen and Nick Hopkins (2001), *Self and Nation*, London: Sage.

Renan, Ernest (1992), *Qu'est-ce qu'une nation?: Et autres essais politiques*, Paris: Presses-Pocket.

Requejo, Ferran (1996), 'Diferencias nacionales y federalismo asimétrico', *Claves de la Razón Práctica* (Jan.–Feb.): 24–37.

Rhodes, Martin (2001), 'The Political Economy of Social Pacts: "Competitive Corporatism" and European Welfare Reform', in Paul Pierson (ed), *The New Politics of the Welfare State*, Oxford: Oxford University Press.

Richer, Karine (2007), *The Federal Spending Power*, PRB 07–36E, Ottawa: Library of Parliament of Canada.

Riley, P.W.J. (1978), *The Union of England and Scotland. A Study in Anglo-Scottish Politics of the Eighteenth Century*, Manchester: Manchester University Press.

Riquer i Permanyer, Borde de (2000), *Identitats contemporànies: Catalunya i Espanya*, Vic: Eumo.

Rodrik, Dani (1998), 'Why Do More Open Economies Have Bigger Government?', *Journal of Political Economy*, 106.6: 997–1032.

Rokkan, Stein (1980), 'Territories, Centres, and Peripheries: Toward a Geoethnic-Geoeconomic-Geopolitical Model of Differentiation within Western Europe', in Jean Gottmann (ed.), *Centre and Periphery: Spatial Variation in Politics*, Beverly Hills and London: Sage.

Rokkan, Stein and Derek W. Urwin (1982), 'Introduction: Centres and Peripheries in Western Europe', in Stein Rokkan and Derek W. Urwin (eds.), *The Politics of Territorial Identity: Studies in European Regionalism*, London: Sage.

—— —— (1983), *Economy, Territory, Identity: Politics of West European Peripheries*, London: Sage.

Romney, Paul (1999), *Getting it Wrong. How Canadians Forgot Their Past and Imperilled Confederation*, Toronto: University of Toronto Press.

Rose, Richard (1982), *Understanding the United Kingdom: The Territorial Dimension in Government*, London: Longman.

Rosie, Michael and Ross Bond (2007), 'Social Democratic Scotland?', in Michael Keating (ed.), *Scottish Social Democracy*, Brussels: Presses interuniversitaires européennes/Peter Lang.

Ross, Duncan M. (2007), 'Diminishing Dividend. The Union and the Economy', in Bob Brown (ed.), *Nation in a State. Independent Perspectives on Scottish Independence*, Dunfermline: Ten Book Press.

Rossiter, David, Ronald Johnston, and Charles Pattie (1997), 'New Boundaries, Old Inequalities: The Evolution and Partisan Impact of the Celtic Preference in British Redistricting', *Regional and Federal Studies*, 7.3: 49–65.

Sassen, Saskia (2001), 'Global Cities and Global City-Regions: A Comparison', in Allen J. Scott (ed.), *Global City-Regions. Trends, Theory, Policy*, Oxford: Oxford University Press, pp. 78–95.

Schmitter, Philippe (1974), 'Still the Century of Corporatism?', *The Review of Politics*, 36.1: 85–131.

Schubert, Carlos Buhigas and Hans Martens (2005), 'Introduction', in Carlos Buhigas Schubert and Hans Martens (eds.), *The Nordic Model: A Recipe for European Success?*, EPC Working Paper 20, Brussels: European Policy Centre.

Scotland Office (2008), *Government Evidence to the Commission on Scottish Devolution*, London: Scotland Office.

Scott, Allen (1998), *Regions and the World Economy*, Oxford: Oxford University Press.

Scott, John and Michael Hughes (1980), *The Anatomy of Scottish Capital*, London: Croom Helm.

Scott, Jonathan (2000), *England's Troubles. Seventeenth-Century English Political Instability in European Context*, Cambridge: Cambridge University Press.

Scott, Paul H. (1992), *Andrew Fletcher and the Treaty of Union*, Edinburgh: John Donald.

Scottish Broadcasting Commission (2008), *Platform for Success. Final Report*, Edinburgh: Scottish Government.

Scottish Council Foundation (1997), *Scotland's Parliament...a Business Guide to Devolution*, Edinburgh: Scottish Council Foundation.

Scottish Executive (2003*a*), *Government Expenditure and Revenue in Scotland (GERS) 2000–2001*, laid before Scottish Parliament by Scottish Ministers, January.

—— (2003*b*), *Government Expenditure and Revenue in Scotland (GERS) 2001–2002*, laid before Scottish Parliament by Scottish Ministers, December.

—— (2006), *Government Expenditure and Revenue in Scotland (GERS) 2004–2005*, laid before Scottish Parliament by Scottish Ministers.

Scottish Government (2007), *Choosing Scotland's Future. A National Conversation. Independence and Responsibility in the Modern World*, Edinburgh: Scottish Government.

—— (2008), *Government Expenditure and Revenue in Scotland (GERS) 2006–2007*, Edinburgh: Scottish Government and National Statistics.

Scottish Social Attitudes Survey (various years), Office of National Statistics. Distributed by the Economic and Social Data Service.

Scruton, Roger (2000), *England: An Elegy*, London: Chatto and Windus.

Seawright, David (1999), *An Important Matter of Principle. The Decline of the Scottish Conservative and Unionist Party*, Aldershot: Ashgate.

Secretary of State for Justice and Lord Chancellor (2007), *The Governance of Britain*, CM 7170, HMSO.

Short, John (1982), 'Public Expenditure in the English Regions', in Brian Hogwood and Michael Keating (eds.), *Regional Government in England*, Oxford: Clarendon.

Smith, Anthony (1999), *Myths and Memories of the Nation*, Oxford: Oxford University Press.

SNP (1999), *Taking Scotland into the 21st Century. An Economic Strategy for Independence*, Edinburgh: Scottish National Party.

—— (2000), *Scotland's 21st Century Opportunity. Government Expenditure and Revenues in Scotland, 2000–2002*, Edinburgh: Scottish National Party.

—— (2006), *Scotland in Surplus – Past, Present and Future*, Edinburgh: Scottish National Party.

Sorauren, Mikel (1998), *Historia de Navarra, el Estado Vasco*, Pamplona: Pamiela.

Spruyt, Hendrick (1994), *The Sovereign State and Its Competitors*, Princeton, NJ: Princeton University Press.

Steel Commission (2006), *Moving to Federalism – a New Settlement for Scotland*, Edinburgh: Scottish Liberal Democrat Party.

Stewart, John (2004), *Taking Stock. Scottish Social Welfare after Devolution*, Bristol: Policy Press.

Storper, Michael (1997), *The Regional World. Territorial Development in a Global Economy*, New York: Guildford.

Straw, Jack (2008), 'Modernising the Magna Carta', Speech at George Washington University, Washington, DC, 13 February.

Streeck, Wolfgang (2006), 'The Study of Organized Interests: Before "The Century" and After', in Colin Crouch and Wolfgang Streeck (eds.), *The Diversity of Democracy. Corporatism, Social Order and Political Conflict*, Cheltenham: Edward Elgar.

Supreme Court of Canada (1998), *Reference re. Secession of Quebec, file 25506*, Ottawa: Supreme Court of Canada.

Surridge, Paula (2003), 'A Classless Society? Social Attitudes and Social Class', in Catherine Bromley, John Curtice, Kerstin Hinds, and Alison Park (eds.), *Devolution – Scottish Answers to Scottish Questions?*, Edinburgh: Edinburgh University Press.

Surridge, Paula (2006), 'A Better Union?' in Catherine Bromley, John Curtice, David McCrone, and Alison Park (eds.), *Has Devolution Delivered?*, Edinburgh: Edinburgh University Press.

Sutherland, Robert (1976), 'Aspects of the Scottish Constitution Prior to 1707', in John P. Grant (ed.), *Independence and Devolution. The Legal Implications for Scotland*, Edinburgh: Green.

Tarleton, Charles (1965), 'Symmetry and Asymmetry as Elements of Federalism: A Theoretical Speculation', *Journal of Politics*, 27: 861–74.

Tarrow, Sidney, Peter Katzenstein, and Luigi Graziano (eds.) (1978), *Territorial Politics in Industrial Nations*, New York: Praeger.

Taylor, Brian (2002), *The Road to the Scottish Parliament*, revised edition, Edinburgh: Edinburgh University Press.

Thatcher, Margaret (1993), *The Downing Street Years*, London: HarperCollins.

Thomson, Ben, Geoff Mawdsley, and Alison Payne (2008), *Powers for Growth*, Edinburgh: Reform Scotland.

————Graeme Blackett, and James Aitken (2008), *Fiscal Powers*, Edinburgh: Reform Scotland.

Tierney, Stephen (2004), *Constitutional Law and National Pluralism*, Oxford: Oxford University Press.

Tilley, James and Anthony Heath (2007), 'The Decline of British National Pride', *The British Journal of Sociology*, 58.4: 661–78.

Tilly, Charles (1975), 'Reflections on the History of European State-Making', in Charles Tilly (ed.), *The Formation of National States in Western Europe*, Princeton, NJ: Princeton University Press.

—— (1990), *Coercion, Capital, and European States, AD 990–1990*, Cambridge, Mass.: Blackwell.

—— (1994), 'Entanglements of European Cities and States', in Charles Tilly and Wim P. Blockmans (eds.), *Cities and the Rise of States in Europe, A.D. 1000 to 1800*, Boulder, CO: Westview.

Trevelyan, George Macaulay (1926), *History of England*, London: Longmans, Green.

Tusell, Javier (1999), *España. Un angustia nacional*, Madrid: Espasa Calpe.

Vicens Vives, Jaime (1970), *Approaches to the History of Spain*, 2 nd edition, Berkeley and Los Angeles: University of California Press.

Walker, David (2002), *In Praise of Centralism*, Catalyst Working Paper, www.catalyst-forum.org.uk.

Walker, Neil (2000), 'Beyond the Unitary Conception of the United Kingdom Constitution?', *Public Law*, Autumn: 384–404.

Ward, Paul (2005), *Unionism in the United Kingdom, 1918–1974*, Basingstoke: Palgrave.

Webster, Wendy (2005), *Englishness and Empire, 1939–65*, Oxford: Oxford University Press.

Weight, Richard (2002), *Patriots. National Identity in Britain, 1940–2000*, London: Macmillan.

Whatley, Christopher (2006), *The Scots and the Union*, Edinburgh: Edinburgh University Press.

Wills, Michael (2008), 'The Politics of Identity', Speech at IPPR, London, 26 March.

Wilson, Charles (1970), 'Note of Dissent', *Scotland's Government. Report of the Scottish Constitutional Committee*, Edinburgh: Scottish Constitutional Committee.

Wright, Alex (2005), *Who Governs Scotland?*, London: Routledge.

Young, Robert A. (1995), *The Secession of Quebec and the Future of Canada*, Montreal: McGill-Queen's University Press.

Zielonka, Jan (2006), *Europe as Empire*, Oxford: Oxford University Press.

Index

Aberdeen 102
acquis communautaire 89, 90, 91, 92, 94
Action Démocratique du Québec 138, 139
administrative devolution 42, 278
Afghanistan 95
Africa 15, 24
Åland Islands 97
Alberta 151
Alexander, Wendy 81. 103
Allaire report 139
Alternative Economic Strategy 50
Amsterdam Treaty 92
ancien regime 127, 174
Anglicization 29
Aragon 19, 127
Argentina 112
Aristocracy 29
Army, British 22, 76, 95
Asia 15, 24, 115
asymmetric shocks 110
Australia 43
Austria 13, 118
Azores 147, 177

balance of payments 111
Balmoral 25
Bank of England 111, 112, 123, 155
Barnett Formula 105, 106, 107, 110, 144, 145,
    149, 152, 157, 184
Basque Country viii, 7, 14, 24, 75, 83, 127,
    137–8, 146–8, 152, 166, 173, 176, 181
BBC (British Broadcasting Corporation) 27,
    28, 76, 156
Belgium 17, 19, 24, 45, 125, 148, 166, 16, 175
Benelux countries 92
Berlusconi, Silvio 92
Berwick-on-Tweed 86
Bible 21
Blair, Tony 46
Bloc Québécois 138
borders 10, 46, 47, 81, 96
    in Europe 57, 92
    and independence 86, 89, 92, 93, 98, 99,
        107, 147, 161, 196, 183
    of Scotland 1, 25, 45, 54, 61, 80, 88, 96, 98

social 48
UK 46
Bosnia 13, 81, 95
Bouchard, Lucien, 96, 138
Boundary Commissions, 23
Bourgeoisie 29, 49
Bretton Woods 111
Britain
    Bank of 155
    defence 165
    club government 56
    constitution 127, 138, 162
    end of, debate 1–5, 58, 61–2, 72
    and Europe 59, 92
    integration 21–5
    and Ireland 121
    judiciary 161
    nation-building 7, 19–20, 26–7, 129
    social union 89, 96
    unionism 30–8, 67–70, 143
British Broadcasting Corporation *see* BBC
British Empire, *see* Empire
British Isles 9, 20, 97, 136
British Medical Association 53
British-Irish Council 97, 137
Britishness vi, 2–4, 17, 20, 24, 27, 29, 30,
    61–4, 66, 67–71, 79, 128, 132, 163, 175
Brittany 24, 186
Brown, Gordon 46, 67, 69, 70, 162, 177, 186
Bruce, Robert 38
Brussels 58, 166, 168, 169
Bundesrat 131, 169
Butler Act, 1944 27

Cabinet 35, 159
Calman Commission, *see* Commission on
    Scottish Devolution
Campaign for a Scottish Assembly 40
Canary Islands 177
Capitalism 47, 51, 101
Catalan language 21
Catalonia vii, 7, 14, 19, 24, 29, 65, 127, 149,
    155, 166, 177,
Catholicism 3, 20, 30, 41, 63, 118
Centralization 23, 56, 70, 128, 135, 145

Centre for Partnership and Performance (Ireland) 121
Chancellor of the Exchequer 159
Channel Islands 77, 177
Charlottetown Accord 164
Charter 88 151, 126, 162
Charter of Rights (British) 131, 134, 164
Charter of Rights, of EU 91, 92, 100
Charter of Rights (Canada) 163, 164
Choosing Scotland's Future 84
Church of England 39, 181
Church of Scotland 25, 39
Citizenship 11, 13, 15
  British 7, 23, 25, 26, 28 68, 70, 87, 88, 131, 143,174
  Canada 125, 163
  European 94, 131
  Puerto Rico 137
  and Scottish independence, 86, 87–9
  social 30, 65, 69, 88, 128, 132, 148
City of London, *see* London
city regions 177–8
city-states 12, 14, 101, 184
civic nationalism 79
civil rights 131
civil service 55, 56, 160
Claim of Right 40
Clarity Bill 84
Clarke, Kenneth 158
class 21, 22, 28–31, 52–7, 61–3, 124, 153, 174
  business 29, 52
  landowning 52
  middle 30, 65
  political 43, 136, 181
  working 29, 30, 38, 49, 60, 61, 65, 74
club government 55–7, 134
collective bargaining 122
collectivism 27, 64
Commission on Scottish Devolution (Calman Commission) 132, 145
Committee of the Regions 167
Common Agricultural Policy 169
Common Fisheries Policy 59, 91
Common Foreign and Security Policy 95
Commonwealth 28, 88, 96, 177
Commonwealth Games 107
Commonwealth Grants Commission 150
Community Allowance 153
competition state 113–18
competitive regionalism 174
concierto económico 138, 146
confederalism vii, 136–41, 143, 159, 160, 161, 162, 164, 166, 172, 176

Confederation of British Industry (CBI) 122
Conservative Party 2, 4, 29, 30, 52–7, 65, 122, 159
  and Europe 4, 58, 92, 22, 163
  and Union 38, 43, 62, 63, 66, 71, 77, 105, 107, 158, 163
consociationalism 120
constitution, of an independent Scotland, 89–90
Constitutional Court, of Spain 83
Constitutional Treaty of EU 59, 83, 92, 94, 167
Convention of Royal Burghs 17, 45
Convention of Scottish Local Authorities 45
Convention on the Future of Europe 58, 138, 167
Cook, Robin 159
Cooper, Lord Justice 39, 182
corporation tax 106, 146
corporatism 118–21
Council of Europe 57, 129, 184
Council of Finance Ministers (Ecofin) 112
Council of Ministers
  of EU 91, 93, 95, 100, 139, 167, 168, 169, 170
  Nordic 97

Dalyell, Tam 40, 156
Darien scheme 24
debt, public 86, 87, 102, 109, 110, 112, 114, 120, 149, 150, 151, 182
decentralization 7, 23, 38, 50, 77, 128, 139, 143, 152
  fiscal 148–9
decolonization 3, 24, 136, 181
defence policy 77, 86, 87, 94, 95, 105, 106, 109, 137, 138, 139, 140, 144
Delors, Jacques 58, 92
Democratization 23, 127
Denmark 94, 95, 97, 112, 116, 117, 176, 177
dependency culture 54
deprivation 5, 117
devolution
  Scotland vii, viii, 14, 20, 24, 43, 52, 61, 67, 71–7, 103–5, 122, 126, 129, 131 132, 133, 139, 143–72, 178
  in 1970s 40, 51, 71–2, 83, 128, 135
  administrative 42, 178
  Conservatives and 53, 65
  and Europe 48, 129, 179
  finance and 104–6, 144, 147–50
  Labour and 65
  SNP and 66. 130

trade unions and 53
Wales 84, 131
and Westminster 134
Dewar, Donald 81
diaspora, Scottish 166
Dicey, Albert Venn 39, 40, 82, 132, 135, 165, 182
Dominions/ dominion status 25, 39, 43, 136, 177
Douglas Home, Alec 158
dual polity 23
Dundas, Henry 35

East Timor 84
Economy 6, 47, 140
  and independence 100, 101–24, 128, 144
  of Union 26–34, 36, 49–52, 154
Edinburgh 17, 38, 49, 85, 107, 155
education
  Scotland 23, 35, 54, 105
  and citizenship 68, 70, 132
  and economic development 50, 117, 119
  and devolution 128, 145, 166
Empire
  British 3, 11, 24–8, 43, 49, 57, 58, 65, 70, 88, 136
  Habsburg 15, 43, 127
  Holy Roman 15
  Ottoman 15, 127
  Russian 13
England
  and broadcasting 155
  Church of 39
  and constitution 70, 130, 133, 135, 136, 160, 162, 164, 171, 175–8
  economy 31–2, 49, 103–5, 151–2
  education 28, 29, 70
  and Empire 24
  and Europe 58, 60, 147, 170, 171
  identity in 61
  and monarchy 42
  MPs 157–8
  nationalism in 1, 29, 28, 162
  political behaviour in 4, 54, 55, 65
  public services in 61, 132, 143, 153
  regionalism 178
  and Scotland 41, 48, 55, 61, 75, 82, 85, 86, 89, 93, 98, 103–5, 107, 113, 133, 151–2, 174, 175
  and Scottish independence vii, viii, 45, 175
  secession of 179
  South-East 178

as synonym for Britain 26, 27, 30, 37, 38, 173
trade unions in 53
and Union 2, 18, 19, 20, 21–2, 24, 36, 71, 98, 178
unionism in 6, 11, 19, 26, 27, 133
Euro 83, 91, 94, 98, 100, 108 112–14, 115, 155, 177
European Union 47, 69, 102, 112, 118, 147
  and Basque Country 138, 147
  competition law 147
  Constitutional Treaty 167
  and devolution 76, 154, 161
  foreign and defence policy 95
  and Ireland 121
  law 88
  majority voting 91, 92, 126
  and Nordic states 97, 177
  Scottish attitudes to 59–61
  and Scottish independence 43, 40, 59, 60, 73, 75, 77, 90–4, 96–7, 98. 99, 100, 130, 137, 138, 139, 155, 167, 171, 174
  sovereignty in 14, 57, 69, 126, 129, 161, 162, 167
  Structural Funds 59, 148
  taxation 146
  trade 113
  Treaty of 167
Europe of the Regions 57, 58, 167, 170, 179
European Central Bank 94, 112, 114, 123
European Convention for the Protection of Human Rights and Fundamental Freedoms (ECHR) 57, 89, 134, 161, 163, 164
European Court of Justice 90, 147
European Economic Area 93, 94, 97
European Monetary Union, *see* monetary union
European Parliament 91, 168
European Single Market 47, 82, 91, 98, 120
Euroscepticism 4, 59–60
exceptionalism vi, 5, 9, 19, 24, 173

Falklands War 65
Faroe Islands 97, 177
federalism vii, 11, 13, 128, 131, 134–7, 147–8, 161, 167
federation, Imperial 25, 43, 135
Festival of Britain 27
Financial Services Authority 112, 158
Finland 13, 95, 97, 116, 117
First World War 22, 23, 27, 28, 29, 32, 40, 42, 43, 51, 101, 182

fiscal decentralization, *see* decentralization
fiscal equalization 139, 146, 148–51, 157
Flanders 141, 166, 176
Flanders Declaration 58
foral system 127, 137
fragments of state 13
framework laws 135, 137, 160
France 2, 3, 8, 9, 17, 19, 20, 22, 24, 68, 125,
    127, 143, 147
Francophonie 166
free trade 14, 31, 49, 96, 97, 101
French Revolution 19, 66
fundamentalists (in SNP) 129

Gaelic 21
GDP, Scotland 31, 33, 104, 106–8, 109, 110,
    111, 115, 116, 124, 184
George IV, King 37
Germany 3, 13, 19, 90, 91, 118, 135, 147
Gladstone, William Ewart 42, 43, 156
globalization 6, 8, 69, 103
Goldsmith, Lord 68, 88
Good Friday Agreement 163
Goschen Formula 104, 105
Governance of Britain, The 67, 162
Government Expenditure and Revenues in
    Scotland (GERS) 106–10
gradualists (in SNP) 129,
Grattan, Henry 70
Greenland 90, 97, 176

Habsburg Empire, *see* Empire
health service 30, 53, 55, 56, 68, 88, 117, 132,
    145, 148, 157, 159, 185
Heath, Edward 54, 56
Highlands 21, 28, 34, 41, 74
historiography 37
Holyrood, *see* Scottish Parliament
home rule
    Irish 82, 135, 156
    Scottish 49, 50, 54, 63, 69, 76, 82, 129, 133,
    135, 171, 182
House of Commons 35, 158, 163
House of Lords 156
Hungary 13

Ibarretxe Plan 13, 137–9, 168
Iceland 13, 97, 98, 116, 176, 184
immigration 12
Imperial federation, *see* federation
imperialism, *see* Empire
income tax 32, 116, 145
independence of Scotland

political economy 101–24
    legality 79–82
    support for 71–7
industrial policy 32, 154
industrialization 2
interdependence 89, 119, 126
intergovernmentalism 91
internal colonialism 5, 21
International Court of Justice 86
International Covenant on Civil and Political
    Rights 81
International Covenant on Economic, Social
    and Cultural Rights 81
inward investment 50, 57, 93, 114, 115, 124,
    154, 165, 166
Ireland
    currency 98
    defence 95
    economy 98, 114, 115, 116, 117, 120
    and Empire 24–5
    Europe 92, 100, 196
    home rule *see* home rule
    independence 3, 82, 88, 98, 136, 177
    nationalism 29
    Northern, *see* Northern Ireland
    public expenditure 31, 32
    social partnership 120–2
    and UK 19, 34, 55, 70, 96
Irish Civil War 25
Irish Free State 25
Irish Party 23
Isle of Man 97, 177
Italy 19, 91, 143

Jacobitism 34, 42, 143
Johnston, Tom 36, 49
Joint Ministerial Committees 160, 170
Judicial Committee of the Privy Council 161
Jugoslavia 84, 91

Keynesianism 8, 36, 102, 118, 119, 128, 185
Kosovo 91, 95, 175

labour markets 88, 89, 92, 100, 114,
    117, 120, 122, 123, 148, 153,
    154, 171
labour movement 28, 29, 43, 50, 53, 58, 67,
    86, 92, 132
Labour Party 28, 29, 43, 50, 53, 58, 67, 86,
    92, 132
Lega Nord 81
legislative regions 58, 129
legitimacy 81, 101

Leipzig agreement 169
Liberal Democrats 62, 83, 129, 135, 145, 181
Liberal Party, UK 23, 30, 42, 43, 135
Liberal Party of Quebec 139
Liberal Unionists 30
Linz–Moreno scale 5, 61
Lisbon, Treaty of 59, 92, 94, 95, 169
Little Englandism 65
Lloyd George, David 32
local government 8, 18. 22, 35. 42, 56, 90, 107, 112
London 21, 30, 56, 85, 98, 104, 106, 107, 112
    Assembly 158, 83
    as capital of UK 49, 59, 112, 135, 170, 171
    City of 55, 111

Maastricht criteria 157
Maastricht Treaty (Treaty of European Union) 92, 105
MacCormick, John 43, 182
MacCormick *vs.* Lord Advocate 182
macroeconomic policy 8, 101, 102, 111, 113, 114, 118, 119, 144
Magna Carta 70
Major, John 81
majority voting, in EU, *see* European Union
Meech Lake Accord 164
military 8, 22, 25, 27, 95
modernization 2, 6, 21, 23, 41, 46, 52, 58, 100, 116, 127, 146
monarchy 14, 15, 18, 19, 24, 25, 68, 89, 127
monetary policy 101, 112, 113, 115, 118, 119, 123, 128, 144, 154, 155
monetary union (European) 98, 102, 120, 154
Monopolies Commission 51
moral economy 64, 65
multiculturalism 66, 67, 68–71, 77, 125
Muslims in Scotland 41
myths 37, 41, 63

nation-building 8, 12, 36, 155, 175
    in Britain 7, 19, 20, 27, 34, 67, 68, 70, 125, 163, 166
    in Catalonia 176, 177
    in Ireland 7
    in Scotland 10. 18, 41, 66, 124, 175
National Assembly for Wales 83, 135
National Association for the Vindication of Scottish Rights 42

national curriculum 70
National Economic and Social Council (Ireland) 121
National Economic and Social Development Office (Ireland) 121
National Economic and Social Forum (Ireland) 121
national identities
    Britain 67–9, 88, 163
    Canada 125, 127, 163
    Scotland 54, 61–4, 67, 71, 74, 124, 128, 143
    USA 125
National Liberals 30
National Plan 36
nationalism 3, 7, 18, 46, 67, 163, 173, 174
    banal 8, 41
    British 4, 38, 58, 65, 66
    Catalan 29, 65
    civic 79
    Irish 43, 77
    neo- 130–2
    Quebec 49
    Scottish ii, 3, 5, 10, 21, 31, 33, 34, 38, 42–4
    Spanish 65
    stateless 64, 94
    'unionist' 38, 44
    Welsh 77
nationalization 27, 29, 101, 166
NATO (North Atlantic Treaty Organization) 94, 95, 129, 165
Needs Assessment Study 106, 150
neo-liberalism 54
neo-nationalism 130–2
neo-unionism 130–2
Netherlands 24
New Deal 153
New Labour 54, 55, 63, 67, 68, 69, 70
new public management 117
new regionalism 47, 140
New Zealand 116
Nokia 97
Nordic Council 97
North American Free Trade Area (NAFTA) 96
North Atlantic Treaty Organization (NATO) *see* NATO
North Britain 26
North Sea Oil, *see* oil
Northern Ireland 45, 68, 82, 83, 88, 97, 104, 135, 146, 160, 162, 163, 176, 177
Norway 94, 97, 110, 116, 118, 176
nuclear power 152, 156

oil, North Sea 36, 46, 50, 86, 87, 104, 107–12, 118, 119, 151, 156, 159, 184
Olympic Games 107
Organization for Security and Cooperation in Europe (OSCE) 95, 129
Orkney 86

Padania 81
paradiplomacy 165–8
Parizeau, Jacques 96, 138
Parti Québécois 138, 164
pay bargaining 32, 120, 121, 122
pensions 86, 87, 88, 93, 105, 146, 152, 154
plurinationalism 67
post-sovereignty vii, 57, 126
Pound Sterling 98, 99 111, 112, 115
poverty 123
Presbyterianism 34
primordialism 40
Private Finance Initiative/ Public Private Partnerships 150
privatization 52, 122
proportional representation 82, 123, 158
protectionism 6, 32, 50, 101
Protestantism 2,3, 20, 63
protodiplomacy 165–8
public choice 102
public expenditure 104–10, 116, 186

Quebec 49, 66, 68, 69, 76, 80, 82, 84–6, 96, 98, 112, 126, 127, 138–9, 140, 141, 152, 163, 164–6, 174, 177, 182

Ravenscraig 50
Reaganomics 115
referendums
    EU 58, 83, 94
    Italy 83
    Northern Ireland 83
    rules for 83, 84
    Scotland vi, 43, 59, 71, 73–5, 77, 81
    Spain 83
    Quebec 84, 96
regional policy 8, 32, 35, 36, 42, 49, 50, 147, 148, 178
regional states 114, 140
regulation, 154–6
Reid, John 159
Republika Srpska 81
Royal Commission on the Constitution (Kilbrandon) 128
Royal Family 25
Russia 26

Salisbury, Lord
Salmond, Alex 103, 130
salt water doctrine 82
Scandinavia 118
Schengen Area 61, 92–3, 96, 97, 100
Scotland Act
    of 1978 128, 153, 154
    of 1998 51, 142, 153, 156, 161, 186
Scotland Europa 58, 168
Scott, Sir Walter 37
Scottish Broadcasting Commission 155
Scottish Council (Development and Industry) 36
Scottish Development Agency 36, 57, *see also* Scottish Enterprise
Scottish Education Department 23, 35
Scottish Enlightenment 34
Scottish Enterprise 151, *see also* Scottish Development Agency
Scottish Government 73, 83, 84, 86, 93, 106, 123, 133, 145, 154, 160, 166, 184
Scottish Government EU Office 168
Scottish Grand Committee 42
Scottish Home Rule Association 42
Scottish MPs 35, 38, 86, 133, 156–9, 186
Scottish National Party (SNP)
    and business 53
    currency policy 112–15
    and devolution 66, 129
    election success 66, 129
    electorate of 61–3, 65
    and Europe 58–60, 91–5, 98, 167, 176
    and finance 107–10, 87, 150, 159
    founding 43
    in government 160–1
    and independence 75, 79, 82–3, 86, 98, 129
    and nation-building 65
    referendum on independence 73, 83
    and security policy 95
    and social democracy 177–8
    and working class 53
Scottish nationalism, *see* nationalism
Scottish Parliament
    demand for 42, 60, 77, 129
    and ECHR 164
    elections 17, 45
    establishment of 133
    and finance 145–51
    and House of Lords 160
    and independence 73–5, 83, 85, 89
    and independence referendum 83, 85

and *MacCormick vs. Lord Advocate* 182
members 52, 87
powers of 60, 135, 141, 152, 156, 161
unionist majority in 83
and Westminster 135, 136, 151, 157, 165
secession
  England 179
  Ireland 82
  Northern Ireland 163
  Scotland 27, 46, 79, 82, 85, 175, 179
  theories of 79–82, 84
Second World War 23, 27, 32, 36, 69, 97,
    101, 105, 136
Secretary of State for Scotland 35, 51, 107
secularization 20, 48
security policy, 94–6
self-determination vii, 79, 81–5, 86, 101,
    130, 141
self-government theory 80, 81, 102
self-government in Scotland
  vs. access to centre 171
  before devolution 35
  campaign for 54
  Conservatives and 54
  and constitution 153, 177
  and Europe 58–9, 130
  and identity 74
  meaning of 76, 89, 126, 143, 144,154
  nationalism and 66
  right to 79
  support for 43, 74–7, 125, 129
  unionists and 38, 105, 133
Shetland 86
Sillars, Jim 58
single market
  European 47,91, 98 120
  UK 1, 88, 98
Sinn Féin 43
Smith, Adam 54
SNP, *see* Scottish National Party
Social Chapter 92
social citizenship 30, 65, 69, 88, 132, 148,
    174, 175, 178
social concertation, 118–23
social democracy 54, 100, 116, 118, 145, 153
social security 35, 62, 88, 105, 110, 123, 137,
    149, 152, 153, 154
social solidarity 6, 10, 19, 30, 31, 47,
    48, 53, 54, 55, 62, 131, 152, 154, 174
social union 89, 96, 97, 99, 130, 174
sovereignty
  in Basque Country 14
  in European Union 14,57, 126, 167

in Northern Ireland 88
parliamentary (Westminster) 37, 38, 39,
    56, 82, 89, 126, 132, 133, 134, 136,
    161, 162, 164, 165
popular 15, 19, 26, 38, 39, 89, 126,
    127, 162
post-, *see* post-sovereignty
pre-modern 127
in Quebec 96
in Scotland 9, 10, 18, 39, 40, 89, 132,
    162,166, 167
shared 14, 58, 134, 143, 167, 174, 177
sovereignty-association 137–9
theory of vii, 11
in United Kingdom 25, 26
Westphalia and 181
Soviet Union 84, 95, 120, 125
Spain 3, 9, 17, 19, 22, 24, 45, 65, 68, 76,
    83, 90, 91, 125, 127, 137, 148, 151,
    160, 161, 169, 175
spatial rescaling 6, 47, 71
Stability Pact 112, 114
state-building 10, 11, 12, 19, 24, 34, 77,
    177
Statute of Westminster 25, 39, 43, 136
Straw, Jack 70
Structural Funds, *see* European Union
Stuart dynasty 42
supranationalism 48, 61, 90, 91, 93, 97, 98,
    126, 137, 169, 170
Supreme Court of Canada 82, 83
Sweden 94, 95, 97, 116, 117
Switzerland 148

teleology 2, 70, 175
territorial management 7, 8, 18, 34, 36, 47,
    56, 105
Thatcher, Margaret 4, 50, 54, 56, 64, 65, 81,
    92, 116, 120, 122
Third Republic, French 3, 68
Third World 24
trade unions 1, 4, 30, 53, 58, 92, 98, 99, 118,
    119, 120
transfer pricing 115
Treasury 105, 106, 107, 111, 150, 151
Treaty of Union 17, 183
Trident missile system 165
Trudeau, Pierre 69, 125, 127, 163

UKREP (UK Permanent Representation in
    EU) 168
unemployment 4, 88, 117, 118, 119, 120, 145,
    146, 152, 153, 154,

UNESCO (United Nations Educational and
    Cultural Organization) 166
Union of the Crowns 96
Union, Acts of 70
unionism 1–5, 15, 33–4, 37–42, 44, 46,
    57, 63, 75, 130, 133, 158, 172, 174–5
unionist nationalism, *see* nationalism
United Nations 79, 81, 128
United States of America 58, 65, 69, 70, 80,
    90, 94, 112, 125, 135, 137, 148, 152, 176
universities 22, 55, 55, 56, 89, 115, 116, 157,
    159
Unlock Democracy 162

value added tax 116, 146, 147
Victoria, Queen 25

wage bargaining, *see* pay bargaining
Wales 19, 21, 23, 29, 31, 45, 61, 68, 69, 79,
    83, 93, 97, 104, 105, 135, 164, 176,
    178, 181
Wallace, William 38
welfare state 3, 4, 19, 27, 30, 32, 36, 53–5,
    58, 92, 106, 114, 116–19, 124, 128,
    131, 132, 145, 151, 152–4, 174, 185
West Lothian Question, 156–9
Western European Union 95
Westphalia, Peace of 3, 11, 181
Whig history 2, 9, 37, 70
Whitehall 42, 58, 107, 145, 151, 160
working class 4, 7, 29, 30, 31, 49, 53, 60,
    61, 63, 65, 74
World Trade Organization 102